Besieged by Behavior Analysis for Autism Spectrum Disorder

Besieged by Behavior Analysis for Autism Spectrum Disorder

A Treatise for Comprehensive Educational Approaches

Eric Shyman

LEXINGTON BOOKS
Lanham • Boulder • New York • London

Published by Lexington Books
An imprint of The Rowman & Littlefield Publishing Group, Inc.
4501 Forbes Boulevard, Suite 200, Lanham, Maryland 20706
www.rowman.com

Unit A, Whitacre Mews, 26-34 Stannary Street, London SE11 4AB

British Library Cataloguing in Publication Information Available

Library of Congress Cataloging-in-Publication Data Available

∞ ™ The paper used in this publication meets the minimum requirements of American
National Standard for Information Sciences Permanence of Paper for Printed Library
Materials, ANSI/NISO Z39.48-1992.

978-1-4985-0808-7 (pbk : alk. paper)

Printed in the United States of America

Contents

Acknowledgments

There are many to whom I owe a tremendous amount of homage and respect. First and foremost, to my two sons and my wife, whose faces and voices keep my focus and passion in check. I owe a tremendous amount of gratitude to the staff at Lexington Books, especially Julie Kirsch, Eric Wrona, Alissa Parra, and Emily Frazzette, without whom the publication of this book would not have been possible. To my former colleagues at Dowling College who took a chance on me before I had truly established myself, and who encourage and support me as I continue to develop as a scholar, teacher, activist, and writer. Also to my new colleagues at St. Joseph's College, who believe in my expertise and value enough to entrust me with their students. To all of my students, be they past, present, and/or future. It is they who keep my intellect alive and my interest fresh. I owe much gratitude to a rich field with much to debate and discuss, as well as whomever is to read this work and engage in discussion about its content whether it is in agreement or disagreement. Further, to all of the scholars who work tirelessly to enhance the quality of life of invaluable individuals with developmental disabilities who have been so grossly devalued in the past. While the approaches and philosophies may vary, the goal and the passion from which it originates is one. I would also like to acknowledge my mother, Wendy Brickman, and my sister, Amanda. Finally, to my late father Paul Shyman who, though never able to see what I've become in this world, forever resides in my heart and whose love is at the core of everything I do.

Introduction

A work such as this presents a significant amount of risk from the very outset. Because it handles two necessarily contiguous issues, the claims of supremacy and exclusivity made by many within the field of Applied Behavior Analysis as well as a subsequent polemic for a comprehensive educational approach to be used for children with Autism Spectrum Disorders instead, there are a number of potential inferential misunderstandings. While those potential misunderstandings will be dealt with deeply and earnestly throughout the work as a whole, it is likely beneficial to handle some of the more potentially divisive ones from the beginning. First and foremost, the argument put forth in this treatise does not, by any means, intend to be a means of "anti-behaviorism." That is, at no point does the polemic suggest that behaviorism is invalid, inutile, or pseudo-scientific. In fact, quite the opposite is proffered. The role that behavior analytic intervention plays in the education of individuals with Autism Spectrum Disorder is indelible and irreplaceable, and must be maintained in any legitimate or potentially effective educational approach for children with Autism Spectrum Disorders. Second, the question of the evidence-basis of Applied Behavior Analysis is not denied. There is undoubtedly a strong evidence-basis for behavior analytic interventions. Rather, it is the boldness and the robustness of claims that are suggested by many proponents of ABA that is censured and tested with rigorous detail.

Those points clarified, a comprehensive work of scholarship and intellect handling the claims of supremacy and exclusivity made by multiple members of the field of Applied Behavior Analysis is long overdue. For several decades now, the authoritative perspective of the field of behavior analysis has been maintained as the dominating narrative in the area of educating individuals with Autism Spectrum Disorders. The reasons behind this largely uncontested phenomenon, especially by the educational field at large, are multiple and varied, but fall directly in line with the undeniable influence, if not full permeation, of the positivistic nature that educational and psychological approaches and interpretations of human behavior have come to highly value. However, this preoccupation with positivistic and outcomes-based approaches coincides quite directly with the de-emphasis of social justice and civil rights in education and the systematic approach toward re-traditionalization of so-called educational reform initiatives. Mirroring the positivistic language of the educational laws, specifically the Elementary and Secondary Education Act (known for a brief time as *No Child Left Behind*) and the Individuals with Disabilities Education Improvement Act, the proponents of the field of behavior analysis have managed to edge out virtually every other legitimate and effective framework for educating individuals with Autism Spectrum Disorder and, in some cases, have even boldly claimed to be the *only* method of intervention that could be deemed evidence-based, crediting itself to such extreme "success" as recovery of individuals with Autism Spectrum Disorder.

This claim of supremacy and recovery is the juncture at which this book takes significant objection and contention. Based deeply in legitimate scholarship and comprehensive research, *Besieged by Behavior Analysis for Autism Spectrum Disorders* outlines multiple arguments to refute such unfounded claims of supremacy made by members of the field of behavior analysis, as well as offering a perspective by which approaches and theoretical frameworks commonly discredited by the field of behavior analysis such as sensory, relationship, and emotionally based models are reintroduced and legitimized on the basis of current information and emerging research findings in multidisciplinary areas including psychology, linguistics, education, and neuroscience as well as an alternate means by which Autism Spectrum Disorder is conceptualized, and uses these as evidence to promote the necessity of a comprehensive model of educating individuals with Autism Spectrum Disorders. Ultimately, this treatise aims to proffer a counter-narrative to the dominant voice of Applied Behavior Analysis in the field of educating individuals with Autism Spectrum Disorders, thus propagating existing discourses as well as generating new areas of theoretical, clinical, and educational discussion.

The danger of claims of supremacy among behavior analysts presents more than simply a paradigmatic threat or one of many examples of a subfield proffering theoretical claims that vastly extend the available evidence. Rather, the by-product of such claims has distinctly deleterious impacts on educational practices, school culture, and the autonomy and dignity of family and individual choice-making. First, Applied Behavior Analysis poses a foundational threat to inclusive opportunities for individuals with Autism Spectrum Disorder by maintaining a qualification-based approach to receiving inclusive educational opportunities. In other words, the methodology promotes the idea that until an individual is "ready" or has "earned" his or her way into a general education classroom, such an environment should not be accessible, thus relegating these individuals, in the meantime (or, in some cases, permanently), to alternative environments such as self-contained classrooms or external school placements that "specialize" in the approach. This perspective reinforces and maintains an ableistic cultural perspective in schools. Furthermore, this approach creates the propagation of the centrality of the conception of "normality" in education, the very basis of ableistic practices. By exercising rhetorical and authoritative control over parental, clinical, and educational decision making processes, maintaining the supremacy of a behavior analytic approach serves to vilify stakeholders who seek or even potentially value additional or alternative means of intervention and education, implying that such decisions of "choosing away" from behavior analytic approaches are unwise and imprudent, if not unethical. The behavior analytic approach capitalizes on the medical model of pathologizing ASD as a "condition" that needs to be "treated," "remedied," and/or "rehabilitated" in order for individuals to be successful, maintaining the deficit-based approach of rehabilitation rather than the biopsychosocial approach of universal design or at least environmental accommodation. Claiming that behavior analysis is the *only* evidence-based practice coupled with the corresponding notion that *only* evidence-based practices should be implemented for individuals with Autism Spectrum Disorder essentially stymies the field of educational research entirely, illegitimating the necessity of continuing to investigate and research any form of intervention other than those that are behavior analytic, including emerging forms of educational interventions based on increasing knowledge of neuroscience in order to continually improve the educational experiences available for individuals with Autism Spectrum Disorders. Finally, the centrality of behavior analysis fosters the perpetuation of the "positivistic" perspective of education, denigrating any attempts to attend to or even address less observable (or unobservable) or less quantitatively measurable (or un-measurable) phenomena, many of which may have distinct significance on the educational experience and quality of life of an individual.

Such claims have scholastic ramifications as well. By over-focusing on one area of research and inquiry, the field becomes imbalanced and one-sided, not only leaving less room for alternative forms of exploration, but creating a scientific and popular culture that is unwilling to consider or accept various perspectives of research and inquiry despite its clear legitimacy. Creating such a hegemonic behavioral culture of research and practice creates a marginalization of other legitimate forms of research and inquiry and, in even more extreme cases, a blatant oppression of those who espouse such differing views, minimizing, if not eliminating the avenues by which such writing and research can be proffered, critiqued, and expanded. This preponderance of single-mode research and inquiry has resulted in a largely pseudo-academic research base for educational approaches in ASD and relat-ed conditions, leaving the extant literature wanting desperately for a more exhaustive, interdisciplinary, and theoretically sound foundation. While there are pockets of such comprehensive explorations of ASD, they remain few and far between and drastically marginalized by the mainstream behavior analytic and positivistic media.

As a former practitioner of "strict" (if not orthodox in some respects) Applied Behavior Analytic approaches in various educational environments for many years, I readily admit that I, too, was lured by the grandeur of the claims purported by the field and became convinced of its effectiveness (and even its supremacy) by what I believed to be observable evidence. That is, I saw the changes in behavior occurring before my own eyes and believed that such changes were due to the simple yet ingenious interventions maintained by simple applications of interventional technology such as the token econo-my and external positive reinforcement schedules, as well as a number of its creative variations. I was convinced that changes in behavior did, indeed, indicate learning and that by changing enough behaviors such individuals would be "more includable" in "regular environments." This is precisely the message of behavior analysis. With more experience, increased awareness of counter-narratives, more understanding of inclusive education and social jus-tice and, perhaps most importantly, an ever-increasing sample of students with whom I worked, I became disheartened, slowly at first, but then quite swiftly, with the limitations of behavior analysis on many different levels. I knew there was more to the individuals with whom I worked than what I could see or measure. I had a hard time legitimizing how motivating an individual to sort by color and shape or engage in other such compliance-based tasks (regardless of how "pre-vocational," "functional," or "job-task based" they were) was truly enhancing his or her quality of life, and why such approaches seemed to require separate, vastly exclusive environments (even some more excluded within the already exclusive school) to be even remotely effective. However, there was no room for such conjecture in the field of Applied Behavior Analysis as it, inevitably, entailed aspects of the individual that were not operational. That is, these qualities could not be observed or measured quantitatively. Somehow I knew this could not be the whole story; that this perspective, while clearly important in achieving cer-tain types of skill acquisition, many of which were vital, could not possibly account for the full spectrum of capabilities and desires that these human beings possessed. Even those researchers who did attempt to address the occurrence of "private" or "inner" events (or any other nominal delineation) did not seem, from my perspective, to reach the true heart of the matter. I did not know, however, where else to turn, as every other approach that appeared to be open to less observable phenomena, such as Developmental Individual-Difference Relationship-Bases or Sensory Integration Therapy was shunned emphatically as being, at best, non-evidence based or, at worst, utter "quackery."

After several years of research, practice, and philosophizing, the potential solution to this dilemma became clearer. Any single mode approach, regardless of the theoretical perspective from which it comes, would be insufficient in wholly targeting the various and complex needs of individuals with ASD. Therefore, the only possible alternative would be a comprehensive approach that espouses and implements methodologies from a variety of theoretical frameworks and perspectives without sacrificing the legitimacy of earnest data analysis and evidence-basis. However, such means of data analysis and evidence-basis need not be based solely in quantitative analysis, but would depend also on a comprehensive means of evaluation.

A book such as this one will require readers to openly question their allegiances to common paradigms in the field of education as a whole, and ASD in particular. We are all more behavioral than we often realize, as our society embodies the very essences of behaviorism and outcomes basis based on tangible reinforcement of one degree or another (money, college degrees, material acquisitions). As such, the reader will be compelled to surrender some of his or her positivistic tendencies to fully appreciate the true value of a more constructive and qualitatively rich perspective. The reader may also have to sacrifice the notion that ASD is a disorder that is to be pathologized and, instead, one that may be regarded as a social construct that does not even necessarily need to be named in order to be addressed. Finally, the reader will have to accept the legitimacy that it is both ethical and clinically necessary to be open to methodological approaches that are theoretically sound but may not yet have acquired the evidence-basis needed to be deemed fully evidence-based (a critique that will be applied directly to behavior analysis itself). By accepting the above perspectives, the reader will be able to understand not only the sensibility, but the necessity of a comprehensive approach for individuals with Autism Spectrum Disorders.

The book is organized into eight chapters. Chapter 1 attempts to delineate the history of the development of the field of psychology, especially that of behavioral psychology, in a concise, though non-exhaustive manner. Drawing on influences ranging from Greek philosophers to theologians and early psychologists such as Wundt and James, through the foundational behaviorist such as Thorndike, Watson, and Skinner, the establishment of the behavioral basis of psychological inquiry is set forth. This chapter also addresses a number of historical paradigmatic dissents with behaviorism from the early 20th century into contemporary times. Chapter 2 serves as a primer for defining and contextualizing some of the main concepts of behavior analysis. Similarly to chapter 1, this chapter is not intended to be presented as an exhaustive investigation of key terminological and conceptual aspects of behavior analysis, but rather serve to present the reader with a working understanding of the foundations of the approach in order to be better equipped to grapple with later critiques. Chapter 3 addresses the continuous development of the concept of autism and/or Autism Spectrum Disorder from both a diagnostic and social constructivist perspective. In this chapter the main argument for regarding ASD not as a diagnostic label but rather as a social construct is delineated. Chapter 4 deeply investigates and interrogates the development of the concept of evidence-based practices from its roots in medicine to its tenuous and often inconsistent application in the social sciences and, ultimately, education. By exploring various types of analytic methods, this chapter will offer an alternative means of understanding evidence-based practices, and call the behavior analytic perspective into serious question. Chapter 5 traces the deep and seemingly natural connection between the field of behaviorism and Autism Spectrum Disorder, beginning from the earliest examples of the relationship in the 1960s through the current. Chapter 6 aims to earnestly interrogate the claims made by the field of behavior analysis, drawing on evidence from various perspectives. The points in this chapter aim to expound on the notion that claims of supremacy and, in many cases, exclusivity proffered by behavior analysts are both unfounded and unethical. These claims are founded upon methodological, theoretical, and philosophical bases. Chapter 7 offers the main polemic for the necessity of a comprehensive educational approach for individuals with Autism Spectrum Disorders drawing on a variety of perspectives including behavioral, relationship-based, socio-emotional, language and communication, and sensory processing. Finally, chapter 8 proposes a "sketch" of how a comprehensive program may be designed, implemented, and evaluated in an applied setting.

It is important to emphasize one point quite strongly. The tenets purported in this book are not, in any way, framed in terms of being anti-behavior analytic. Quite the opposite, in fact, the arguments put forth in this book will maintain the importance, if not centrality, in some cases, of the behavior analytic approach. Indeed, the behavior analytic approach must invariably be a component of any legitimate comprehensive program for individuals with Autism Spectrum Disorder. Furthermore, the book seeks to de-emphasize the significance of methodological labeling altogether. That is, that categorizing of paradigms itself is a deleterious process by pervading artificial boundaries between approaches that are all designed for the same purpose: to target and address the needs of individuals with Autism Spectrum Disorder in a way that enhances their value to society, their inclusivity, and ultimately their quality of life. Further, the critiques proffered of the behavior analytic research design is not intended to be illegitimating. Rather, the aim to address a very important and overlooked notion in the field: that these research efforts do not match the claims being made at their behest, and that giving credence to such claims is entirely unethical.

It is important to emphasize that this book is intended to be one written from a scholastic and academic perspective as well as a practical and clinical one, and will therefore handle a number of the issues raised from a position of dense and deep research and philosophical explanation. However, the essential message and the utility of the book in terms of application must not be underestimated, as a number of its chapters deal with the practice of such an approach directly. Therefore, readers who are less interested in the academic or scholastic underpinnings of the ideas expressed in this book and are more interested in its practical and applicable utility may benefit most from reading chapters 5, 6, 7, and 8 on their own, as these chapters handle directly the shortcomings of utilizing behavior analytic methodologies alone and present a means of incorporating a more comprehensive means of educating individuals with ASD.

Essentially, the discussion involving the appropriate means of educational approaches for individuals with Autism Spectrum Disorder has grown stale, stagnant, and overrun with hackneyed repetitions of a distinctly limited research design. What was once an earnest attempt at producing a canon of innovative and practical research studies has become a seemingly endless compendium of studies offering now only quantity at the expense of quality. The pressures of the "publish or perish" perspective and an outcomes-based educational policy agenda combined with a rhetorical need to maintain the legitimacy of a relatively simplistic approach in the context of pluralistic and highly technical research methodologies in the field of ASD itself has created what has amounted to more of an "armory" than a canon of research.

The intention of this book is to be bold and unapologetic. The main message is twofold. First, to expose the truth that the inflated claims being made by behavior analysts are not only inaccurate, but a legitimate threat to the educational opportunities and social justice of individuals with Autism Spectrum Disorder and the autonomy of their families. Second, it seeks to exemplify the idea that comprehensive practices are more widely and soundly supported by research and are, indeed, evidence-based when they are designed, approached, and applied within a sound, systematic, and carefully planned framework. It is my hope that this book becomes but one of many works that earnestly seeks to expand the legitimacy of educating individuals with Autism Spectrum Disorder from empirically sound and humanistic comprehensive perspectives. Indeed, this is the only means by which these individuals are to become valued and truly functional civic members of society.

Chapter One

The History and Development of Behaviorism

Delineating the development of a subfield within the context of a larger and equally as elusive greater field is a difficult scholastic task. When the field in question is one in the context of social science, the task becomes even more daunting as the development of social phenomena and its associated modes of study can be traced from multiple and even debatable roots. Such is the case of the development of behaviorism within the field of psychology. However, the demarcation and discussion of both historical events and their corresponding social developments is an imperative part of any work involving social progress. The focus of this initial chapter, then, is not to attempt to present a comprehensive or exhaustive history of psychology in any sense, as such a task could only be attained in a much larger dedicated work. It is, however, intended to situate the reader within a particular historical and social context in preparation for following a later polemic that aims to show why the behavior analytic perspective (the moniker that will be used to denote the application of behaviorism in practice) alone is not sufficient in educating individuals with Autism Spectrum Disorder. That is, the history is being presented primarily to address the types of problems and questions that have been addressed by psychology and, subsequently, education, which in a Western context are inseparable; how such problems and questions have been addressed by various modes of thinking and investigation; and what behaviorism and, in the context of educating individuals with Autism Spectrum Disorder, behavior analytic intervention in particular has offered that is, indeed, different than other paradigms.

This chapter will primarily employ the investigation of such a history from the perspective of historiography. According to Furay and Salevouris, historiography is:

The study of the way history has been and is written—the history of historical writing. . . . When you study historiography you do not study the events of the past directly, but the changing interpretations of those events . . .[1]

As such, it is not sufficient that names, dates, and ideas are simply denoted in a chronological fashion and claim to be a historical investigation. Rather, such information will be used only in relation to the actual effect and influence they had on the social structure and activity of the society and culture itself, either localized or global.

A BRIEF HISTORY OF THE GENERAL FIELD OF PSYCHOLOGY

There are various socially significant reasons as to why the field of psychology itself came into development to begin with, and why the fulfillment of its purpose is essential to the continued journey toward the understanding of the human experience, including learning processes. However, studying psychology or any other single discipline alone can create single-modal or unilateral thinking, thus divorcing it from the very important contextual connections to other modes of thinking such as history and philosophy, among others, all of which contribute directly to educational thought and practice. As such, designing a study that explores interdisciplinary connections is essential in the ability to present comprehensive ideas, which yield comprehensive polemics by broadening and deepening the purview under which it functions.[2] This notion being offered, it begs reassurance that the following exploration will be comprised of only a sampling of psychological perspectives and developments, and in no way attempts to offer anything near an exhaustive or even comprehensive account of the development of the field of psychology.

In what way and using which functions does psychology inform social science and contribute to the effort toward understanding the myriad aspects of the human condition? The main mode by which psychology does so is by the delineation of scientific and/or philosophical theories, which organizes the employment of empirical observations and acts as a guide for future observations.[3] When this information is gathered and organized sufficiently enough it will lead to confirmable and practicable propositions. As such, much thought in psychology, especially thought which will eventually coalesce into what becomes the field of behavioral psychology, has taken the form of determinism, or the idea that everything that occurs is a result of a finite number of causes. If those causes were each known, all action could be predicted with accuracy.[4] This history of determinism can be traced to the very beginning of formalized thinking in the Western-based society.

The Greek and Early Christian Philosophers

Because the Greeks had such a profound impact on the development of thought and philosophy of all types in subsequent Western civilizations and cultures, the beginning of any such discussions must invariably begin with an historical account, if only a brief one, of Greek thinkers and philosophers. Thales (634–546 B.C.E.) is often credited as being the first philosopher, though not nearly as well known as some of his successors. Thales purported the notion of *cosmology*, which suggested that all components of the universe consisted of natural substances and, as a result, were governed by natural principles and not the whims of the gods, a vastly controversial idea given ancient Greece's deific social context. More specifically, Thales regarded water as the primary substance in all matter, an astonishingly accurate insight that would soon be shown to be true for many earthly substances. Thales also developed processes by which eclipses could be predicted, navigation could be facilitated using observable planetary positions, and geometric principles could be applied to measure heights of buildings, which was important in both architectural design and construction. Espousing a somewhat contradictory idea to what many ancient Greeks likely thought, Thales became known as an early example of Greek thinkers called "physicists," or those who relied on physical explanations of earthly actions, as opposed to godly or supernatural ones. Perhaps most importantly, however, Thales was thought to be highly interested in proffering his ideas as a matter of speculation and engaging in discussion and debate about them, laying the groundwork for one of the first forms of scholastic theorizing and discourse processes.[5]

Democritus (460–370 B.C.E.) may be seen as the next major figure in the development of Greek philosophy, and is also thought to be among the last of the cosmologists who looked more to the physical nature of the universe rather than that of inner human workings and phenomena. Often credited with the first explanation of atomic theory, Democritus purported that all matter was made up of tiny particles which were unchangeable. However, he further explained that different organizations of these particles were what caused differences in physical attributes such as shapes, colors, sizes, among many other potential physical differences. Most interestingly, however, he believed that humans, too, were comprised of such particles. Essentially, he espoused what came to be known as elementism (known also as reductionism),[6] or the notion that all physical things, regardless of complexity can be broken down into an atomic structure.

Hippocrates' (460–377 B.C.E.) influence on modern Western thought and medicine cannot be overstated and will not be fully captured in this section by any means. However, one of the most significant contributions to science that Hippocrates offered was his meticulously detailed and accurate documentation of diseases, treatments, and patients, which led to an early means of data collection, analysis, and data-based decision making (relative to the types of decisions and treatments of the time). From Hippocrates' records, he concluded that all disorders, both mental and physical, were caused by natural factors such as susceptibility, organic injury, and/or an imbalance of bodily fluids. He was also the first noted practitioner to recognize the concept of a "brain" which served a central function in human processes. Ultimately, Hippocrates was one of the earliest noted and, arguably, most well-regarded opponents to the idea of supernatural or metaphysical explanations of disease. Hippocrates' contribution to what would become, over millennia, the "medical model" was unmistakable, and would have a distinct influence on psychology and education alike.[7]

Around the same time the concept of Stoicism became relatively well-known. Stoicism purports that a system known as *logos*, which is rational, guides the universe in all of its aspects. Furthermore, Stoics suggested that there is a cyclical nature to the universe consisting of repeating phases of creation and dissolution, creating a potential for constant search for philosophical and physical truths throughout such cycles. Finally, Stoics emphasized that there was an important difference between the concept of emotion and that of self-reflection. Specifically, emotions were clouded perceptions of reality which could be distracting from the truth, whereas self-reflection and self-control were far more facilitative of such a quest, an early example of operationalization despite its focus on internal processes. The Stoic approach, in many ways, can be seen as quite similar to the later conceptions of behaviorists, specifically in the area of distrust of emotions.[8]

After Hippocrates' time came the three most noted Greek philosophers whose canons of work could be attributed to influencing almost every facet of contemporary Western thought, from theology to physics and everything in between. Socrates (470–399 B.C.E.), is perhaps the most widely noted philosopher, and is often regarded as the "father of modern philosophy." To summarize Socrates' philosophy and influence in a mere paragraph or even a few pages is an impossible and even dishonorable task and, as such, will not be attempted. However, the method that Socrates developed (or at least popularized and systematized) is among his most important contributions to the general development of any field involving inquiry into any aspect of the human experience, be it physical, mental, or otherwise. Known most commonly as the "inductive method" (and by some as the "Socratic method"), Socrates purported that the most valuable and essential means by which to engage in the pursuit of a truth is by starting with a basic concept and, through intense questioning and dialogue, work toward a specific and universal definition of that concept. The universal definition devised can ultimately be seen as the "essence" of the concept, or what constitutes *all* that makes up such a concept. By seeking and attaining knowledge, Socrates thought, one will be led, necessarily, to morality.[9]

Plato, Socrates' student, was instrumental in the preservation and transmission of his teachings through a primarily oral means. Plato himself was, in his own right, a foundational figure in the development of modern systematic inquiry. While Plato's early efforts focused almost entirely on recording and promoting the ideas of Socrates, he eventually founded his own school within which he began to develop and teach his own philosophies, some of which differed from those of Socrates. While again risking an oversimplification, Plato's main philosophy purported that beliefs, in and of themselves, do not constitute knowledge or truth (as he demonstrated with his well-known and powerful parable of the *Allegory of the Cave*), but rather there is a difference between what is truth and what is perceived *as* truth. More specifically, sensory experiences, those physical interpretations upon which humans often rely most, can be misleading. As such, Plato believed that all knowledge is innate, and can be learned only through a process of deep introspection, or what came to be called the "reminiscence theory of knowledge." This idea would become essential to the later Determinists such as Descartes, who would echo it closely while developing it immensely. [10]

Aristotle (384–322 B.C.E.), who was a main pupil of Plato, eventually founded what would be regarded as the world's first university. Known as the *Lyceum*, it was an institution possessive of several teachers, students, and a considerably well-stocked library, especially given the time's strong focus on oral transmission of ideas. Aristotle's philosophical prowess is almost inconceivable, as his writings and work cover a massive breadth and depth of topics including memory, sensation and perception, dreams, and learning. For the purpose of this inquiry, however, it must suffice to say that Aristotle can be seen as the Greek philosopher whose work had the most direct influence on the field of Western psychology and especially education. In Aristotle's day most systems of education were deeply connected to war or, at the very least, a function of nationalism and militarism as demonstrated by the fact that schooling was provided primarily to young men undergoing military training for the purpose of national defense and patriotic preservation. The only other form of formal training outside of militaristic training was for athletics, and was available only to those families of means who could afford such services. Athens eventually adopted a more formal system of democratic institutions known as "letter schools," in which reading, writing, and math were also taught, most commonly utilizing the methodology of group lessons; but these, too, were also reserved for those families of means who could afford to send their children to these institutions. These social changes, however, were of significant importance to Aristotle, who took a direct interest in the role that education plays in society. As he wrote, "[n]o one will doubt that the legislator should direct his attention above all to the education of the young."[11] More so, Aristotle believed that the educational system should be an entity that is publicly supervised, and function directly out of "politics," contextually meaning the direct benefit of the *polis*, or city. According to Aristotle, ". . . it is [politics] that ordains which of the sciences should be studied in a polis, and which each class of citizens should learn and up to what point they should learn them."[12] Therefore, to Aristotle education was a public entity which was obligated to serve a deeply important public function. However, all levels and aspects of education were not provided to all citizens, relegating one class as an educated class and another as an uneducated class. To Aristotle, however, this separation of classes was not to be determined based on financial or aristocratic means, but rather on natural proclivity for learning (that is, an "intelligent" educated class and an "unintelligent" uneducated class).

As social development proceeded perceptions and means of explaining and investigating human behavior changed in a variety of ways, especially after the influence and interpretations of the teachings attributed to Jesus Christ and the eventual establishment of Christianity both as religion, philosophical and social conceptualization, and an institution in the context of the Church. Theological influences, in multiple ways, returned the thought processes and postulations of many philosophers to those of supernatural (or divine) influence on the human condition, a trend that would be so deeply socially engrained and so philosophically important that it would penetrate the most prolific philosophers and philosophies to one degree or another. It also, in certain respects, served to cohesively connect foundationally different perspectives such as those of the Judeo-Christian theological philosophies and that of the Greeks'. One of the most influential early theological philosophers whose work became widely known was St. Augustine (354–430 C.E.), who concentrated his voluminous philosophical output on the connection between human spirituality and society. According to St. Augustine, there was little that needed to be known about the physical world as it was all created by God. Therefore, the truly important matters lie in the mind, the spirit, and the soul. For humans, the progression was linear, beginning with body's awareness to sense perception toward the internal knowledge of forms, or what were referred to as universal ideas and, ultimately, to the awareness and belief in God.[13] A consistent theme in St. Augustine's philosophy was the separation between God and man, functioning almost as a persistent reminder to people that they were not God. One such example that St. Augustine used to solidify this separation was humans' dependency on the concept of time as essential in understanding the world, whereas God is timeless, lacking the need for time or any other such relational concept. Because humans were so dependent on such relational concepts, this alone (though there were other examples), was proof enough that they were not God, and God was, indeed, superior. Finally, St. Augustine made a significant contribution in the area of duality, specifically, that there are mechanisms of the physical world, such as sight, sound, and other sensory experiences, and there are mechanisms of the metaphysical world, such as time, space, and, in some cases, emotion.

St. Thomas Aquinas (1225–1274), perhaps the only other Christian philosopher credited with a distinct influence on Western philosophy beyond theology, lived and wrote at a time during which the works of Aristotle were translated into Latin and published more widely, which resulted in the reopening of questions involving the relationship between faith and reason and, essentially, the foundation upon which many societies, including that of St. Thomas Aquinas', had been built. St. Thomas Aquinas was a traditionally educated man, having attended university at Montecassino and later at the University of Naples, where he met other members of the newly forming Dominican order of Catholicism. What makes St. Thomas Aquinas particularly interesting as both a theologian and a philosopher is that he appears to make a concerted effort to frame his ideas from the standpoint of both theological and philosophical perspectives. That is, he does not necessarily control for one or the other, or present different arguments or handle different topics depending on which vantage he is presently engaging. Rather, he seeks to reconcile both in a way that is satisfactory. However, he does appear to genuinely understand the difficulty of such an endeavor, and the resistance that many who read him may display in their quest to be either one or the other. As he states:

> The believer and the philosopher consider creatures differently. The philosopher considers what belongs to their proper natures, while the believer considers only what is true of creatures insofar as they are related to God, for example, that they are created by God and are subject to him, and the like.[14]

However, it becomes St. Thomas Aquinas' strength, albeit a complicated one, that is to be able to handle the delicate questions of both theology and philosophy as a single discipline. He does so, in some respects, by regarding both as a form of science. He does not in any way strip theology of the centricity of God or intellectualize unnecessarily by doing so. Rather, what he aims to do is present and facilitate a means of discussing both from a systematic point of view, one that retains all necessary tenets of each, but allows for a universally available discussion. Essentially, he draws similarity between the modes of thinking, distinguishing between their "grounding" and what is regarded as their subject matter as opposed to mutually exclusive disciplines. As he further states:

> Thus it is that divine science or theology is of two kinds, one in which divine things are considered not as the subject of the science but as principles of the subject and this is the theology that the philosophers pursue, also called metaphysics. The other considers divine things in themselves as the subject of the science, and this is the theology which is treated in Sacred Scripture. They are

both concerned with things which exist separately from matter and motion, but differently, insofar as they are two ways in which something can exist separately from matter and motion: first, such that it is of the definition of the things said to be separate, that they can never exist in matter in motion, as God and the angels are said to be separate from matter and motion; second, such that it is not part of their definition that they exist in matter and motion, because they can exist apart from matter and motion, although sometimes they are found in matter and motion, for example, substance, potency and act are separate from matter and motion because they do not require matter in order to exist as mathematicals do, although they can be understood without sensible matter. Philosophical theology treats of things separate in the second way as its subject and of things separate in the first way as the principles of its subject. But the theology of Sacred Scripture treats of things separate in the first way as its subject, although in it some things which exist in matter and motion are considered insofar as they are needed to make the divine manifest.[15]

St. Thomas Aquinas also respects and embraces the idea that different ways of questioning will, in themselves, provide different ways of knowing. That is, there are many different ways to know God, many different ways to seek truth, and many different ways to grapple with philosophical problems, and the mode of investigating such ways will not necessarily bear different ultimate truths, but will create different means of knowing the same truth from different perspectives and under different types of language, thought, and conception. As he states:

> It should be noted that different ways of knowing (*ratio cognoscibilis*) give us different sciences. The astronomer and the natural philosopher both conclude that the earth is round, but the astronomer does this through a mathematical middle that is abstracted from matter, whereas the natural philosopher considers a middle lodged in matter. Thus there is nothing to prevent another science from treating in the light of divine revelation what the philosophical disciplines treat as knowable in the light of human reason.[16]

As such, the method of investigation or even analysis does not change the nature of truth and, even further, it is possible to attain the same level of truth regardless of specific beliefs, as truth is truth regardless of the perspective of the investigator. Therefore, it appears that for St. Thomas Aquinas, the ontology of the matter is far more important, if not independent, of the epistemology and the methodology. This notion becomes very important in the later attempt at organizing different modes of science as having different purposes, and different modes of science being more or less applicable in the field of education. Ascribing to Aquinas' view, there is not likely to be a more or less supreme science, as all sciences are progressing toward the same unchangeable truth in different terms and by different means. St. Thomas Aquinas believes that philosophy and the act of philosophizing depends upon prior knowledge which, in itself, will differ in quantity, quality, and perspective, depending on the background through which such knowledge was attained. As such, St. Thomas Aquinas warns both the believer and the philosopher in the same way to not accept bad proofs and unlikely explanations based solely on their congruence with their orientation. That is, genuine seekers of truth are to hold all explanations up to the same rigorous skepticism before they are accepted from any vantage. To St. Thomas Aquinas, the quickness with which explanations are accepted is likely more explanatory of why there are such discrepancies between philosophers and theologians and, *ipso facto*, theology and philosophy, as one's background and biases are more influential than that which a path to truth will actually provide.

The Western Philosophers

A major philosophical paradigm shift came underway at the turn of the 16th and 17th centuries, with no better example than the observations and reports of Galileo Galilei, who was in the process of developing a novel and vastly controversial system of physics. This new system sought to understand the physical world in a formalized and mathematical fashion; a conception that was seen as distinctly heretical to the predominating Christian views of the previous several centuries. According to this new mode of physics, key concepts of the universe such as movement and change could be understood by applying mathematical formulas. Most significantly, Galileo sought to proffer an alternative system to that suggested by Aristotle, which was still the dominating theory of the natural sciences during the time, creating what was called by some the "new sciences" and to many scholars later on, the scientific revolution. What made Galileo's perspective so objectionable to the Church, however, was the increasingly formalized notion that the Sun, rather than the Earth, was the center of the universe. Though this theory had been offered earlier by Copernicus, it was demonstrated far more convincingly by Galileo's methods of systematic observation aided by advanced technology such as the telescope, which could observe the solar system to distances as far as Jupiter. This revelation was seen as heretical to the message of the Bible and God's teachings, causing some to question the legitimacy of the "dominion of man," a creature of a non-central planet. Acquiescing to the vast political pressure of the Catholic Church, Galileo publicly refuted his own claims, though few believe that he, indeed, truly intended to rescind his ideas but rather sought only to comply with orders under duress. According to Galileo himself:

> I have been judged vehemently suspect of heresy, that is, of having held and believed that the sun is the center of the universe and immovable, and that the earth is not at the center of same, and that it does move. Wishing, however, to remove from the minds of your Eminences and all faithful Christians this

vehement suspicious reasonably conceived against me, I abjure with a sincere heart and unfeigned faith, I curse and detest the said errors and heresies, and generally all and every error, heresy, and sect contrary to the Catholic church.[17]

The controversy surrounding Galileo's ideas as well as his subsequent rescinding of his views influenced the development of science both in practice and philosophy for centuries to come and, in many ways does still. By raising some of the most important questions that scientists of various paradigmatic perspectives and fields still disagree about and conceive of differently, such as what the nature of truth really is and by what means truth can be known or demonstrated, Galileo truly did revolutionize not only the study of science, but also the practice of scientific inquiry.

Around the same time Rene Descartes (1596–1650) began to publicize his contextually unusual but influential philosophy. Descartes, like St. Thomas Aquinas, emphasized a dichotomy between the mind and the body, but he expanded this idea by suggesting that despite being separate, there is a reciprocal relationship between the body and the mind, such that the body can affect the mind and the mind can affect the body. Furthermore, Descartes suggested that the mind and body, though connected, are each governed by entirely different sources, with the body being governed by "mechanistic laws" while the mind is governed by reason.[18] What made Descartes' philosophy somewhat unusual was that it was dependent both on mathematical explanation as well as theological explanation; in a sense, an attempt to unite the two prevailing but distinctly different explanations of the workings of the universe at the time.[19]

Descartes' first and, arguably, most famous work, at least foundationally, came in the form of the *First and Second Meditations*, in which he universally questions how one can truly be certain of anything at all. Specifically, Descartes expressed skepticism of humans' tendency to rely entirely on sensory experiences in attempts to truly "know." According to Descartes, this reliance results in a misinterpretation of the process of understanding, in that sensory experiences are actually mental, not physical processes, as they often appear and are thought to be at the time (a notion that, with even basic neuroscience, is shown to be true).[20] Ultimately, Descartes' famous saying *cogito ergo sum*, or "I think, therefore I am" (translated in a number of different ways) comes to be the most apt summary of his philosophy. Descartes' definitive example comes in the form of the Wax Argument. As Descartes states:

[T]he wax itself never really was the sweetness of the honey, nor the fragrance of the flowers, nor the whiteness, nor the shape, nor the sound, but instead was a body that a short time ago manifested itself to me in these ways, and now does so in other ways. But just what precisely is this thing that I thus imagine?

Let us focus our attention on this and see what remains after we have removed everything that does not belong to the wax: only that it is something extended, flexible, and mutable.[21]

Basically, what Descartes attempts to represent is that though there is a clear physical difference between solid wax (which is white, solid, cold, etc.) and melted wax (which is clear, liquid, hot, etc.) one knows that it is, indeed, the same substance regardless of their direct opposite states of appearance, just differing in physical form. Had one relied on sensory experiences alone, then one would have determined that the two substances were, indeed, different. Knowing, cognitively, that they are the same is possible only by using cognitive perception beyond sensory faculties. Therefore, Descartes contends clearly that what distinguishes humans' ability to perceive the world and truly "exist" is the ability to rely not on senses for understanding but, rather on cognition and perception.

John Locke (1632–1704) offered one of the next major paradigmatic arguments in the quest for understanding the human condition in a school of philosophy most often termed as *empiricism*. According to Locke, humans were not born with any innate understanding and the human mind and capacity was, essentially, a "blank slate," or *tabula rasa*. As such, knowledge is acquired through two distinct forms of experience: sensation, or the processes of understanding the external world, and reflection, or the process of understanding one's own mind, leading to consciousness of such aspects of the mind as thought and emotion. Ultimately, it is the purpose of the senses to observe and perceive simple stimuli through sensation, a passive process, while the mind combines those stimuli into more complex ideas through reflection, a more active process. As such, Locke's philosophy ultimately contends that there is nothing that exists in the intellect that was not, at some point, initially present in the senses. Therefore, the existence of complex thought is built upon the combination of several simplistic sensory perceptions. This idea has significant ramifications for understanding aspects of the human mind, especially in the way of the existence of potentially innate principles such as morality, ethicality, belief, and even God. As Locke states, "the truest and best notions men have of God were not innately imprinted, but acquired by thought and meditation and a right use of their faculties."[22]

What Descartes and Locke, in particular, added to and exemplify in the context of the discussion was a likely precursor for what the established field of psychology would later experience in the 20th and 21st centuries: the question between nature, or the centrality of the mind and its predispositions, as is often explored through cognitive realms of psychology, and nurture, or the importance of the environment and, specifically, the consequences of the environment.

Later in the 18th century the groundwork for the eventual advent of social psychology was laid by the discovery and subsequent writings involving the "Wild Child of Aveyron" (also known as Victor of Aveyron), a feral child who emerged from the woods into Aveyron, a small town in France. While it is apparent that he was received well by the townspeople, he was soon taken in by scientists for study and documentation. Interestingly, this situation took place at a time in social development during which there appeared to be an increasing interest in what was known as the "new science of human nature" concerned with looking for the "laws" that governed it.[23] Around the same time Louis-Françoise Jaufferet established what became known as the *Societe des Observateurs d l'Hommes* (Society of the Observers of Man), an early example of a professional philosophical organization that attracted a variety of distinguished French intellectuals from a large cross-section of fields including linguistics, history, exploration, and philosophy, among others. Adopting a motto of "know thyself," the main goal of the *Society of the Observers of Man* was to attempt to establish a body of empirical studies (those based on systematic observation and data collection) that investigated various questions concerning the human experience such as the relationship between animal and human nature, differences in humans based on ethnic and regional origins, and what became known as *physiognomy*, a now defunct and discredited but nonetheless contributive method of inquiry that made diagnostic posits based on facial features.[24] Many scientists, however, opposed such a practice for its apparent lack of validity, leading to a growing skepticism of what become known as "popular science" by intellectuals, an interestingly portentous example of what appears to be happening with behaviorism currently (e.g., "pop psychology").

The field of psychology as a bona fide area of academe, however, is thought to have been established by Wilhelm Wundt in 1879, who is credited with having created the first laboratory for psychological research at the University of Leipzig in Germany. According to Wundt, only the immediate experience, that is, something that is mutually exclusive from prior knowledge or previous experience was directly observable and available for systematic study. As a result, Wundt's work concentrated almost entirely on human perception, specifically, what he called "internal perception," or focusing on the experience of the sensation itself, not the *interpretation* of the sensation. Wundt posited what he referred to as the "table metaphor," in that a perception influenced by past experience, known as a mediate, would be described as the formal understanding of the object (e.g., a table), while the immediate experience would not (e.g., a flat plane with four cylindrical supports). As such, if one is viewing such a "flat plane" as a table they are clearly interpreting the experience, making it difficult, if at all possible, to study it systematically and thus, empirically. Wundt's perspective soon came to be known as *structuralism*, in that it espoused the notion of looking to investigate phenomena at the most basic and primitive of its states: its essential structure. Proposing that psychology, as a study of the mind, was simply an extension of natural science, Wundt believed it could be studied using the same modalities used by other natural sciences. Specifically, Wundt believed that the process of introspection should not be defined as an "armchair" process of simply thinking about oneself and one's feelings, but rather a psychological exercise that can be controlled, manipulated, measured, and systematically studied in a laboratory setting.

This newly established field would come to make a distinct difference in America shortly after its establishment by Wundt, marked especially by Edward Titchener's arrival at Cornell University and the increasing dissemination of the ideas of William James of Harvard University. Titchener was the main pupil of Wilhelm Wundt who, at first, followed his ideas quite stringently until he began to develop his own, which he also called *structuralism*. Titchener, like Wundt, believed that introspection was the only valid means by which to study the workings of the mind, but believed more specifically that only specially trained "introspectors" were qualified to do so. According to Titchener's methodology of introspection, structuralist researchers (who were, themselves, the introspectors as well) were only to report their inner states with specific regard to sensations, images, and affect. Through this process, Titchener believed that psychologists could discover the elemental structure of consciousness itself, hence, *structuralism*.

Titchener broke with some of the other emerging psychologists on two main tenets. First, because Titchener held that the purpose of the study of psychology was to investigate human consciousness in particular, he blatantly rejected any forms of psychology and experimentation that were conducted using animals, as many of the earlier forms of what was to become behaviorism would be (e.g., Thorndike and Skinner). Instead, Titchener valued only those forms of investigation that dealt with the human condition and experience directly. Second, Titchener was interested in what consciousness *was,* as opposed to what consciousness *was for*, as many of his contemporaries were, likely as a result of the call for the utility of science as opposed to seeking merely theoretical discoveries. Titchener did not believe, as many of his contemporaries did, that psychology had to have a distinctly social purpose but could be a mode of scientific discovery in and of itself, an early example of the distinction between basic and applied research. As structuralism is itself defined, the purpose of such study is to analyze the structure and elementary processes of the mind and consciousness and to isolate them in order to determine their formation.

Despite his focus on the human condition, however, Titchener was staunchly positivist in that he focused entirely on what he believed were observable experiences, at least as they were "structurally defined" and reported by the introspectors. This process was not to explain or identify causality, but rather to provide empirically sound descriptions of the human experience for the sake of understanding itself.

William James, a contemporary of Titchener, characterized both the purpose of psychology and the human condition quite differently. James, regarded in many cases as the propagator, if not the founder of the school of thought known as *pragmatism*, was intently focused on the utility of psychology as well as many other forms of human thought processes. According to James:

> The pragmatic method is primarily a method of settling metaphysical disputes that otherwise might be interminable. Is the world one or many?—fated or free?—material or spiritual?—here are notions either of which may or may not hold good of the world; and disputes over such notions are unending. The pragmatic method in such cases is to try to interpret each notion by tracing its respective practical consequences.[25]

Therefore, the purpose of such data gathered from the study of psychology according to James was opposite to that of Titchener. James cites C.S. Peirce as the primary originator of these ideas that would soon be regarded as pragmatism. According to Peirce:

> From all these sophisms we shall be perfectly safe so long as we re-ect that the whole function of thought is to produce habits of action; and that whatever there is connected with a thought, but irrelevant to its purpose, is an accretion to it, but no part of it. If there be a unity among our sensations which has no reference to how we shall act on a given occasion, as when we listen to a piece of music, why we do not call that thinking. To develop its meaning, we have, therefore, simply to determine what habits it produces, for what a thing means is simply what habits it involves. Now, the identity of a habit depends on how it might lead us to act, not merely under such circumstances as are likely to arise, but under such as might possibly occur, no matter how improbably they may be. What the habit is depends on when and how it causes us to act. As for the when, every stimulus to action is derived from perception; as for the how, every purpose of action is to produce some sensible result. Thus, we come down to what is tangible and practical, as the root of every real distinction of thought, no matter how subtle it may be; and there is no distinction of meaning so one as to consist in anything but a possible difference of practice.[26]

James ultimately situates pragmatism within the greater auspice of empiricism, but in a way that he believes to be more applicable to the social sciences in particular. As James explains:

> A pragmatist turns his back resolutely and once and for all upon a lot of inveterate habits dear to professional philosophers. He turns away from abstraction and insufficiency, from verbal solutions, from bad a priori reasons, from fixed principles, closed systems, and pretended absolutes and origins. He

turns toward concreteness and adequacy, towards facts, towards action, and towards power. That means the empiricist temper regnant, and the rationalist temper sincerely given up. It means the open air and possibilities of nature, as against dogma, artificiality and the pretence of finality in truth. [27]

James clearly supported the tenets of what would become an applied behaviorist approach, specifically, conditions and behaviors which were observable and measurable and clearly served a social purpose as being central to the study and application of psychology. Rooting even more deeply in Peirce, James steered the nascent field toward what would eventually become a widespread preoccupation with operationalization, leading to many future iterations and definitions.

THE BIRTH OF BEHAVIORISM

As aforementioned, determining the beginning of any historical occurrence is challenging, as separating the actual formation of the area of interest itself from its precursors and catalysts almost invariably results in debatable conclusions. The challenge is no different in attempting to determine the history of psychology and behaviorism's place within it. The impetus, if not purpose of any new paradigm of thought is a perceived need for improvement resulting from a gap in explanation by the current dominant approach. According to John A. Mills the formation of behaviorism was no different and, as such, was born out of four basic needs. First, there was a need for a practical application to the advances in the scientific field of psychology, as James earlier indicated. Second, there was a largely unacknowledged need in psychology for philosophical and scientific respectability. Third, there was a need to generate a specifically "behavioral" (or behavioristic) body of literature to contribute to this general philosophical and scientific validation. Finally, there was a need to provide an empirical basis for animal studies and its potential application to humans, the ultimate area of research that is most closely connected to the development of behavioral psychology. [28] Ultimately, there was a growing belief, largely attributed to the Progressives, that social science, a term growing in popularity and applicability, should somehow serve the greater social good. In this case "good" was defined most commonly as material comforts and economic success, as it is often conceptualized in capitalistic societies such as that of America. [29] The early proponents of behaviorism also offered an idea that was, at the time, largely unheard of. That is, that it is practice that should inform theory, not vice versa. In other words, it was what people were already doing that should serve as the data that inform the theories, and that the social application and practicality would serve as the ultimate test of that theory. In many ways, this was an apt extension of American society's preoccupation with pragmatism at the time, especially in the social realms and, in many ways, as a social response to a developing societal meritocracy as opposed to a lingering aristocracy.[30] Around this time a small circle of intellectuals that came to be referred to as "The New Realists" who insisted that scientific investigation was predicated on the idea that observations made and used in scientific investigations need to be verifiable in order to be acceptable, began to express thoughts that could be seen as being in accordance with what become known as behaviorism. Other influential thinkers such as Edward Cary Hayes and Luther Lee Bernard published some theories in the early 1900s that were quite comparable to Watson's later behavioral ideas.[31] Ultimately, around the turn of the century, much of what would later be characterized as methodologically psychological research was being investigated in a distinctly "problem-driven" manner as opposed to a "theory-driven" manner, an important setting for a paradigm such as behaviorism to flourish. According to Wesley Clair Mitchell:

> Psychology is moving rapidly toward an objective conception and a quantitative treatment of their problems. Their emphasis upon stimulus and response sequences, upon conditioned reflexes; their eager efforts to develop performance tests, their attempts to build up a technique of an experiment, favor the spread of the conception that all of the social sciences have a common aim—the understanding of human behavior; a common method—the quantitative analysis of behavior records, and a common aspiration to devise ways of experimenting upon behavior.[32]

The concept of behaviorism, then, became a valiant force in many areas of social science, including economics, sociology, history, public policy, and political science. This trend is made quite obvious by Floyd Allport, who contends:

> [G]overnment itself is behavior. Conceived as a structure, or an institution, it is behavior of a different sort from those more obvious and spectacular processes . . . it consists of deeper, more stable, and more generalized attitudes. But it is, nonetheless, behavior.[33]

Max Meyer was largely responsible for the growing public awareness of behavioral psychology, however, by the publication of his influential manifesto *The Psychology of the Other One* (1921),[34] in which Meyer extended the notion of behaviorism to language, an idea that was to be recapitulated far more successfully by B.F. Skinner in his work *Verbal Behavior* (1957). In this work Meyer insisted that psychology and psychological investigations deal only with behaviors that were both overtly observable and of relevant social interest and function.

In any case, the stage was clearly set for a successful infusion of behavioral theory into the nascent though quickly developing field of psychology, and there were a handful of truly key contributors to this development. As Morris states:

> Behavior analysis can be understood not only in terms of its internal practices, and the external contrasts those practices make with psychology as a whole, but also in terms of how those practices and contrasts developed historically. Just as the behavior of an organism is a function of its history . . . so too is the activity of a scientific discipline a function of its scientists. . . . Not only does the study of the history of a science seem inevitably to clarify its philosophy, but such study also contributes to the further development of that philosophy.[35]

The Behaviorists: Pavlov, Thorndike, Watson, and Skinner

There are some clearly important players whose work created not only the foundation but the research basis for the establishment of the field of behaviorism, among the most foundational being Ivan Pavlov, Edward L. Thorndike, John B. Watson, and B.F. Skinner (though there are most certainly numerous other researchers who played important contributive roles as well). All of these men conducted research and proffered writings which would not only shape but ultimately define what would become the clearly distinct and contributive field of behaviorism and, eventually, behavior analysis. While many of the preceding scientists contributed theories and set foundations for later work, it was these theorists and researchers whose work solidified the behavioral field as one regarded as a bona fide means of systematic inquiry.

Perhaps the most significant event in the formation of behaviorism occurred when a physiologist who was not only disinterested in behaviorism, but disinterested in human behavior altogether, Ivan Pavlov, a Russian natural scientist turned physician, observed behavioral responses quite accidentally. Initially, Pavlov and his colleagues were attempting to conduct research on the properties of digestion as they connected to saliva, using canines as their main subjects. Curiously, however, in the midst of the process Pavlov began to notice that the dogs would begin salivating even in the absence of edible items. Over time, Pavlov observed that the salivation activity was not necessarily due only to an autonomic process, but was influenced by seemingly unrelated environmental factors as well. As such, Pavlov termed the phenomenon a "learned response," concluding that the initial non-edible stimulus for salivation was his research assistants' white lab coats (or, perhaps, their mere presence or their smell, ideas that were not entertained in the ultimate research but equally as potentially explicable). Regardless of identifying the environmental source the dogs were clearly salivating in the absence of food. Through increased experimentation with other non-edible items and entirely unrelated stimuli such as metronomes and bells, Pavlov concluded that dogs could learn to engage in a biological action in response to a nonbiological or even merely contextually related stimulus. Thus, the concept of classical conditioning was proffered.[36]

Through this research Pavlov became a significant contributor to not only the theoretical foundation of behaviorism, but also to the philosophy of science and systematic investigation. Pavlov came to believe that positivism, or attention only to what is directly observable, was the most logical and effective way to engage in scientific investigation as opposed to theories, which left far too much room for philosophical explanation in the absence of facts. Essentially, Pavlov became a proponent for the idea that psychological constructs are most effectively and accurately studied in terms of their relation to physiological responses. This idea became foundational to his concept of the *cortical mosaic*, or the notion that there is a biological system that is responsible for determining how an organism responds to its environment, solidifying the essential connection between environment and behavior.[37]

Edward L. (E.L.) Thorndike was responsible for extending Pavlov's theories specifically in the realm of animal learning by directly investigating the specific roles that consequences play in the acquisition of various behaviors and skills. Initially, Thorndike was most interested in investigating the notion of whether animals show evidence of reasoning in order to solve problems, as humans appeared to do. Devising the now well-known "puzzle box," Thorndike placed cats in locked crates with passages that were opened only by sequentially manipulating a series of strings, levers, and latches in the correct order which, when done so, would open the latch, allowing the cat to escape and access a small bit of food. Based on the series of experiments, Thorndike concluded that though the cats became more fluent in opening these latches with repeated exposure, he claimed to have not observed any direct evidence of reason or insight. Rather, the cats were successful based on a random series of behaviors which eventually, based solely on probability, opened the latch. Thorndike did concede, however, that the cats becoming more adept at unlatching the box doors through repetition did evidence that learning was possible without insight, a key concept in the later application of behavior analysis to human learning, especially as applied to individuals with intellectual and developmental exceptionalities for whom naturally or socially occurring insight may be distinctly limited.[38]

In an attempt to formalize his findings, Thorndike offered the label of *associationism* to his proposed paradigm, and proffered its two foundational laws. First, the *law of association* was postulated as the concept that learning was (or at least could be) achieved by associating certain responses with certain consequences, regardless of the learner or whether the learner has the capability of employing insight or reasoning to the task. Second, the *law of effect* stated that as behaviors became consistently followed by a more satisfying state of affairs they would be strengthened, making them more likely to occur again in the future by the same organism (conversely, those followed by an undesirable state of affairs would be weakened, making engagement in them less likely).

Around the same time as awareness of Thorndike's research grew, John B. Watson became a distinct force within the field of social sciences as a whole, but especially in the context of psychology. Known for his bold statements and even bolder experiments, Watson would almost single-handedly change the course of the systematic inquiry into human behavior, claiming that behaviorism, the name he would ultimately give to the field in a 1913 paper, would act as a ". . . fresh, clean start."[39] Watson's main claim was that all data previously represented in psychology, namely those pro-cured in the context of the developmental or psychoanalytic fields, were entirely false. Watson's behaviorism is described by many as radical (though quite a few writers challenge the characterization), seemingly because it unequivocally rejects the study of mental processes altogether. Given the time frame in which Watson proffered his ideas (in many ways at the height of American nationalism in response to an ever-increasing influx of immi-grants and growing fascination with individualism and "results-based" capi-talistic success), Watson's theory came to be known as a patently "American" psychology as it was pragmatic, fact-based, outcome-oriented, and professional.[40] Within only a few decades, the term "behavioral psychol-ogy" seemed to be interchangeable with, if not entirely replacing, the term "experimental psychology." As such, Watson promulgated clearly that psychological investigations must deal only with information gathered di-rectly from observation and produce results that were applicable to human behavior and social organization.[41] Put clearly by Watson, "psychology's theoretical goal is the prediction and control of behavior."[42] Therefore, psychological investigation must be predicated on demonstrating behavioral phenomena, not just observing it, leading to behavioral synthesis, or the notion that simple behaviors combine to form seemingly more complex be-haviors, concepts that came to later be termed as shaping and chaining, both instrumental in the application of behavior analytic intervention.

Perhaps the most crucial player in the eventual clinical application of behaviorism was B.F. Skinner, to whom the field, at least in its contemporary context, is attributed to almost entirely. Though Skinner spent much of his undergraduate career at Hamilton College and some of his post-collegiate career interested in literature and, specifically, creative writing, he found little success in this endeavor and became more interested in the fields of philosophy and, ultimately, psychology, after reading Bertrand Russell's book *Philosophy*.[43] Upon entering Harvard as a graduate student he was also exposed to the works of Pavlov and Watson, adding significantly to his interest in behavioral psychology specifically. Most significantly, perhaps, was Skinner's reading of Francis Bacon, whose work challenged the authorities in the field of philosophy for unabashedly appealing to Plato and Aristotle as philosophical bases, if not muses. Skinner likened Bacon's criticism of philosophy to that of Watson's criticism of psychology: that it was rife with discussion but devoid of evidence. According to O'Donohue and Ferguson, Skinner was significantly influenced by Bacon in the following ways: (1) Skinner emphasized empirical observation and experimentation as the ideal way to gain knowledge; (2) Skinner regarded the scientific method as the ideal way to gain knowledge; (3) Skinner believed that science should create technologies that could truly help people; (4) Skinner preferred to read books of "nature" rather than literature (contrarily to his younger years) so as to not be influenced by people and their thoughts but, rather, the irrefutable laws of the world; and (5) Skinner questioned deeply the notions of "idols" and "authority."[44]

But what ultimately made Skinner the "new" face of behaviorism when the field seemed to be indelibly credited to Watson? That is, what was Skinnerian behaviorism, also known as radical behaviorism, as opposed to Watsonian behaviorism? According to Herrnstein:

> [Skinnerian behaviorism was a] movement dedicated to the study of behavior, to environmentalism as opposed to nativism, and to a primacy of the law of effect in guiding the behavior of organisms, especially human beings. It is a movement whose controversiality has grown along with its influence.[45]

Ultimately, Skinner proposed that the entirety of behavioral plasticity is explained through operant and respondent conditioning processes alone. Furthermore, there was a vast difference between the way in which Watson and Skinner viewed "private" events. Watson distinguished between the "treatable" public events and "untreatable" private events, indicating his belief that though private events do indubitably occur, it is not possible to address them in a behavioral paradigm. Skinner took deep opposition to this notion, referring to this idea as "methodological behaviorism." Contrarily, Skinner chose the term "radical" to describe his form of behaviorism to indicate that private events such as thinking and feeling were not only nonexistent, but were merely "grammatical" verbal constructs that were entirely deniable.[46]

HISTORICAL DISSENTS WITH BEHAVIORISM

As is the case in any field of thought, be it physical science or social science, the seemingly popular or general acceptance of it is, in no way, an indication that the tenets of that field are to be deemed correct or validated by the greater professional field. While widespread acceptance may be used as a cultural indication of progression of a field, especially in an area of social science that can garner public support in its application to fields such as mental health or education, this does not necessarily indicate its scientific or clinical comprehensiveness. There are always qualified and informed members of a field who dissent with good reason with the prevailing opinions regardless of how widespread and popularly accepted they may be (this is as true currently as it has ever been historically). As James admonishes despite being a staunch pragmatist:

> If you follow the pragmatic method, you cannot look on any such word as closing your quest. You must bring out of each word its practical cash-value, set it at work with the stream of your experience. It appears less as a solution, then, than as a program for more work, and more particularly as an indication of the way in which existing realities may be CHANGED. THEORIES MUST BECOME INSTRUMENTS, NOT ANSWERS TO ENIGMAS, IN WHICH WE CAN REST [caps in original]. We don't lie back upon them, we move forward, and, on occasion, make nature over again by their aid.[47]

According to Uttal, there has been a distinct transformation that is ever-present in the field of psychology from one that was almost entirely behavioral (at least in terms of widespread acceptance of validity) to one that is, at least simultaneously, cognitive. The questions began to change from focusing on whether the mind existed, a question deemed far too philosophical and impossible to demonstrate behaviorally, to what the workings and the processes of the mind were, and whether or not they were accessible or amenable to systematic study without reducing the processes to only their outcomes or components, such as behaviorism appeared to do. According to Uttal:

> Behaviorists generally argue that all responses (or behaviors) are measures of the totality of the experience or awareness of the behaving organism and are the resultant of a combination of many different stimulus, organism, and response variables as well as the past experience experience . . . of an individual.[48]

Quite succinctly, radical behaviorists do not believe that behaviors indicate underlying mental processes in any meaningful or analyzable way. Furthermore, behaviorists suggest that when people do report mental states, they are necessarily obscured, if not entirely contaminated by their own personal perspectives and preoccupations yielding entirely unreliable and inutile data. To non-behavioral scientists, however, specifically those who work within the realm of cognitive science or even neuroscience, such elements of the mind can, indeed, be accessed without having to engage in reductionist observations of mere outcomes and components. Further, such outcomes, if they are the only data accessible at a given time, can be used to infer underlying mental states or processes if analyzed within the correct methodology.

While James' endorsement, or at least, re-introduction of pragmatism (as per Peirce) was a powerful precursor to the proliferation of the behavioral perspective, particularly such as the brand espoused by Watson, Titchener's frame of thought remained very much central to the still developing though not nearly as widespread science of the mind, or what would later become the field known by the rather liberal and deleteriously imprecise term "cognitive science." As Titchener emphasized, analysis of introspection, when correctly applied and used, was capable of allowing the inner workings of the mind to become measurable and that actual display of behavior was not the only means of remaining positivistic. To Titchener, the role of language and its ultimate connection, if not demonstration of, the workings of the mind were essential, and needed to remain central to the study of psychology.

William MacDougall represents what may be considered as the first scholarly retort to the growing "movement" of behaviorism as spearheaded by Watson. To MacDougall behaviorism, especially the mode espoused by Watson, is a vast oversimplification. This oversimplification, however, MacDougall claims, is exactly what makes it so appealing to the masses, including other psychologists. As he states:

> Dr. Watson's views are attractive to many persons, and especially to many young persons, by reason of the fact that these views simplify so greatly the problems that lie before the student of psychology: they abolish at one stroke many tough problems with which the greatest intellects have struggled with only very partial success for more than two thousand years; and they do this by the bold and simple expedient of inviting the student to shut his eyes to them, to turn resolutely away from them, and to forget that they exist. [49]

This oversimplification, MacDougall contends, represents the terminal point of behaviorism as a theory. By focusing especially on Watson's notion of the unimportance of thought (what Skinner called "private events" or "experiences within the skin"), MacDougall calls upon experiences of individuals with brain injury as his chief retort. As MacDougall states:

> [Watson claims] . . . all that is called thinking is merely the mechanical play of the speech-organs . . . this view of the thinking-process is rendered untenable by a multitude of familiar facts . . . there are many cases on record of patients rendered aphasic, that is speechless, by injury, not of the peripheral speech-organs, but of the cerebral speech-organs; yet many such patients think very well; they know very well what they want to say, but cannot say it. Some patients can play such a game as chess, even though their cerebral speech-organs are so far destroyed that, as well as finding it impossible to utter coherent speech, they cannot understand written or spoken language. [50]

The tenets of keeping the concept of mind and language central to the purview of psychology remained very much alive in the field, though suppressed in many ways by the ever-growing behaviorist movement, with few scholars being as outspoken as MacDougall in the throes of Watson's greater influence. In 1948, however, there seemed to be forming a more structured and systematized counter-movement to the seemingly virulent fascination with behaviorism as a result of the wide dissemination and popular availability of Watson's work. In 1948 a conference entitled *Cerebral Mechanisms of Behavior* held at the California Institute of Technology catalyzed this counter movement with a counter narrative to the behaviorist ideology. This conference focused primarily on emerging fields that study human behavior and the "mind" as well as new directions in established fields, such as the role of mathematics in "computers" and advances in neuroscience. Karl Lashley, a noted early neuroscientist and major contributor to the understanding of cerebral mechanisms in learning and memory, though at one point very much a behaviorist-harshly criticized the notion of behaviorism in a now famous speech entitled "The Problem of Serial Order in Behavior." In this oration, Lashley offered some early notions for the need of a more cognitively-based science, challenging the central idea of behaviorism that the environment played the most major role in human behavior rather than internal thought processes and cognitive ideation. Lashley's main concern with the effect of the behavioral perspective of psychology and other social sciences was that it appeared to be creating a climate in which scientists could not engage in systematic investigations and discourses involving the mind at all without being ostracized if not overtly silenced. Those who engaged in such investigations would either be forced to keep such conversations and research efforts to themselves or within small and furtive circles, or to cloak such topics in behavioral language so as to gain acceptance and readership for their studies. Overall, a behaviorally imperious environment was created that severely limited the breadth and quality of scholarly discourse that was permitted in a field that was far too young to be so censored. As Lashley states:

> Thus it appears that the current formulations of behaviorism have not made good their claim to exclusive possession of the field of psychology. Methodological behaviorism has all the faults of psychophysical parallelism plus that of intolerance. It admits the existence of certain phenomena called conscious, admits that it can not fit them into its system, and denies to others the right to study those phenomena and to seek to formulate them into a science. [51]

It is important to recognize, however, that Lashley did not eliminate the relevance of a behavioral perspective, but rather re-contextualized it as an outcome of more intricate cerebral processes rather than a learning process in and of itself. Ultimately, it was Lashely's perspective that behaviorism offered far too simplistic of an explanation for complex processes such as learning and language acquisition. Heeding the opportunity to use his show-case at the symposium to re-infuse the importance of the language of cognition into the field, Lashley stated, "[t]he problems raised by the organization of language seem to me to be characteristic of almost all other cerebral activity."[52] This was the proverbial "shot" that was heard around the world of social science, and boldly reintroduced the ever important perspective of the science of the mind. What was equally as jarring to the field was Lashley's explanation for such a trend in the sciences. According to Lashley, many scientists of the time, as well as those who had come before, were equally as conversant and educated in the areas of the humanities (such as philosophy, classics, and literature) as they were in the physical and social sciences, which yielded their ability to engage in thought and experimentation with a broader and more grounded basis. The new scientists, however, especially those functioning under the auspices of behaviorism, were trained almost entirely in the field of psychology itself, and behavioral psychology at that, which eliminated the presence or purpose of any other exposure to areas outside of it. As a result, topics that were quite central in other areas of the humanities and the broader, non-behavioral social sciences, like consciousness and the mind, were deemed irrelevant by the more narrowed perspectives of trade behavioral psychologists.

The events that transpired at the *Cerebral Mechanisms* symposium reignited the ever important mission and focus of the nascent but far less influential field of cognitive science. Though cognitive science, especially as applied to psychology is itself distinctly threatened conceptually by a number of significant weaknesses including poorly devised definitions and challenging circumstances under which evidence for its ideas cannot be convincingly demonstrated within strictly positivistic limitations, the tenets and catalytic philosophies espoused by the field are relevant and important, and deserve to be investigated and applied, especially in terms of its direct responses to behaviorism. According to Gardner, one of the foremost advocates, practitioners, and researchers in the field of cognitive science, it can be defined as ". . . a contemporary, empirically based effort to answer long-standing epistemological questions—particularly those concerned with the nature of knowledge, its components, its sources, its development, and its deployment."[53] Gardner suggests that there are five main features of cognitive science: (1) it is necessary to speak about mental representations and to posit a level of analysis that is wholly separate from that of a biological and/or neurological standpoint on one end of the spectrum, and sociological and cultural on the other; (2) central understanding of the human mind is analogous to that of the computer; (3) the conscious decision to de-emphasize certain aspects that may be important to cognitive functioning but confounding to cognitive science, such as emotions, historical and cultural factors, and the background context within which thoughts occur; (4) much is to be gained from interdisciplinary studies (philosophy, psychology, artificial intelligence, linguistics, anthropology, and neuroscience); (5) the same set of issues that have interested thinkers for centuries (that is, a new way to look at older ideas).[54]

The importance of cognitive science for this treatise lies not as much in its specific theories, but rather in its reframing of behavioral perspectives and its specific objections to the reductionist approach employed by behavioral sciences such as rendering vastly important conceptions such as the mind and emotions utterly useless. Boulding's statement frames it clearly:

> In the case of humans we have a key to opening the black box of our minds in our capacity for reflection and communication. It seems the height of absurdity to dismiss this as "operant control" of "vocal musculature."[55]

While many in the field are still quite quick to dismiss a perspective such as that which is offered by cognitive psychology in favor of one that is more behavioral (in the sense of its focus on observable and measurable outcomes), there are still many opposing voices. Pablo Gomez responds to one such instance in his response to an article by Eileen Pizzurro who, among other things, claims that behaviorism is a theoretical perspective that has certain methodological advantages over other perspectives, yielding its dominance and widespread acceptance legitimate. Gomez contextualizes a number of points that created a scientific environment for this dominance to take hold, however he does not attribute such points to genuine strength in understanding of human behavior, but rather strength in conveying its own message. First, Gomez points out that by focusing only on observable behavior, behaviorists had the ability to operationalize to begin with, and therefore convey in direct language all aspects of their theory, eliminating, or at least minimizing the descriptive ambiguities with which other fields of inquiry struggle. The elimination of descriptive ambiguities, however, was not a genuine elimination of the respective phenomena's nebulous or ambiguous existence, but rather an elimination of the need to describe them, as they were discounted by the theory itself. Secondly, Gomez asserts that behaviorism is not an explanatory theory, but rather a theory that highlights outcomes only. That is, there is less information as to *why* a behavior takes hold, but more so that it does and *what* it looks like. At the time of Watson's initial theorizing, this perspective addressed a particularly "American" means of thinking; one that was unduly fixated on outcome over process (a social scientific form of the "ends justifying the means"). Thirdly, during the time that behavioral psychology was founded and proliferated, there was a limited means of advanced interdisciplinary information from which to borrow or reapply theories. Therefore, as Watson himself declares, a "clean, fresh start" was imposed, one that broke from all precedents and created not only its own language but, eventually, its own means of evaluation and research (as will be discussed in more detail later on). These historical and cultural conditions, rather than scientific strengths, bear a more legitimate explanation of the perceived success of behaviorism.[56]

Additionally, the legitimate strengths of mind-based science can also be touted. First, Gomez cites that cognitive science is as empirically based as behaviorism, but one that concerns itself with ". . . much more interesting and rich phenomena."[57] Additionally, with new sciences such as computer science, artificial intelligence, and neuroscience (strengthened by the ever-advancing capabilities of neuroimaging techniques), cognitive science was able to form its own language to empirically and convincingly address phenomena that were seen before as ambiguities.

Perhaps fewer scholars took such vociferous and fervent issue with Skinner's theories, especially those involving language acquisition and use, than Noam Chomsky, the well-known MIT professor, linguist, and political commentator. Centered prominently on the idea that Skinner's theories were based, at best, in pseudoscience and were vastly influenced by the cultural and nationalistic climate of the United States at the time, Chomsky issued a scathing critique, primarily of Skinner's book *Verbal Behavior*, in 1959, and again toward his general theories in 1971. Regarding the very controversial nature of Skinner's work, Chomsky states:

> The public reception of his work is a matter of some interest. Skinner has been condemned as a proponent of totalitarian thinking and lauded for his advocacy of a tightly managed social environment. He is accused of immorality and praised as a spokesman for science and rationality in human affairs. He appears to be attacking fundamental human values, demanding control in place of the defense of freedom and dignity. There seems something scandalous in this, and since Skinner invokes the authority of science, some critics condemn science itself, or "the scientific view of man," for supporting such conclusions, while others assure us that science will "win out" over mysticism and irrational belief.[58]

Therefore, Chomsky's critiques of Skinner covered not only scientific inadequacies, but also the interplay of scientific influence on society in an industrial and capitalistic culture. As Chomsky states, Skinner's theory is characterized as being ". . . quite vacuous . . . as congenial to the libertarian as to the fascist."[59] By this Chomsky suggests that science, in and of itself, appeals to the concept of authoritarian control that thrives in any modern industrial society, despite the form of governance it claims to implement. In particular, Chomsky is critical and dubious of the notion of "behavioral control" that Skinner claims can be achieved through application of his operant methodology. It is the notion of control itself that Chomsky finds particularly disturbing, especially in Skinner's focus on the locus of the environment as the source of control, as Skinner states ". . . all control is exerted by the environment."[60] Furthermore, Chomsky finds it disturbing that Skinner claims these behavioral approaches can take the place as fact over previous attempts to explain human behavior including ". . . personality theory, states of mind, feelings, traits of character, purposes, and intentions."[61] While Chomsky states rather bluntly that neither Skinner, nor any other behaviorists, possess any real evidence to support these bold claims, the more important critique forwarded by Chomsky is that, even if Skinner's prediction of behaviorism as inexorable fact comes true, it would be "inherently limited" and therefore use only its authoritarian quality to be accepted and regarded as truth, not actual evidence as would be necessary to be accepted by the greater scientific community. Skinner does so, in Chomsky's view, by not only claiming what the purpose of behaviorism is but, further, what the purpose of scientific investigation itself should be. As Skinner states:

> the task of a scientific analysis is to explain how the behavior of a person as a physical system is related to the conditions under which the human species evolved and the conditions under which the individual lives.[62]

Chomsky agrees only in basic part, conceding that the purpose (or at least one of the purposes) of scientific inquiry is to discover and explain facts. However, this basic purpose is not, in itself, the explanation of the scientific process. Chomsky points out in opposition to Skinner that, with special regard to human behavior, the purpose of scientific inquiry is not to determine the effects of the types of conditions that he regards (e.g., the environment and consequences within it), but whether or not these conditions have an effect at all. In this sense, Chomsky accuses Skinner of "starting in the middle." That is, he has already accepted that the conditions to which he pays most attention are most significant, and is concerned now only with building evidence in its favor. Chomsky, however, does not contend that the conditions on which Skinner concentrates have, in fact, been evidenced at all. His ability, therefore, to convince many within the social science community as well as the general public is based not on scientific evidence or legitimate demonstration, but on the authoritarian power of the field of psychology at the time and its "assistance" in the national zeitgeist of environmental control of human behavior and preoccupation with observable outcomes. It is Skinner himself who advises his reader that the public has ". . . [no] need to know the details of a scientific analysis of behavior . . ."[63] As Chomsky states clearly:

> Skinner does not comprehend the basic criticism: when his formulations are interpreted literally, they are clearly false, and when these assertions are interpreted in his characteristic vague and metaphorical way, they are merely a poor substitute for ordinary usage. Such criticisms cannot be overcome by

verbal magic, that is, by mere reiteration that his approach is scientific and that those who do not see this are opposed to science, or deranged.[64]

Other critiques came from within the field of behaviorism itself, one of the most well-known being that of Breland and Breland (1961), direct intellectual descendants of Skinner himself and well-known animal behavior researchers. Breland and Breland grew ever more suspicious that studies of animal behavior alone could be generalized to human behavior. As they state, "[t]here seems to be a continuing realization by psychologists that perhaps the white rat cannot reveal everything there is to know about human behavior."[65] This idea developed through multiple observations of animals behaving in unexpected and behaviorally counter-intuitive ways, specifically in purportedly conditioned situations in which an animal appears to have strong instinctive drives and choosing such instinctive behaviors in place of the conditioned one despite reinforcement. The researchers termed this phenomenon "instinctive drift" and were clear that such an observation did not denigrate entirely the theory of behaviorism, but rather demonstrated that the theory itself had distinct weaknesses and could not be viewed as an exhaustive and axiomatic paradigm. As they suggest:

> The notion of instinct has now become one of our basic concepts in an effort to make sense of the welter of observations which confront us. When behaviorism tossed out instinct, it is our feeling that some of its power of prediction and control were lost with it. From the foregoing examples, it appears that although it was easy to banish the Instinctivists from the science during the Behavioristic Revolution, it was not possible to banish instinct so easily.[66]

Therefore, as illustrated by the initial critiques of Lashley followed by those of MacDougall, Breland and Breland, Chomsky, and Gomez, the centricity of behaviorism in social science and education has been both overstated and de-contextualized. While historically a formidable case has been made, this overstatement will be revisited methodologically throughout this work. Essentially, however, the groundwork has been laid to demonstrate that though behaviorism, as a mode of investigation, does offer an essential part of the framework within which exploration into human behavior and subsequent treatment of such behavior can be applied, it does not, by any means, universally or comprehensively satisfy an ever-increasing understanding of individuals with Autism Spectrum Disorders.

NOTES

1. Furay and Soulaveris, *The Methods and Skills of History: A Practical Guide*, 1988, 223.
2. Man Cheung Chung and Michael Hyland, *History and Philosophy and Psychology*.
3. B.R. Hergenhan, *An Introduction to the History of Psychology*.

4. Ibid.
5. Ibid.
6. Ibid.
7. Ibid.
8. Daniel Robinson, *An Intellectual History of Psychology.*
9. Hergenhan.
10. Ibid.
11. Plato, *Politics*, Book VIII, 1337a 10–11.
12. Ibid., 1094a28-b2.
13. Ibid.
14. St. Thomas Aquinas, *Summa Contra Gentiles*, Bk. II, Chapter II.
15. St. Thomas Aquinas, *Exposition of Beothius' On the Trinity*, q.5, a.4.
16. St. Thomas Aquinas, *Summa Theologiae*, Ia. Q., 1, a., ad 2.
17. Stanford Encyclopedia of Philosophy, http://plato.stanford.edu/entries/galileo/#3.
18. Ibid.
19. Ibid.
20. Ibid.
21. *Meditations on First Philosophy*, Second Meditation, 30–31. Translated by D. Cress.
22. John Locke, *An Essay Concerning Human Understanding*, Retrieved on October 10, 2013, from http://www.earlymoderntexts.com/pdf/lockess1.pdf.
23. Gustav Jahoda, *A History of Social Psychology: From the Eighteenth Century Enlightenment to the Second World War.*
24. Ibid.
25. William James, *Pragmatism: A New Name for Some Old Ways of Thinking*, 1907.
26. C.S. Peirce, *Popular Science Monthly* 12 (1878), 286–302.
27. James, 1907.
28. John A. Mills, *Control: A History of Behavioral Psychology.*
29. Ibid.
30. Ibid.
31. Ibid.
32. Ibid., 30.
33. Ibid., 32.
34. https://archive.org/details/cu31924031214442.
35. Edward K. Morris et al., "The History of Behavior Analysis: Some Historiography and a Bibliography," *Behavior Analyst*: 13 (2) 131–58, 1990, 133–34.
36. Hock, R.R. (2002). *Forty Studies that Changed Psychology: Explorations into the History of Psychological Research* (4th ed.).
37. B.R. Hergenhahn, *An Introduction to the History of Psychology.*
38. Don H. Hockenbury and Sandra E. Hockenbury, *Psychology.*
39. Watson, 1924, as cited by Edward K. Morris et al., "The History of Behavior Analysis: Some Historiography and a Bibliography," *Behavior Analyst*: 13 (2), 131–58, 1990.
40. William O'Donohue and Richard Kitchener, *Handbook of Behaviorism.*
41. Ibid.
42. Watson, 1913, as cited by O'Donohue and Kitchener, 32.
43. William T. O'Donohue and Kyle E. Ferguson, *The Psychology of B.F. Skinner.*
44. Ibid.
45. R.J. Herrnstein, *The Evolution of Behaviorism*, http://jpkc.ecnu.edu.cn/fzxlx/jiaoxue/The%20Evolution%20of%20Behaviorism.pdf, 593.
46. Susan M. Schneider and Edward K. Morris (1987), "A History of the Term *Radical Behaviorism*: From Watson to Skinner," *Behavior Analyst*, 10, 27–39.
47. James.
48. William R. Uttal, *The War Between Mentalism and Behaviorism: On the Accessibility of Mental Processes*, 5.
49. William MacDougall (1929). "Fundamentals of Psychology—Behaviorism Examined." From http://psychclassics.yorku.ca/Watson/Battle/macdougall.htm.
50. Ibid.

51. Karl Lashley, "The Behaviorist Interpretation of Consciousness" (1923). From http://psychclassics.yorku.ca/Lashley/consciousness.htm.

52. Lashley, 1951, as cited by Gardner, *The Mind's New Science*, 12.

53. Howard Gardner, *The Mind's New Science*, 6.

54. Ibid.

55. Boulding, as cited by Pizzurro, http://www.personalityresearch.org/papers/pizzurro.html.

56. Pablo Gomez, "Why I Am Not A Behaviorist,' http://www.personalityresearch.org/papers/pizzurro.html.

57. Ibid.

58. Noam Chomsky, 1971, "The Case Against B.F. Skinner." From http://www.chomsky.info/articles/19711230.htm

59. Ibid.

60. Ibid.

61. Ibid.

62. Ibid.

63. Ibid.

64. Ibid.

65. Keller Breland and Marian Breland (1961), "The Misbehavior of Organisms," *American Psychologist*, 16, 681.

66. Ibid., 684.

Chapter Two

A Primer on the General Concepts of Behavior Analysis

The focus of this chapter will be to delineate the main concepts of behavior analysis that apply directly to practice and intervention in educational settings, particularly for individuals with Autism Spectrum Disorder. The purpose for such a chapter is not, by any means, to present a complete picture of behavior analysis, neither is it to oversimplify the theory nor the practice. Rather, it is to ensure that the reader gains a base level, working understanding of the general tenets and terminology of behavior analysis, such that the reader can be better grounded to understand the later critiques. In order to maximize the legitimacy and accuracy of the information presented in this chapter, the concepts delineated and their corresponding definitions and contextualization are derived entirely and directly from trade texts authored by known behavior analysts, specifically Alberto and Troutmann (2010) and Martin and Paer (1999), among other incidental peer-reviewed works. As such, this chapter will be presented, quite intentionally, as encyclopedic. While the methodologies will be more closely investigated and critiqued in a later chapter, they will be presented in a technical fashion only in this section. As the breadth and depth of behavior analysis should not and cannot be truncated in order to fit entirely within a single chapter of a book, it is important to note that the definitions for each concept will serve only to familiarize readers with basic understandings. When applicable, practical clinical or classroom-based examples of such concepts will be offered for better contextualization.

BASIC TERMINOLOGY AND CONCEPTS IN
BEHAVIOR ANALYSIS

According to behavior analytic theory, all behavioral sequences can be segmented into three distinct components: the antecedent, known also as the discriminative stimulus (S^D), the behavior, known also as the response (R), and the consequence, known also as the reinforcing/resultant stimulus (S^R). A common example of such a sequence is: question (antecedent/S^D); the student engages in such as raising their hand, evading eye contact, or calling out (behavior/R); and the student is addressed one way or another, either by being selected to answer the question or not being selected to answer the question (consequence/S^R). This sequence, known also as ABC (Antecedent—Behavior—Consequence) assessment, forms the basis of all learning and behavior according to behavior analysis. The ABC process assists both in the formulation of operational definitions, or means of describing specific behaviors in observable, measurable, and replicable terms as well as in the determination of the function of behavior.[1,2]

As Skinner contextualized the exhibition of behavior in terms of probability, the concepts by which behaviors either increase or decrease are known, respectively, as *reinforcement* and *punishment*, each with their own respective quantitative sub-categories of *positive* and *negative*. Reinforcement:

> describes a relationship between two environmental events, a behavior (response) and an event or consequence that follows the response . . . only if the response increases or maintains its rate as a result of the consequence.[3]

More specifically, *positive reinforcement* is the provision of a consequential stimulus (that is, something preferred is provided) that increases the probability that a behavior will be exhibited again. Positive reinforcement is described as:

> if, in a given situation, somebody does something that is followed immediately by a positive reinforce, then that person is more likely to do the same thing again when he or she next encounters a similar situation.[4]

A common example that applies to a clinical or classroom situation is the use of token boards or token economies for the demonstration of appropriate target behaviors (social, functional, or academic). If an individual engages in a desired or, as is often referred to, a "socially appropriate" behavior, then that individual receives a reinforcer, or a stimulus that is preferred or enjoyed, such as a preferred food item or a token (a common form of currency that can be collected and redeemed for subsequent reinforcers at a later time).

Conversely, negative reinforcement is the withdrawal of a consequential stimulus (that is, something non-preferred is taken away) that increases the probability that a behavior will be exhibited again in the future. More specifically, negative reinforcement is described as, ". . . the contingent removal of an aversive stimulus immediately following a response that increases the future rate or probability of the response."[5] In the context of a clinical or classroom situation, an individual may be told that a demand will be removed contingent upon completion of a certain amount of responses (e.g., once the individual reads one page of a book aloud he or she may put the book away). Typically, negative reinforcement is used successfully with a demand that is likely to be aversive but is being attempted to be systematically increased by building tolerance of engagement in the behavior.

Remaining with the notion that Skinner conceptualized these ideas in the context of probabilities, punishment is:

> a consequent stimulus that (a) decreases the future rate or probability of occurrence of behavior; (b) is administered contingently on the production of the undesired or inappropriate behavior; and (c) is administered immediately following the production of the undesired or inappropriate behavior.[6]

Sub-categorized identically to reinforcement, punishment comes in two forms: positive and negative. As such, positive punishment is the contingent addition of an aversive stimulus in order to decrease the likelihood that the behavior occurs again in the future. In the classroom, a common use of positive punishment is the contingent requirement of additional work following an inappropriate behavior. For example, if a student protests a demand to work and engages in non-compliance, additional requirements are demanded (e.g., extra examples on a worksheet). Conversely, negative punishment indicates the contingent withdrawal of a preferred stimulus in order to decrease the likelihood that the behavior occurs again. A common example of negative punishment in the classroom is the removal of recess or recreation time as a consequence for engaging in inappropriate behavior. A vastly important concept to emphasize is the common but grossly inaccurate confusion between negative reinforcement and punishment, be it positive or negative. While the field is rife with erroneous references to the concept of "negative reinforcement" in order to indicate what is actually punishment (likely due to the misconception of the word "negative" which, in behavior analysis is of quantitative value, not qualitative value), it is imperative that anyone who is to truly understand even the basic concepts of behavior analysis is aware of this clear and vital difference.

While the above concepts refer, ultimately, to environmental manipulations that are contingent upon the demonstration of particular behaviors, there are specific guidelines to which skilled behavior analysts (or teachers skilled in behavior analytic methods) abide in order to determine the appropriate methodologies that are to be used in the classroom context. The main process by which behavior analysts determine what approaches are to be used in a behavior intervention plan (BIP; to be defined more specifically later) is a functional behavior assessment (FBA) or, if possible or necessary, a more precise though more complex process of functional behavior analysis. A FBA "involves asking (a) what are the antecedents . . . for the behavior, and (b) what are the immediate consequences for the behavior?"[7] FBAs are most typically conducted in the form of questionnaire-based assessments and, if possible, a direct observation of the individual in a variety of situations which can be more reliable and useful in the design of a BIP. Essentially, the purposes of a FBA are threefold.

The first purpose is aimed toward determining and constructing an operational definition for the behavior sought to be changed. An operational definition, as aforementioned, consists of defining a target behavior in observable (that is, a way in which the behavior can actually be seen) and measurable (that is, a way in which the behavior can be directly measured in a quantitative fashion). This determination allows for clear and accurate measurement of the demonstration of the target behavior. The formation of an operational definition is an essential component of achieving the goal of behavior analysis: accurate assessment of observable behaviors in terms of their change in occurrence as the result of environmental manipulations.

The second purpose of a FBA is the determination of function for the behavior. For the most part, this stage of the process focuses primarily on the problem behavior; that is, the behavior which will be sought to be replaced through an intervention plan because it is either maladaptive or inappropriate by social, functional, or academic standards. The first category of problem behavior is those maintained by attention from others, known also as social positive (in the qualitative sense) reinforcement. These behaviors are maintained when individuals receive attention in one form or another as a result of engaging in the target behavior. It is, however, important to note that under extreme deprivation, individuals may also become reinforced by disciplinary (or negative, in the qualitative sense) attention. The second category of problem behavior is those maintained by self stimulation, known also as internal sensory positive reinforcement. These behaviors are maintained based on their natural pleasure, and may, at times, involve sexual reinforcement (such as masturbatory behaviors, especially in pubescent individuals). The third category of behavior is those maintained by environmental consequences, also known as external sensory positive reinforcement. These behaviors are maintained based on pleasure gotten from preferred items in the environment. The fourth category of problem behavior is those maintained by escape from demands, known also as social negative reinforcement. These behaviors are maintained based on relief of demand acquired from an undesired situation being withdrawn. The fifth and final category is those maintained by medical explanations, such as tic disorders, pre-menstrual issues, or changes in behavior based on illness or biological factors of any kind. [8]

The third purpose of a FBA is to lead to an accurately and appropriately designed Behavior Intervention Plan which accounts for the function of the individual's behavior, known by a number of other names including behavior treatment plans, intervention programs, as well as other such similar monikers. Martin and Paer suggest a set of guidelines when using a FBA to devise a treatment plan including defining the goal and the target behavior as well as the desired amount of stimulus control, identifying those who can assist in controlling the relevant stimuli and reinforcers, consider capitalizing on existing means of stimulus control, determining the modes of teaching such as shaping, fading, and/or chaining, the selectable nature of the S^Ds, using what methods will a behavior be decreased, if applicable, what the details of the reinforcement system will be, specifying the setting in which the training will take place, how generalization will likely take place, and by what means will all of the aspects of the behavior plan be documented (e.g., data collection products, graphs, formalized intervention plans, signed documents, etc.). [9]

Despite the individually based BIP that is likely to be derived from the FBA process, there is a clear prescriptive process for conducting a FBA, including defining the problem in operational terms, identifying antecedent events, identifying consequences that typically follow the behavior, form hypotheses about the consequent events that are believed to maintain the problem behavior, collect data on all aspects of the behavior including antecedents and consequences in the natural environment, complete a FBA, design an intervention for replacing the behavior, and analyze the data to determine if there appears to be a relationship. [10]

As the key factor in any behavior analytic program is accurate assessment of observable target behaviors, especially in the context of whether such behaviors have changed in the intended direction, the methods of data collection are an imperative concept to address. While there are many methods that are possible to implement in any given behavior intervention plan, this section will approach these methods based on three main categories within which various specific methods of data collection can be delineated: (a) event recording; (b) temporal; and (c) descriptive data collection methodologies.

The first category, known as event recording, consists of frequency, rate, and interval recording. Frequency, "refers to the number of instances of the behavior that occur in a given period of time." [11] While this methodology is able to monitor behavior both accurately and with great detail if such behaviors are exhibited at moderate rates, it can be considerably challenging to capture behaviors that occur excessively or at particularly high intensities with any accuracy or detail at all. Further, frequency is not appropriate for measuring time-based behaviors (such as time spent attending or time spent in tantrum), effectively limiting the types of behaviors for which frequency data collection is appropriate. A variation of frequency data collection is applied by calculating a rate. That is, measuring the number of times a behavior occurs within equally divided time intervals, and then converting that measure to a ratio indicating the number of occurrences per the context of the interval (for example, contextualizing a behavior in terms of number of times exhibited per hour when multiple hour-long intervals were used to measure the behavior).

While lacking the level of detail that can be attained from frequency and rate data collection, interval data collection can be applied to frequently occurring behaviors without sacrificing its accuracy.[12] In general, there are three subtypes of interval data collection. Partial interval data collection requires that the behavior be exhibited for any part of the interval in order to be counted as an occurrence. A limitation of partial interval data collection is the likelihood of an overestimation of the occurrence of the behavior. Whole interval data collection is essentially the opposite of partial interval, in that it requires that the behavior persist for the entire duration of the interval in order to be counted as an occurrence. A challenge with whole interval data collection is the likelihood of an underestimation of the occurrence of the behavior. Finally, momentary time sampling uses a pre-specified time for a direct observation of behavior. If at the moment of that pre-specified time the individual is observed engaging in the target behavior, it is counted as an occurrence. Conversely, if at the moment of that pre-specified time the individual is not observed engaging in the target behavior, it is not counted as an occurrence. This type of data collection may either overestimate or underestimate the occurrence of the behavior depending on a variety of factors.[13]

The second category of data collection is temporal-based methods. Within this category, there are two main methodologies: duration and latency. Duration data collection consists of, "recording the amount of time between the initiation of a response and its conclusion."[14] For example, the amount of time an individual spends on a particular task is best measured in terms of duration of minutes and/or seconds. Latency data collection, the other form of temporal data collection, is defined as "the time between the occurrence of a stimulus and the beginning of a response."[15] For example, the amount of time it takes an individual to begin complying with the task demand is best measured in terms of latency of minutes and seconds.

The third and far broader category of data collection methodology, though in no way exhausting the available methodologies within behavior analytic practices, is to be considered descriptive. Among the various possible methods to engage in descriptive measures of data collection, the more common forms include topography, locus, and intensity. Topography is in many ways similar, if not potentially identical to the "B" phase in ABC data collection. Topography indicates "the form of a particular response"[16] such as the specific description of bodily movements, particular words or sounds uttered aloud, etc. Locus data collection is used to determine where or, in other cases, with whom a behavior is more likely to occur, allowing for better prediction of behavior as well as information providing for a means of differential reinforcement in environments that appear to be more aversive or less reinforcing than others. For example, individuals may have a more aversive reaction to noisier locations than quieter ones and, when monitored, locus behavior data collection will identify this tendency. Intensity, though likely the most subjective form of observable data collection methods, is used when analysts determine the importance of a level of behavior in terms of severity. For example, if an individual engages in aggressive behavior toward others, but varies in the type of aggression and the force with which he or she aggresses, intensity behavior data collection can give an indication of such differences in severity. While there are a number of different means by which intensity can be monitored, including high-technological approaches which can determine exact measurements of certain elements of intensity such as volume or force, one of the more applicable clinical methods is a Likert-type scale, with lower numbers indicating lower intensities while higher numbers indicate higher intensities. A clear but complicated challenge to intensity behavior data collection is the subjectivity with which individuals are likely to rate intensity depending on a number of variables including size, strength, as well as experience with aggressive individuals. [17]

Data collection alone, however, is by no means enough to accurately measure the effectiveness of a behavior intervention. Once the data are collected, some type of systematic analysis must take place in order to determine if the intervention that was implemented was, indeed, effective, or if any changes need to be made in order to increase the effectiveness. There are multiple designs that behavior analysts may use to evaluate interventions, with some being stronger than others as well as serving distinctly different purposes between them. There are two main methods, however, in determining what behavior analysts consider to be rigor and effect in such analysis: the establishment of interobserver agreement and functional relationship, respectively.

Interobserver agreement, known also as inter-rater reliability and interobserver reliability, among other terms, is the primary means by which reliability is measured in single-subject designs. Interobserver agreement is "the consistency of data collection reports among independent observers."[18] This measure is most often expressed as a percentage using the calculation of dividing the number of agreements by the total number of observations and multiplying by 100 (A/A+D x 100). There appears to be a general consensus in behavior analysis that an interobserver agreement measure of 80 percent should be seen as a bare minimum of acceptability. In general, interobserver agreement is collected in a percentage of the clinical sessions or trials, rather than for each individual response.

A functional relationship is said to exist if the dependent variable system-atically changes in the expected and desired direction as a result of the manipulation of the independent variable, or intervention. Functional rela-tionships can only be confidently demonstrated within intervention designs that possess replicable conditions; that is, if a behavior analyst can show, through repetition of some kind that the same, or at least similar, results are observed across the repetitions, then the functional relationship may be claimed with increased confidence. [19]

Functional relationships, however, are only attainable by using certain types of intervention designs. While there are a number of different interven-tion designs available to use within the context of behavior analysis, focus in this chapter will be maintained on the following more commonly used de-signs: AB design, ABAB (or reversal) design, and multiple baseline design.

The AB design, also known as the teaching design, though common in classrooms, is not a particularly strong framework for determining the effec-tiveness of an intervention and, in fact, cannot determine whether a function-al relationship exists. This design consists of only two phases: the baseline phase followed by the intervention phase. The baseline phase is characterized by data collection in the absence of the proposed intervention (either with no intervention at all or a different intervention) to which the proposed interven-tion is to be later compared. In general, baseline data are collected for at least three or four points until data are stable. Unstable baseline data are inutile as they reduce the comparability with the intervention data, making interpreta-tion of the intervention's effectiveness difficult and unreliable, if at all pos-sible. For example, if a teacher is interested in determining whether a token economy system will increase a student's engagement in hand-raising with-out calling out, that teacher will first measure the amount of times the indi-vidual raises his or her hand in the absence of the token economy system. This is the A, or initial baseline phase. Once stable baseline data are attained, the teacher will then start the B phase, or intervention, in this case, the token economy. During the intervention, the teacher will regularly collect on the same behavior and in the same fashion as in the baseline phase, and plot the data on a graph (e.g., number of times the student raises hand without calling out). If the amount of times the student raised his or her hand during the B phase does increase, the teacher may be apt to conclude that the intervention was effective which may, indeed, be true. However, the teacher cannot make such a claim with confidence as there is no means of determining a function-al relationship in AB design, as it lacks a replication. Therefore, while practi-cal and relatively easy to implement in a classroom, the AB design is not capable of determining functional relationships and, therefore, not a reliable measure of intervention effectiveness. [20]

The ABAB, or reversal design, consists of two baseline phases and two intervention phases which are implemented alternately in successive sessions. Essentially, the reversal design consists of two successive teaching (AB) designs. The main difference is a subsequent return to baseline (the second A phase) followed by a final return to intervention (the second B phase). This repeated sequence allows for a replication. If the levels of behavior in the second A phase return to levels similar to that of the first A phase, and the levels of the behavior in the second B phase return to levels similar to that of the first B phase, then it can be said that a functional relationship exists, as it appears that it is the intervention that has stimulus control over the target behavior since it is reduced when the intervention is removed. However, if the behavior remains at the intervention level in the absence of the intervention (such as in the second A phase), then a functional relationship cannot be said to exist, and there is another confounding factor besides the intervention that has gained stimulus control over the target behavior. The ABAB design is far more reliable in terms of claiming a functional relationship. However, this design can be very difficult to implement in a classroom situation as it requires much organization, as well as being dependent on a behavior that is actually reversible, which may not apply to many academic skills (that is, one cannot simply "unlearn" what has already been learned such as sight words, counting, etc.).[21]

The multiple baseline design also possesses the capability of demonstrating a functional relationship through replication. Multiple baseline design permits the behavior analyst to analyze the relationship between an independent variable and a dependent variable across multiple conditions. For some examples, a behavior analyst can monitor the effect of a single intervention on more than one behavior within an individual student, the effect of a single intervention on one behavior across multiple students, or the effect of a single intervention for one student across multiple environments, among other possibilities of application. In a multiple baseline design, baseline data are collected across all conditions initially. Once baseline data are stable across conditions, the intervention is implemented in the first condition, while baseline data continue to be collected in the other conditions (that is, the intervention is only implemented in one of the conditions while no intervention is implemented in the others). Once an effect is seen in the first intervention condition, it is implemented in a second intervention condition, while baseline data collection continues in the remaining condition(s). This gradual implementation of interventions is continued until all conditions include the intervention. If the conditions that remain in baseline maintain stability while the conditions that are under the intervention trend in the desired direction across multiple conditions, then a functional relationship can be determined, as each subsequent phase can be regarded as a replication. The more dramatic the difference in data between the baseline and intervention conditions, the more confidence one can have in the functional relationship.

Finally, it is important to note that the way in which much, if not most, behavior analytic data are analyzed employs the process of visual inspection as opposed to statistical evaluation, with only some instances of the calculations of even basic descriptive statistics when applicable. It is important to note, however, that statistical analysis, even if conducted at the basic level in the context of single-subject designs, would have to be very carefully contextualized, as single-subject designs, as a rule, use a very low number of subjects, for which most statistical methods are not accurate or applicable.[22] This issue will be explored more deeply later in the work.

BEHAVIOR MODIFICATION TECHNIQUES

Now that the basic terminology in behavior analysis has been established and defined, this section will focus on the methodological means of changing behaviors. Specifically, this section will deal with the concepts of differential reinforcement strategies, shaping, fading, chaining through task analysis, and extinction.

One of the more useful and important strategies for changing behaviors in behavior analysis is manipulation of environmental consequences through differential reinforcement, of which there are four main types: differential reinforcement of low rates of behavior (DRL), known also as differential reinforcement of latent behavior; differential reinforcement of other behavior(s) (DRO); differential reinforcement of alternate behaviors (DRA); and differential reinforcement of incompatible behavior (DRI).[23] Differential reinforcement of latent behaviors (DRL) is when a specific schedule of reinforcement is applied in order to decrease the rate of behaviors that, though tolerable or desirable in low occurrences are inappropriate when they occur too often or rapidly.[24] For example, if a student with Autism Spectrum Disorder engages in excessive conversation (or vocalization) during work time, a teacher may use a DRL in order to maintain the conversational skill while also teaching that conversation is only acceptable during socially appropriate times, such as during leisure activities, lunch, or in between task demands. Differential Reinforcement of Other Behaviors (DRO) occurs when a reinforcing stimulus is provided contingently on the absence of the target behavior for a specified period of time.[25] For example, if a student gets out of his seat excessively during work time, the student will be specifically reinforced for staying in his seat in order to emphasize this appropriate behavior over other inappropriate behaviors that may be competing. Differential Reinforcement of Alternative Behaviors (DRA) reinforces the occurrence of a behavior that is a topographical alternative to the behavior targeted for reduction.[26] For example, if an individual engages in yelling when presented with a non-preferred demand, he or she would be reinforced for asking for a two-minute break in place of the yelling. This is an alternative behavior because the two behaviors *can*, topographically, be performed simultaneously (that is, one *can* yell and ask for a break simultaneously). Finally, Differential Reinforcement of Incompatible Behaviors (DRI) reinforces a behavior that is topographically incompatible to the behavior targeted for reduction.[27] For example, a student who excessively taps their pen, pencil, or fingers on the table can be taught to squeeze their hands under their desks tightly instead. These two behaviors are topographically incompatible, in that they cannot be physically performed simultaneously.

Shaping and fading are two similar processes in modifying behavior toward being more independent. Shaping is defined as:

> a procedure used to establish a behavior that is not presently performed by an individual . . . by the successive reinforcement of closer approximations and the extinguishing of preceding approximations of the behavior.[28]

Shaping can be used and capitalized on in various ways, and can even occur somewhat naturally in the environment. As explained by Martin and Paer:

> Sometimes a new behavior develops when an individual emits some initial behavior and the environment (either the physical environment or other people) then reinforces slight variations in that behavior across a number of trials. Eventually that initial behavior may be shaped so that the final form no longer resembles it.[29]

A common example of such naturally reinforced shaping cited by behaviorists is the development of language in a baby, who begins by babbling, which slowly transforms into one-word utterances, two-word utterances, and eventually sentences and fully functional and grammatical language (a concept explored and explicated in-depth in *Verbal Behavior* by B.F. Skinner). Behavioral theory of language (which will be explained in more detail later) suggests that such development takes place as a result of a combination of reinforcement of approximations from initial sounds to words, when the reinforcement is provided only for the more sophisticated form of behavior (such as "ma ma" becoming "mommy" or "da da" becoming "daddy").

Shaping can take place on four main components of behavior: (a) topography; (b) amount; (c) latency; and (d) intensity (or force). Topography refers to physical requirements and spatial configurations of a particular behavior, such as printing a word and writing the same word in cursive. Though the end result is the same, the topography of both the final product and the accompanying process is distinctly different. The amount of a behavior refers to the measurement of how it occurs, usually in the context of frequency and/ or duration of the emission of the behavior. Depending on the goal, the frequency or duration may be increased or reduced. Latency refers to the time between the provocation of a behavior by a stimulus and when the individual begins to engage in that specific behavior. Finally, the intensity of a response refers to the physical force that behavior has on the environment.[30]

Essentially, the process of shaping consists of four factors that are necessary to consider:[31]

1. Specifying the final desired behavior (terminal behavior)
2. Choosing a starting behavior
3. Choosing the shaping steps
4. Moving along at the correct pace

Fading refers to "the gradual change, on successive trials, of a stimulus that controls a response, so that the response eventually occurs to a partially changed or completely new stimulus."[32] It is important to keep the distinction between shaping and fading (and, eventually, chaining as well) in mind in order to have a clear understanding of each process. Shaping focuses on approximations of behaviors which lead an individual closer to the final desired behavior, focusing primarily on the final response being perfected. In fading, however, the focus is on reinforcing the final response in the presence of closer approximations of the desired stimulus, focusing primarily on the stimulus being perfected. As explained by Martin and Paer, "shaping involves the gradual change of a response while the stimulus stays about the same; fading involves the gradual change of a stimulus while the response stays about the same."[33] While the distinction may seem based only on small details, it is a significant distinction nonetheless. Fading, therefore, is used when a stimulus exerts a significant amount of control over a response, but it is a stimulus that is less naturalistic and, therefore, inhibitive of true independent performance of the behavior.[34]

As most processes are in behavior analysis, the fading process occurs along changing dimensions of behaviors, most notably by the use of various types of prompts, or "supplemental stimuli that control the desired behavior but that are not part of the final desired stimulus . . ."[35] There are multiple types of prompts, and the means by which various behavior analysts present and define them may differ, though despite the terminological differences, most are relatively similar to one another at a fundamental level. Verbal prompts are types of stimuli that supplement the final desired behavior using spoken words. For example, if a student often forgets to close their locker when they are done exchanging their materials the teacher may say, "close your locker," assisting in the performance of the desired response. Gestural prompts are types of stimuli that supplement the final desired behavior using bodily motions, often with one's hand. For example, in the same situation as above, instead of providing a verbal prompt, the teacher may point to the locker door as a reminder for the student to close it. Modeling prompts are types of stimuli that consist of the teacher enacting the identical behavior that is desired from the individual. For example, if there is an open locker in the proximity of the student, the teacher can close that locker as a model for the student to do the same to their own. Physical prompts are types of stimuli in which the teacher physically manipulates the individual's relevant body parts and motions in order to provide guidance toward completing the target behavior. For example, the teacher either pushes the elbow of the student to initiate contact with the locker (partial physical prompt) or physically guides the student through the entire process (full physical prompt). Finally, environmental prompts, a broader category, are types of stimuli in which the environment is altered in order to make the completion of the final desired behavior more likely. For example, having a locker with a special hinge that automatically closes but does not fasten the locker can be an example of this type of prompt. Once the prompting procedures are determined, the behavior analyst will then determine a plan to systematically fade, or decrease the intensity of assistance implemented in order to increase the student's independence. Once the fading process begins, close attention must be paid to the student's progress to ensure that the process is being implemented at the correct pace, neither too quickly nor too slowly. [36]

Chaining is a behavior analytic procedure that is also stepwise and dimensional in nature, as well as potentially combinative of both the shaping and fading process. In general, there are three specific methods in chaining: forward chaining, backward chaining, and total-task chaining. Before chaining is understood, however, the process of task analysis must first be defined and delineated. A task analysis is "the process of breaking a task down into smaller steps or component responses to facilitate training . . ."[37] While the actual steps included as individual components are somewhat subjective based on a number of factors, including the individual's familiarity with the skill, gross and fine motor skills, and history of skill acquisition, the end result of the task analysis should be the same, which is the full engagement of the target behavior. Once the task analysis is constructed, the behavior analyst will then decide which type of chaining will be used to teach the final target behavior.

In the first method, total task teaching, "the [individual] attempts all the steps from the beginning to the end of the chain on each trial and continues with total task trials until all steps are mastered."[38] For example, if the behavior chain being taught is a vocational task of sorting mail in employee mailboxes, the individual would be prompted through all steps required to complete the final desired behavior. The second method, backward chaining, "constructs the chain in a reverse order from that in which the chain is performed . . . that is, the last step is established first, followed by the next-to-last step . . . and so on, progressing backward to the beginning of the chain."[39] For example, if an individual has an aversion to dressing (such as putting on pants), the behavior analyst will complete all steps leading up to the final step, requiring the individual to complete only the last step (such as buttoning the pants). The third method is forward chaining in which "the initial step of the sequence is taught first, then the first and second steps are taught and linked together . . . and so on until the entire chain is acquired."[40] Activities of Daily Living are a common example, such as teaching independent engagement in the initial step of "turning on the water" first in a sink-based activity. Despite the type of chaining chosen, Martin and Paer offer some guidelines for its effective use:[41]

1. Construct a task analysis by identifying the units of the chain that are simple enough to be learned without difficulty.
2. Ensure the units are taught in proper sequence, ensuring that stimulus control (what controls the elicitation of the behavior) is maintained.
3. Determine a fading procedure to decrease the likelihood that extra prompting is needed.
4. If forward or backward chaining is used, ensure that the individual is completing all steps up to the current step.
5. Ensure that consistent and sufficient reinforcement is used early in the teaching procedure to maximize correct performance throughout the entire teaching sequence.
6. Ensure that all reinforcement is used correctly and effectively, avoiding any inadvertent reinforcement or inadvertent prompting.

While the previous methodologies all handle increasing behaviors to one degree or another, extinction addresses the occasional need to decrease a behavior. Extinction is a process that states:

> (a) if in a given situation, an individual emits a previously reinforced response and that response is not followed by a reinforcing consequence, then (b) that person is less likely to do the same thing again when he or she next encounters a similar situation.[42]

While many mistakenly refer to the process of extinction as "ignoring" (or, in some instances, "planned ignoring"), this is a vast misconception. Ignoring is primarily a passive process (that is, when someone is ignored, their behavior is no longer attended to at all, whether it persists or not), while extinction is an active process by which the undesired behavior of the individual is consistently attended to, though not reinforced, in order to determine when it is no longer being emitted, and its absence is then reinforced. When used effectively, extinction is likely to bring about a significant decrease of the undesired behavior (often after a temporary significant increase called an extinction burst), with a possibility of additional temporary resurgences known as spontaneous recovery.

SPECIFIC TEACHING METHODOLOGIES WITH THE BEHAVIOR ANALYTIC APPROACH

It is important to remember that the aforementioned concepts are part of the theory of behavior analysis which is, at its heart, a theory of learning. The concepts take practical shape, however, once the principles are applied to specific methodologies of teaching, of which there are multiple examples. This section will focus on four main methodological frameworks within the field of behavior analysis: Discrete Trial Instruction, Applied Verbal Behavior, Pivotal Response Training, and Picture Exchange Communication Systems.

Discrete Trial Instruction (DTI), known also as Discrete Trial Training or Discrete Trial Teaching (DTT) as well as the "Lovaas Method" in some literature, is one of the most widely used but also widely mischaracterized methodologies within behavior analysis. Its mischaracterization stems from the notion that many in the greater field of education, specifically special education, use DTI and ABA synonymously, when DTI is actually only one distinct methodology under the auspice of the greater learning theory of ABA. The purpose of DTI is to break tasks down into simple, single-step subcomponents. Typically, DTI sessions are conducted in compartmentalized or at least highly non-distractible environments, often with well-defined boundaries and clear delineations of areas of personal space. Ultimately:

> DT[I] breaks down skills into small sub-skills and teaches each sub-skill intensely, one-at-a-time. It involves repeated practice with prompting and fading of prompts to insure the child's success. DTT then uses reinforcement to help shape and maintain positive behaviors and skills. [43]

The method of DTI is a prescriptive, five-step sequence. Each sequence has a particular purpose, and is generally applied invariably. The sequence is: [44]

1. The discriminative stimulus (S^D) is when the instruction or cue is provided in order to evoke the target behavior.
2. The prompting stimulus (S^P) is an optional phase in which a prompt is provided in order to supplement the behavior.
3. The response (R) is the skill or behavior elicited by the discriminative stimulus.
4. The reinforcing stimulus (S^R) is a consequence designed to increase the likelihood of the behavior occurring again upon the presentation of the same or similar discriminative stimulus.

While there are distinct strengths to DTI, there are a number of challenges and risks that are imperative to address. First, while DTI is an effective means at teaching single-steps or sub-components of a greater skill, the process is particularly slow, yielding the potential for little overall progress despite long engagements in teaching. Secondly, the DTI process requires a very contrived, controlled, and restrictive environment, which is not likely to represent the typical classroom setting with its distractions, shared space and materials, and more complex instructions. Third, if implemented incorrectly, the use of DTI can result in a responder that is rigid and limited in both types of response as well as responsiveness to multiple discriminative stimuli if they do not match exactly, or similarly enough, to the teaching stimulus. Fourth, but certainly not exhaustively, individuals who receive instruction predominantly through DTI may come to be significantly prompt dependent, with little means of initiation as a result of the clear teacher direction that comes with DTI.

Some of the main weaknesses of DTI, specifically the lack of connection between the response and the reinforcement, as well as the overwhelming teacher directedness of the methodology, are directly addressed by a method known as Pivotal Response Training, or PRT. Developed primarily by Robert and Lynn Kern Koegel of the University of California, Santa Barbara, PRT capitalizes heavily on systems of reinforcement, though in a very different manner than that of DTI. PRT is an approach that capitalizes on pivotal behaviors, defined as "those [behaviors] that, when changed, generally produce large collateral improvement in other areas."[45] These behaviors include increasing motivation and responding to complex social, linguistic, and academic interactions in the form of multiple cues, child choice, self-management, and self-initiation, among others. Ultimately, PRT posits three main goals:[46]

1. To teach the child to be responsive to many learning opportunities and social interactions that occur in the natural environment.
2. To decrease the need for constant vigilance by an intervention provider.
3. To decrease the number of services that remove the child from the natural environment.

These procedures are based on action upon establishing operations and stimuli from the natural environment itself, decreasing the need to alter the environment in order to maintain reinforcement opportunities for responding. By capitalizing on the natural environment and a variety of reinforcers and learning situations that use multiple exemplars, PRT methodologies offer to the child a far greater amount of choice in both reinforcement as well as learning opportunities. PRT is also expansive of DTT as it not only attempts to teach basic behavioral skills, but has also been shown to be effective at increasing individual's engagement in more cognitively and emotionally based activities such as symbolic play and socio-dramatic play.[47]

Applied Verbal Behavior (AVB) has many similar foundations and practices as DTI and PRT, such as the intensity of treatment protocols, hierarchically designed curricula, and the use of operant conditioning.[48] There are, however, a number of differences between the approaches as well. First, AVB typically capitalizes more on the natural environment (with a sub-methodology referred to as Natural Environment Teaching), which maintains the focus on continuous language training in the presence of the actual stimuli as well as motivating variables. This capitalization of the natural environment strengthens the connection to the "real" environment which should eventually have the stimulus control if treatment is to be generalizable. Ultimately, the AVB approach "employs a functional account of language (a) to teach children multiple functions of language and (b) to teach each function using the ultimate controlling variables specific to that function."[49] The AVB approach focuses so specifically on language:

> Because language underlies most learning in the typical child and is so conspicuously defective in children with autism, developing language skills is seen as a major goal of any training program. In most such programs, the training consists of the application of the behavioral technology described above to what is usually called communicative behavior.[50]

Though AVB is often credited as being an applied outcrop of Skinner's 1957 work *Verbal Behavior*, this may be a vast overstatement. As Michael (1984) states:

> Interestingly, this extensive body of research makes almost no use of the concepts, terms, and analyses that appear in Skinner's (1957) *Verbal Behavior*. Although the term verbal behavior had become widespread, the recent trend is toward increased use of the traditional term, language, in spite of its implication of a common process underlying kinds of behavior that differ considerably from one another, such as speaking and listening . . . the research could have easily been conceived without the benefit of the distinctions Skinner makes.[51]

While the components and the theory of AVB cannot be stated in their entirety in the context of this chapter, the main tenets regarding the types of verbal functions in which an individual can engage can be divided into five basic categories in hierarchical order from most simplistic to most complex. The basic level of verbal functioning is the *echoic*, or a verbal response to another verbal interaction most often in the form of a verbal imitation. That is, if a teacher requests that a student repeat a word (such as "water") or points to an object (a bottle of water) while stating the word, the individual will engage in echoic by repeating that word back. The second level is the *tact*, which is the verbal labeling of an object evoked by the presence or property of a particular object or event. For example, if an individual sees a bottle of water and verbally acknowledges its presence (not necessarily indicating wanting to access it), the individual will engage in a tact by indicating its presence verbally by stating its proper name (or whatever approximation of that name that he or she is able to utter). The third level of verbal functioning is the *mand*, a diminutive of the words "command" or "demand," which is a verbal function in which stating the label results in reinforcement in the form of access. For example, if the individual is thirsty the individual will engage in a mand by indicating the presence of the water bottle in order to express the intention of accessing it. The fourth level of verbal functioning is the *intraverbal*, which is a mode of verbal output based out of previous knowledge of the existence of an object or event that is not present in the immediate environment. For example, the individual will engage in an intraverbal by indicating the recollection of a person who is not present or an event that took place previously. The statements are often conceptualized as basic declarative statements, and are the first step toward more abstract and conversational forms of social interaction. Finally, the *autoclitic*, which is the most sophisticated form of verbal behavior, is dependent on the speaker's own awareness of his or her ability to engage in verbal behavior and using such awareness to engage in verbal behavior that can serve a completely abstract function, such as conversation without the indication of accessing needs. For example, if an individual makes the statement "I'm sure it is going to rain," this statement has less to do with the rain itself and almost entirely to do with the speaker's interaction with another for social purposes.

The Picture Exchange Communication System (PECS), though likely to be regarded as predating the outcrop of AVB as a specific approach was, in many ways, based on the same types of principles and has been adapted and updated, in many ways, along with AVB, especially in the area of Augmentative and Alternative Communication (AAC), or electronic devices with voice outputs that supplement or replace the "voice" of the individual. The basis of PECS was careful to distinguish the notion of language from communication. Communication:

> can be characterized as the relaying and receiving of information, needs, or thoughts in a shared medium that has communicative intent to affect the receiver's behavior in some way. [52]

Developed initially by Bondy and Frost (1994), the PECS system became a widely used and adapted form of low technological alternative and augmentative communication. In recent years this approach has been adapted to high technological instrumentation such as voice output communication systems utilizing PECS pictures. The PECS system was designed with six distinct phases, each increasing in complexity hierarchically in order to provide individuals with ASD and other communication-based disabilities with a mode of communicative output (and, potentially, input). The ultimate goal of PECS is to enable students with communicative disabilities to attain communicative competence, defined as, "having the knowledge of what communication patterns are and how they are used appropriately in specific situations."[53] This definition was expanded by Light (2009), who suggested four specific areas for communication competence specifically for individuals using AAC systems: expressing needs and wants, developing social closeness, exchanging information, and fulfilling social etiquette reinforcements.

The main mode of PECS capitalizes on the use of pictures to allow individuals to express language in communicative ways by exchanging pictures in return for a change in the receiver's behavior. The exchange of the picture is to be regarded as equivalent to a verbal (or vocal) request, and is to be responded to accordingly. For example, if an individual who uses PECS exchanges a picture of water with a receiver, he or she should be given access to water once the exchange is completed. These exchanges can, at least theoretically, be used for any type of communication, be it inquisitive or declarative. This approach is particularly different than past approaches as it allows the individual to be not only a responder, as they are in DTT and, in some ways, PRT, but also an initiator, allowing for more communicative control and the potential for increased communicative independence.

There are, however, some distinct challenges to the PECS system. First and foremost, since the system is based on physical pictures, an increased vocabulary results in an increase in pictures. Therefore, a means to organizing such pictures needs to be determined. A historical difficulty was that the physical pictures also ran the risk of being lost, damaged, or destroyed, as well as becoming part of a large and cumbersome binder. This issue has been addressed by the increasing use of electronic AAC devices. However, new challenges arise with these higher technological quality machines, including mechanical failures, software bugs, as well as expense.

NOTES

1. Martin and Paer, *Behavior Modification: What it Is and How to Do It?* 1999. 6th ed.
2. Alberto and Troutman. *Applied Behavior Analysis for Teachers*, 2012.
3. Ibid., 216.
4. Martin and Paer (1999), 27.
5. Alberto and Troutman (2012), 254.
6. Ibid., 282.
7. Ibid., 258.
8. Ibid.

9. Ibid., 289–90.

10. Ibid., 268.

11. Ibid., 243.

12. Alberto and Troutman, 2012.

13. Ibid.

14. Ibid., 424.

15. Martin and Paer (1999), 250.

16. Alberto and Troutman (2012), 242.

17. Ibid.

18. Ibid., 426.

19. Ibid.

20. Ibid

21. Ibid.

22. Veronica M. Ximenes et al. (2009). "Factors affecting visual inference in single-case designs."*Spanish Journal of Psychology*: 12 (2), 823–32.

23. Alberto and Troutman (2012).

24. Ibid.

25. Ibid.

26. Ibid.

27. Ibid.

28. Martin and Paer, 62.

29. Ibid., 62.

30. Ibid.

31. Ibid., 66.

32. Ibid., 113.

33. Ibid., 115.

34. Ibid.

35. Ibid., 118.

36. Ibid.

37. Ibid., 137.

38. Ibid., 134.

39. Ibid., 134.

40. Ibid., 135.

41. Ibid.

42. Ibid., 47.

43. Paulina Peng-Wilford and Xuejun Kong, "Behavioral Treatment for Children with Autism." 2011. *North American Journal of Medicine and Science*. 18–163.

44. Ibid., 160.

45. Lynn Kern Koegel et al. (1999), "Pivotal Response Intervention I: Overview of Approach," *JASH*, 24(3) 174–85, 174.

46. Ibid., 174.

47. Karen Pierce and Laura Schreibman. "Increasing Complex Social Behaviors in Children with Autism: Effects of Peer Implemented Pivotal Response Training." *Journal of Applied Behavior Analysis*, 28, 285–95.

48. James E. Carr and Amanda M. Firth, "The Verbal Behavior Approach to Early Intensive Behavior Intervention for Autism: A Call for Empirical Support." *Journal of Early Intensive Behavioral Intervention*, 2 (1) 2005.

49. Ibid., 19.

50. Mark L. Sundberg and Jack Michael. "The Benefits of Skinner's Analysis of Verbal Behavior for Children with Autism." *Behavior Modification*, 25 (5) 2001 699.

51. Michael, 1984, as cited by ibid., 701.

52. Cheryl Ostryn, et al. (2008). "A Review and Analysis of the Picture Exchange Communication System (PECS) for Individuals with Autism Spectrum Disorders Using a Paradigm of Communication Competence." *Research & Practice for Persons with Severe Disabilities*, 33, v. 1–2, 13–24.

53. Ibid., 14.

Chapter Three

From Diagnosis to Social Construct

The Creation of Autism Spectrum Disorder

Tracking the development of a condition or a diagnosis can be elusive as it is dependent on determining not only when the particular condition was first named, but equally as importantly when it began to be noticed as distinct from other conditions. To do this presents a formidable challenge, as the name of the condition itself is often indicative of the definition, and vice versa. Diagnostic criteria compel observers and diagnosticians to mark particular traits and characteristics of individuals in order to determine whether or not they fit a diagnosis, or at least approximate the conceptualization of a condition. Therefore, even with spectral conditions, as the current diagnostic criteria represent Autism Spectrum Disorder to be, those individuals who do not meet the predetermined criteria are not considered as being part of the group. How then, before such criteria exist, is a field to identify the existence of a condition? This is the challenge that will be addressed in this chapter.

In addition to attempting to demonstrate the existence of ASD before its distinction as a clinical description or diagnosis, the further argument will be made that ASD has extended beyond being a mere psychiatric diagnosis, but rather a social construct with social consequences and social criteria in and of itself. As such, the way in which ASD is not only diagnosed, but the way in which the condition and the individuals who possess the diagnosis, or at least engage in the symptomatology associated with it, are perceived and treated by society, its institutions (especially schools) and its individual members will be contended as being entirely socially based. Therefore, it will be argued that there is a far greater importance and consequence attributed to the *development* of the diagnosis than the diagnosis itself, in that the occurrence and the diagnosis of ASD is not simply a matter of diagnostic precision or clinical understanding, but rather the creation of a social system of treatment that has deeply permeated society's medical and educational institutions. Diagnostic labels, then, function not merely as means of organizing individuals for the sake of treatment and/or educational service provision. Rather, they are a social construct in its deepest sense, as the labels themselves as well as the subsequent "treatment" of the people that results directly from receiving the label are directly indicative of the value systems of the society that employs them.

AUTISM IN THE PAST: THE HISTORICAL PERSPECTIVE OF DIAGNOSTIC DEVELOPMENT

Superimposing contemporary diagnoses on past individual cases is an interesting though precarious practice, especially when considering the diagnostic label themselves. Capturing a historical account of something such as autism (or Autism Spectrum Disorder) is distinctly challenging as it spans vast generations, cultural contexts, and definitions and, as Canguilhem states, historians often have "the tendency to see the history of the subject in light of today's truth, which is easily confused with eternal truth."[1] More specifically, Verhoeff points out that, "a history of the concept of autism will always remain an imperfect approximation of a general (scientific) sense of the meaning of autism at a particular moment in time."[2] Grinker astutely adds to this dynamic discussion by pointing out that naming a condition or an experience does not, by any means, give it "life," nor does it eliminate the possibility that such a condition existed before it was formally named by whatever institutional body is responsible for doing so. Furthermore, some cultures have no name for the diagnoses and pathological conditions that Western "modernist" societies have created in large part from the "Western" medical perspective that it puts so much stock in. As such, with the absence of a "diagnostic label" comes also an implicit social narrative that the condition is neither pathological nor "disordered," and therefore does not need distinction, much less treatment or correction.[3]

That being said, there are historians who do believe that some clear cases of ASD can be identified in the past. One such example is the "green children" as described by William of Newburgh in the 12th century, who spoke of one boy and one girl with green skin who were unable to communicate and did not appear to know how to follow social customs. The Little Flower of St. Francis was described as a man who could not understand people whose opinion differed from his own, a potential indication of Asperger's Disorder. The "blessed fools" of Russia ("blessed," in this context, referred to "feebleminded," or intellectually disabled by current nomenclature), were described as people who were preoccupied with engaging in repetitive behaviors, needed to be confined so they did not wander, had seizures, and were either echolalic or mute. Other historians believe that the variety of feral children described throughout history such as Victor of Aveyron, Wild Peter of Germany (though some medical historians believe Peter likely had Pitt-Hopkins Syndrome), and Kamala and Amala of India were also potential examples of individuals with ASD who, perhaps, were spurned by their parents as a result of their abnormality and incorrigibility (the custom of leaving children who were "diseased" or "defective" in the wild is a historically common practice that can be traced as far back as the ancient Greek practice of exposure).[4]

In terms of perspectives that bear more similarity to Western diagnostic traditions, perhaps the first reference to what would become Autism Spectrum Disorder was by J. Langdon Down in 1887 (contrary to both Bleuler and Kanner, each of whom is often credited with the first description of autism). While best known for his identification of Down's Syndrome as well as the unfortunately named "idiot savant," Down divided intellectual disability into two distinct categories: "congenital" and "accidental;" Down also described a third category of "feeble-minded" individuals who defied clear classification based on his diagnostic nomenclature. Referring to it at the time as "developmental retardation," which is now likely Autism Spectrum Disorder, Down suggested that this type of intellectual disability was comprised of individuals who lacked the physical aspects of the other types, had developed normally though later underwent a sudden regression marked by "lost wonted brightness" and lost speech, as well as the "suspension of normal intellectual growth." Further, Down described these individuals as "living in a world of their own . . . spoke in the third person . . . [had] rhythmical and automatic movements . . . [and] lessened responsiveness to all endearments of friends."[5] What Down was describing appears to very likely be the condition now known as Autism Spectrum Disorder.

Many accounts of the eventual diagnostic attention to Autism Spectrum Disorder begin with the systematic observations of the condition by Leo Kanner, a Viennese physician working at Johns Hopkins in the 1940s. At the time, almost all children who presented with behaviors analogous to what is currently deemed Autism Spectrum Disorder were diagnosed with childhood schizophrenia, a very rare, if not nearly defunct diagnosis currently. Unconvinced that some of the individuals that he observed were, indeed, correctly diagnosed, Kanner began to record more systematic observations of such differences, which he ultimately described as:

> [an] inability to relate themselves in the ordinary way to people and situations from the beginning of life. Their parents referred to them as having always been "self-sufficient." . . . There is, from the start an *extreme autistic aloneness*

[italics in original] that, whenever possible, disregards, ignores, shuts out anything that comes to the child from the outside.[6]

While the term "autistic" was borrowed by Kanner from Eugene Bleuler, a
Swiss psychologist, initially to describe patients with dementia who with-
drew from the "real world" into a "fantasy" world, Kanner used it to describe: (1) a profound lack of affective contact and (2) elaborate, repetitive,
ritualistic behavior in the absence of psychotic symptoms.[7] Kanner began to
describe this distinct disorder based, initially, on a case-by-case report of
eleven individuals. While there were clearly differences between each individual, Kanner was able to distill a number of common characteristics, described as:

> a unique "syndrome," not heretofore reported, which seems to be rare enough,
> yet is probably more frequent then is indicated by the paucity of observed
> cases. It is quite possible that some such children have been viewed as feeble-
> minded or schizophrenic. In fact, several children of our group were intro-
> duced to us as idiots or imbeciles, [one was] . . . feebleminded, and two had
> been previously considered as a schizophrenic.[8]

As such, Kanner clearly dissents from the notion that these individuals are
schizophrenic or have intellectual disabilities of the "generic" type, concur-
ring with Down's suggestion proffered at the end of the 19th century. His
descriptions of the fundamental elements of the condition he observed consisted of the following:

> The outstanding, "pathognomonic," fundamental disorder is the children's *in-
> ability to relate themselves* [italics in original] in the ordinary way to people
> and situations from the beginning of life. . . . This is not, as in schizophrenic
> children or adults, a departure from an initially present relationship; it is not a
> "withdrawal" from formerly existing participation. There is, from the start an
> *extreme autistic aloneness* [italics in original] that, whenever possible, disre-
> gards, ignores, shuts out anything that comes to the child from the outside. . . .
> Almost all the parents reported . . . that the children had learned at an early age
> to repeat an inordinate number of nursery rhymes, prayers, lists of animals. . . .
> Aside from the recital of sentences contained in the ready-made poems or
> other remembered pieces, it took a long time before they began to put words
> together. Other than that, "language" consisted mainly of "naming." . . . The
> fact that the children echo things heard does not signify that they "attend"
> when spoken to. It often takes numerous reiterations of a question or command
> before there is even so much as an echoed response. . . . Everything that is
> brought to the child from the outside, everything that changes his external or
> even internal environment, represents a dreaded intrusion . . . *loud noises and
> moving objects* [italics in original] . . . are reacted to with horror. . . . Yet it is
> not the noise or motion itself that is dreaded. The disturbance comes from the
> noise or motion that intrudes itself, or threatens to intrude itself, upon the

child's aloneness. The child himself can happily make as great a noise as any that he dreads and move objects about to his heart's desire. . . . The dread of change and incompleteness seems to be a major factor in the explanation of the monotonous repetitiousness and the resulting *limitation in the variety of spontaneous activity* [italics in original]. . . . The children's *relation to people* [italics in original] is altogether different. Every one of the children, upon entering the office, immediately went after blocks, toys, or other objects, without paying the least attention to the persons present. . . . Even though these children were at one time or another looked upon as feebleminded, they are all unquestionably endowed with good *cognitive potentialities* [italics in original]. . . . The combination of extreme autism, obsessiveness, stereotypy, and echolalia brings the total picture into relationship with some of the basic schizophrenic phenomena. . . . But in spite of the remarkable similarities, the condition differs in many respects from all other known instances of childhood schizophrenia.[9]

Kanner's remarkably detailed and astute definition of what would later become a formal diagnosis in and of itself was instrumental in the nascent process of systematic observation of both particular human behaviors and a method of systematizing diagnostic processes through itemizing traits. However, in the case of autism, it took quite some time for this to happen and, even when the term autistic was beginning to be accepted in the descriptive analyses and nomenclature of clinical psychology and psychiatry, it was not yet included in the Diagnostic and Statistical Manual, the official guide for diagnosing psychiatric conditions, maintaining the only diagnostic option for such individuals being "Schizophrenia, childhood type."

Perhaps equally as importantly, however, Kanner described each individual's ability to improve and learn in his original paper. Even in the throes of eugenics and mass institutionalization, where diagnosis beyond "feeblemindedness" had little importance since such individuals were largely damned to institutional confinement, the individuals who participated in Kanner's program were systematically observed and reported to have distinct improvements in behavior and communicative development.

At nearly the same time, though largely unaware of Kanner's work due to the restrictions on information of the Nazi regime, Hans Asperger, also an Austrian, began to relate observations of a similar type of individual, though markedly different in key ways than Kanner's eleven cases. According to Asperger, maladaptive characteristics of individuals with the disorder that he came to call "autistic psychopathy" often went undetected within the first three years of life, as the development of speech was deemed relatively normal despite some common errors such as the use of improper or reversed pronouns. Despite this relatively unremarkable linguistic aberration, other more distinct indications of linguistic difficulties, including the imperceptions of subtle verbal jokes and nonverbal difficulties in both perception and production (e.g., facial gestures, body language, etc.) were observed. More

obvious, however, was the individuals' distinct difficulties with social interactions, which were often marked by intense one-sided interests as well as a
general disregard for the rules governing social interaction such as gestures,
posture, movement, eye contact, and physical proximity, among others characteristics.[10]

As a direct consequence of sequestration of intellectual pursuits during
the Nazi regime, Asperger's work was entirely unknown to American and
other European audiences outside of Austria and Germany until 1981, when
it was discovered and disseminated by Lorna Wing, an English researcher,
and her colleagues.[11] It was around this time, as well, that Asperger learned
of other researchers' work in related areas, namely Kanner's. Described by
Asperger (1979) when he later learned of Kanner's characterization of the
"autistic symptomatology":

> Kanner's infantile autism is a near psychotic or even psychotic state, though
> not identical with schizophrenia. Asperger's typical cases are very intelligent
> children with extraordinary originality of thought and spontaneity of activity
> though their actions are not always the right response to the prevailing situa-
> tion. Their thinking, too, seems unusual in that it is endowed with special
> abilities in the areas of logic and abstraction and these often follow their own
> cause with no regard for outside influences.[12]

Despite Asperger's indication of the difference in observations between he
and Kanner, a study of his 1944 paper "Autistic Psychopathy in Childhood"
reveals that their descriptions are strikingly similar, namely in the area of
challenged social interaction and the presence of stereotyped behavior. Furthermore, Asperger concurred with Kanner's indication that autistic characteristics differed from those of schizophrenia in that their symptoms were not
apparently regressive, but stable, though continually challenged over time.[13]
The main difference, however, was in Asperger's perception of the root of
the disorder. While Kanner was not particularly clear offering, at times,
multiple suggestions for etiology, Asperger was explicit in his belief that
Autistic Psychopathy was a personality disorder that merged into the "normal
continuum," made up of a group of eccentric and withdrawn though gifted
individuals who manage, albeit in odd and questionably effective ways, social interaction and means of communication. Though he submitted that the
individuals he described corresponded to those described by Kanner in general ways, his sample was distinct in that he deemed the condition as being
marked by a stable personality, though lifelong, without the progressive
"fragmentation" as noted in schizophrenia and, he believed, in the cases
Kanner described.[14] It is important to note, however, that there appears to be
some distinct misunderstanding by Asperger about Kanner's descriptions,
which is evident in his contradictory statements about them.

Following Kanner's work in America and Asperger's work in Austria more individuals became involved with the increased interest and study of this burgeoning clinical concept. Despite increased discourse, however, there remained significantly varying interpretations and assertions about the nature of autism (still not a diagnosable condition as per the DSM), allowing grounds for various explanations and, thus, various modes of treatment for such individuals. Bruno Bettelheim, who remains one of the most contentious figures in the history of autism, was one such individual whose ideas and practices are deemed questionable, if not entirely unethical despite their distinct attainment of popularity and common practice. Bettelheim's conceptions and treatments were rooted deeply in the supposed psychoanalytic understanding that autism was "nothing less than the emotional withdrawal of an infant at the hands of a cold and emotionally distant parent . . . ,"[15] the concept that came to be known as the infamous "refrigerator mother theory." Though it is often forgotten that the analogy of the refrigerator was first expressed by Kanner, who suggested in an early portrayal of autism that parents of children with autism kept their children "neatly in a refrigerator that did not defrost,"[16] it was later de-contextualized and over-generalized by Bettelheim in his 1967 book *The Empty Fortress: Infantile Autism and the Birth of the Self*, in which he explained that the "refrigerators" were mothers in particular who directly caused their children's autism.

Bettelheim's personal history, in itself, is one greatly influenced by his proclivity for deception. He was a Holocaust survivor who was released from the concentration camp in Buchenwald in 1939 as a result of an amnesty enacted in honor of Hitler's birthday, during which he immigrated to the United States. Though he was neither credentialed nor qualified in the practice of psychoanalysis and possessed only some training in philosophy from the University of Vienna, he managed to parlay this bit of training into a directorship of the Orthogenic School, a residential facility for children with mental illness affiliated with the University of Chicago. Some of the residents of the school seemed to fit the descriptions of autism that were emerging from Kanner and garnering increased attention. Drawing on his experience in concentration camps, Bettelheim first suggested that autistic children suffered "extreme situations" as did prisoners of the camps in the Holocaust, specifically that of "maternal deprivation."[17] As such, his proposed therapy, which he called "milieu therapy," consisted of regaining a connection with a "cold and hard" mother by both hugging and kissing a statue representative of the mother which, also, was "cold and hard as stone," but also by hitting, kicking, spitting, and, allegedly urinating on the statue in order to release repressed anger leading to a remission of the autistic characteristics.[18] Astonishingly, this perspective and therapeutic intervention was widely viewed as both acceptable and sensible within the greater field, as well as receiving mainstream attention through media such as *Ladies Home Journal*, *Playboy*, and *Scientific American* magazines. His status as a legitimate practitioner became so significant that he even received a considerable grant from the Ford Foundation in 1956 to admit, service, and observe a number of supposedly autistic children at the Orthogenic School. It was through one of these children, Joey (later known as "Joey the Mechanical Boy") that Bettelheim developed and, putatively, vetted his "refrigerator mother" theory. In his description of Joey's mother:

> [Joey's] birth, she said "did not make a difference. . . . I did not want to see or nurse him" his mother declared. "I had no feeling of actual dislike—I simply did not want to take care of him." For the first three months of his life Joey cried "most of the time." A colicky baby, he was kept on a rigid four-hour feeding schedule, was not touched unless necessary and was never cuddled or played with. The mother, preoccupied with herself, usually left Joey alone in the crib or playpen during the day . . . Joey's mother impressed us with a fey quality that expressed her insecurity, her detachment, from the world and her physical vitality. We were struck especially by her total indifference as she talked about Joey. This seemed much more remarkable than the actual mistakes she made in handling him. . . . Joey's existence never registered with his mother.[19]

While Bettelheim's prominence was maintained for several years, stories of Bettelheim and his questionable past began to surface after his suicide in 1990. Though information about his lack of qualification in psychoanalysis was made public and the case reports in *The Empty Fortress* were either mischaracterized or entirely fabricated, more concerning was increasing reports of his abuse of residents during his directorship at the Orthogenic School.[20]

In direct response to the charade created by Bruno Bettelheim, Eric Schopler, a student at the University of Chicago during Bettelheim's tenure, began to construct an alternative conceptualization of autism, one that not only entirely vindicated parents from any causal responsibility, but deemed them as essential participants in the therapeutic process. Based out of his dissertation research concerning perceptual problems among individuals with autism, Schopler became a pioneer in the now common, if not overtly accepted belief, that autism is a treatable and dynamic condition. His protocol, eventually known as TEACCH (Treatment and Education of Autistic and related Communication Handicapped Children) grew out of a five year grant funded by the National Institutes of Mental Health in the 1960s. The distinguishing factor of this approach was the centricity of two novel aspects: (1) the view of parents as participants in the therapeutic and educational process, and (2) the conceptualization of autism not as a deficiency, but as a culture. Developed by Schopler and his colleagues, the culture of autism is:[21]

1. Relative strength in and preference for processing visual information (compared to difficulties with auditory processing, particularly of language).
2. Heightened attention to details but difficulty with sequencing, integrating, connecting, or deriving meaning from them.
3. Enormous variability in attention (individuals can be very distractible at times, and at other times intensely focused, with difficulties shifting attention efficiently).
4. Communication problems, which vary by developmental level, but always include impairments in the initiation and social use of language (pragmatics).
5. Difficulty with concepts of time including moving through activities too quickly or too slowly and having problems recognizing the beginning or end of an activity, how long the activity will last, and when it will be finished.
6. Tendency to become attached to routines and the settings where they are established, so that activities may be difficult to transfer or generalize from the original learning situation, and disruptions in routines can be uncomfortable, confusing, or upsetting.
7. Very intense interests and impulses to engage in favored activities and difficulties disengaging once engaged.
8. Marked sensory preferences and aversions.

What Schopler offered was a perspective of autism that not only decried the psychoanalytic vilification of parents, namely mothers, but regarded the condition as a positive set of circumstances that, when capitalized on, could be utilized in order to treat the condition and enhance both the functionality and quality of life of the individual.

THE AGE OF DIAGNOSIS

Despite the strong effort the early researchers made in distinguishing autism from childhood schizophrenia and proposing the groundwork for some potential interventions, the general trend in the nascent field of psychiatry in the 1950s and 1960s was to continue characterizing such individuals as schizophrenic. It is important, therefore, to note again, that though the term "autistic" was used increasingly commonly in the description of individual behavior, it was not yet a formal psychiatric diagnosis, still only appearing in the description of childhood schizophrenia in the first two versions of the Diagnostic and Statistical Manual. Records from Bellevue, the first public hospital in the United States quite well-known for its psychiatric facilities, indicate this tendency quite clearly. While there are many such case studies from which to choose, one of the more well-known cases that is cited to demonstrate the likelihood of individuals who were most likely autistic being diagnosed as schizophrenic is that of "Arnold" in 1959. When Arnold was four-and-a-half years old he was brought to Bellevue by his parents, who were no longer able to control him. He was described by his parents as a child who did not speak, was a "loner," had no bowel control, and played compulsively with the toilet.[22] As Arnold was described by the main doctor on his case, who remains unidentified:

> He was mute or echolalic, though he knew and could repeat the words of innumerable popular songs. He had severe tantrums in which he would withdraw completely, suck his thumb, make odd guttural sounds and be completely inaccessible. . . . His development was apparently unremarkable until the age of 11 months when he would rock in his crib. . . . There were no indications of organic pathology.[23]

Grinker, among others, suggests the idea that this trend was an early example of what would eventually be termed "diagnostic replacement" (though autism was not yet a formal diagnosis, it was demonstrated as being different from schizophrenia in a relatively clear way) or the notion that a disorder that is diagnosed under one name begins to be more commonly diagnosed by another name, resulting in a low representation or decrease of the former diagnosis and a high representation or increase of the latter one. This phenomenon does not truly represent a genuine increase in incidence, but rather just a change in diagnostic nomenclature and transfer of frequency from one label to the other. This will become a significant issue again during the 1990s until the present. In the context of the 1950s, it is suggested that individuals who were previously diagnosed under the various guises of "feeblemindedness" (usually according to the nomenclature of the *Textbook of Mental Deficiency* of the time such as *idiocy, lunacy, insanity, or feeble-mindedness* from the 1908 version or *idiot, imbecile,* and *moron* from the 1963 update) were now being diagnosed as schizophrenic based on a better "understanding" of the various idiosyncratic symptoms. The occurrence of diagnostic replacement is supported by the case notes of Loretta Baker, a psychiatrist at Bellevue, who reported over 600 cases of pediatric schizophrenia in the 1950s alone, increasing to roughly 2,000 by 1966. It begs reprisal that under the current state of pediatric psychiatry, a diagnosis of schizophrenia is almost entirely unheard of, while diagnoses of Autism Spectrum Disorder appear to be increasing steadily. Equally as importantly, in the first two versions of the DSM, the word "autistic" was used as a descriptor for the diagnosis of "Schizophrenia—Childhood Type." Therefore, to display autistic symptoms was to be diagnosed, *ipso facto*, as schizophrenic, creating the condition to be one and the same, at least from a diagnostic perspective.[24]

It was during this time, concurrent with the increased interest in defining the condition of such individuals as "autistic" despite its existence as a formal diagnosis, that the field of psychiatry was, itself, undergoing a distinct metamorphosis; one which continues into the current time. With an increase in the use of psychoactive medications to treat various psychiatric disorders, the field began to transform from a nearly entirely Freudian psychoanalytic perspective to a more medical psychopharmacological-based perspective.

Also marking this metamorphosis was the stylistic change with which the DSM was organized. Though the inception of the DSM dates back to 1952, the systematic, checklist-style delineation of psychiatric diagnostic criteria was not implemented until the DSM-III in 1980, under the direction of Robert Spitzer.[25] This change was part of a global attempt to transform the field of psychiatry from a more philosophical foundation to a medical-symptomatological-based foundation. The significance of this change cannot be understated in the resultant changes in various aspects of the mental health field including, but not limited to, treatment options, insurance coverage, and educational placements.

The DSM-III, published in 1980, was particularly significant for ASD as it was the first version in which autism was included as a bona fide diagnosis distinct from schizophrenia, characterized under the newly created category of Pervasive Developmental Disorders (PDD). The characterization of the diagnosis was based largely on Rutter's categorization methodology, which specified onset by the age of 30 months, marked by impaired social development, impaired communication, and unusual behaviors including, but not limited to, repetition of action. According to the DSM-III criteria, autism was to be organization in the context of deficits in social interaction, social-communication, and social/symbolic play, being divided into two categories for diagnosis: *infantile autism*, which was defined as onset of symptomatology by 30 months of age, and *late-onset autism*, which was defined as onset of symptomatology after 30 months of age. In 1987, a revised version of the DSM-III (DSM-III-R) was released that widened the criteria of Pervasive Developmental Disorders in order to facilitate the diagnosis according to variability in the degree of deficits, especially for children with more subtle symptoms. This new conceptualization was based on a more well-defined spectrum of: (1) reciprocal social interaction; (2) communication (verbal and nonverbal); and (3) repetitive, stereotyped, or ritualistic behavior. It was in this version that the subtype of Pervasive Developmental Disorder-Not Otherwise Specified (PDD-NOS) was added in order to account for individuals who did not fully meet the original stringent diagnostic criteria due to the lesser severity of their symptoms. At the time of the DSM-III-R the diagnosis of PDD-NOS was predicted to remain as a low incidence diagnosis, though common enough to merit a separate diagnostic representation.[26] Furthermore, the DSM-III-R included "high functioning autism" as an additional

subtype. In 1994, with the release of the DSM-IV, the contemporary conceptualization of the autism spectrum began to take shape with the inclusion of
Asperger's Disorder as its own subtype (replacing High Functioning Autism)
within the Pervasive Developmental Disorders category, and the label of
"infantile autism" was revised to "autistic disorder."[27] In 2000, a revised text
version of the DSM-IV (DSM-IV-TR) was released which did not change
diagnostic criteria per se, but rather reorganized specific diagnoses using a
five-part axial system. Under this version of the DSM, which remained the
most influential in the diagnosis of autism until 2013, the "autism spectrum,"
as it was known only colloquially within the field, though not in diagnostic
terms, likely consisted of Autistic Disorder, Asperger's Disorder, and Perva-
sive-Developmental Disorder-Not Otherwise Specified (PDD-NOS).

Perhaps, at least in part, due to the limitation and translation of Asperger's work, it remains unclear as to whether the diagnostic definitions in both
the DSM-IV-T-R and DSM-5 were influenced as much by Asperger as Autistic Disorder was by Kanner. While there are undoubtedly similarities,
newer and more adapted ideas of such characteristics were suggested by
other diagnosticians since Asperger's original writing. Beginning with the
aforementioned work by Wing and colleagues, an extended conceptualization of what she referred to as "Asperger Syndrome" (though the diagnosis,
when included in the DSM-IV, was termed Asperger's *Disorder*) was presented. Wing's main contribution of the initial understanding of autism as a
spectrum disorder, of which Asperger's Disorder was a part, was her delineation of the Triad of Impairment (which was revised over the years):[28]

1. *Impairment of social interaction.* This refers to the marked reduction
   of non-verbal signs of interest in and pleasure from being with another
   person—making eye contact, initiating and responding to smiling, initiating, and responding to affectionate physical contact such as hugging, kissing, greeting, and waving good-bye. The beginning of social
   interaction can be seen in sociable children from birth, long before
   language develops, and can be seen in sociable, severely disabled
   children and adults who have no language, even in those who are non-
   mobile.
2. *Impairment of social-communication.* This refers to the decreased
   ability to "converse" non-verbally and verbally with another person,
   sharing ideas and interests or to negotiate in a positive friendly way.
   The earliest manifestation of social-communication in typically developing children is joint referencing to share an interest, seen in the last
   part of the first year. People in the autism spectrum also often have
   problems understanding what is said to them, tending to interpret
   things literally.

3. *Impairment of social imagination.* This is the decreased capacity to think about and predict the consequences of one's own actions for oneself and for other people. In typical development it does not develop until after 3 years of age. Impairment of this ability is perhaps the most important and disabling of all the consequences of having an autism spectrum condition of any kind. We believe that it should not have been ignored by the designers of the DSM-IV or the DSM-5 (and ICD-10). The DSM instead introduced repetitive behavior patterns, not the impaired social imagination, as the last leg of the triad.

Since Wing's original publication in 1981, there has been a consistent and ever-changing controversy regarding the distinctions between the sub-typed organization in the DSM-III through the DSM-IV-TR, as well as the very definition of some of the subtypes themselves, specifically that of Asperger's Disorder. Rutter and Schopler argued:

> As there is an obvious research need to compare autism with Asperger syndrome, we suggest that there is a need for a . . . category for Asperger syndrome in order to encourage and facilitate that research. [29]

Therefore, it appears that the diagnostic category itself was used to facilitate research in the differences between the two potentially different conditions rather than truly define it as a diagnosis. As a result of this research, which was conducted by a number of different clinicians, multiple descriptions and possible criteria for diagnosing Asperger's Disorder were devised. Among the more well-accepted versions, though in no way an exhaustive account, are those of Tantamand colleagues, Szatmariand colleagues, and Gillbergand colleagues. Tantam suggested that the five criteria by which Asperger's Disorder can be identified are: [30]

a. language used freely but not adjusted to the social context
b. the wish to be sociable but failure to relate to peers
c. clumsiness
d. idiosyncratic but engrossing interests
e. marked impairment of non-verbal communication

Szatmari and colleagues suggested the following more parsimonious though less well-defined criteria: [31]

a. solitariness
b. impaired social interactions
c. impaired non-verbal communication
d. odd speech

Finally, Gillberg's criteria, which are, arguably, the most highly regarded amongst practitioners consist of the following:[32]

a. social impairments
b. narrow interests
c. repetitive routines
d. speech and language peculiarities
e. non-verbal communication problems
f. motor clumsiness

These initial debates soon developed into an overarching concern with the organization of the Pervasive Developmental Disorder category, specifically regarding the behavioral phenotypes it delineated. In the first decade of the 2000s, an increased concern over the diagnostic legitimacy of the sub-typed structure of autism gained significance in the greater field, garnering much discourse as well as scientific investigation. Since the inception of autism as a diagnostic category in the DSM-III, and the various permutations of the specific diagnostic labels throughout each revision, there was no truly standardized way of diagnosing the condition aside from the availability of some instrumentation, none of which was required for a diagnosis to be made. While several means of diagnostic instrumentation existed, such as the Autism Diagnostic Interview (ADI), the Autism Diagnostic Observation Scale (ADOS), the Childhood Autism Rating Scale (CARS), and the Gilliam Autism Rating Scale (GARS), to name only a few, the process of diagnosis was implemented by what is known as the "clinical best estimate." Clinical best estimate refers to the ability of the clinician to utilize his or her interpretations of available instrumentation and clinical knowledge in order to choose the most appropriate diagnosis for the individual. As a result of this concern, a notable study principally authored by Catherine Lord sought to investigate whether there was clinical legitimacy to the DSM-IV (and the virtually identical ICD-10) behavioral phenotypes of Autistic Disorder, Asperger's Disorder, and Pervasive Developmental Disorder-Not Otherwise Specified. By recruiting competent clinicians with expertise in utilizing validated diagnostic instruments throughout twelve university-based diagnostic centers, significant variation in actual diagnostic practices was observed. That is, there appeared to be more of a regional significance to the actual diagnosis of behavioral phenotype given as opposed to a clinical, phenotypic one. There are a number of possible explanations for this finding, but the outcome is virtually undeniable: there is not likely clinical legitimacy to the sub-typed organization of Pervasive Developmental Disorders as designated by the DSM-IV-TR (and, presumably, the previous versions either).[33]

As such, there appears to be a legitimate clinical need for a re-evaluation and re-definition of Autism Spectrum Disorders. Resultantly, a subcommittee of the DSM-5 Work Group for Neurodevelopmental Disorders, including many well-known and diverse individuals in the field of Pervasive Developmental Disorders, was established. Using the Simons Simplex Data set, a sizable and putatively reliable collection, the work group began to reassess the organization of the DSM-IV-TR. Based on a vast amount of meetings and committee projects, the Work group significantly revised the diagnostic label and criteria for what was formerly known as Pervasive Developmental Disorders, officially released in the DSM-5 in May of 2013.

As it is stated in the DSM-5, there is now a single diagnostic category known as *Autism Spectrum Disorder*, with two symptom domains: (1) social-communication domain; (2) restricted interest and repetitive behavior domain. Diagnostically, individuals must meet the following in their current condition, or based on an accurate historical account:

Persistent deficits in social-communication and social interaction across contexts, not accounted for by general developmental delays, and manifested by all three of the following:

a. Deficits in social-emotional reciprocity
b. Deficits in nonverbal communicative behaviors used for social interaction
c. Deficits in developing and maintaining relationships

Restricted, repetitive patterns of behavior, interests, or activities as manifested by at least two of the following:

a. Stereotyped or repetitive speech, motor movements, or use of objects
b. Excessive adherence to routines, ritualized patterns of verbal or nonverbal behavior, or excessive resistance to change
c. Highly restricted, fixated interests that are abnormal in intensity and focus
d. Hyper-or hypo-reactivity to sensory input or unusual interest in sensory aspects of environment.

Symptoms must be present in early childhood (but may not become fully manifest until social demands exceed limited capacities).

Symptoms together limit and impair everyday functioning.

There is, however, another sub-diagnosis within the category that has been both questioned and criticized significantly by the greater field. Labeled as *Social Pragmatic Communication Disorder*, these individuals display:

1. Persistent difficulties in the social use of verbal and nonverbal communication as manifest by deficits in the following:

a. Using communication for social purposes, such as greeting and sharing information, in a manner that is appropriate for the social context;

b. Changing communication to match context or the needs of the listener, such as speaking differently in a classroom than on a playground, communicating differently to a child than an adult, and avoiding use of overly formal language;

c. Following rules for conversation and storytelling, such as taking turns in conversation, rephrasing when misunderstood, and knowing how to use verbal and nonverbal signals to regulate interaction;

d. Understanding what is not explicitly stated (e.g., inferencing) and nonliteral or ambiguous meanings of language, for example, idioms, jokes, metaphors, and multiple meanings that depend on the context for interpretation.

2. Deficits result in functional limitations in effective communication, social participation, social relationships, academic achievement, or occupational performance.

3. Onset in the early developmental period (but deficits may not become fully manifest until social-communication demands exceed limited capacities).

4. Deficits are not better explained by low abilities in the domains of word structure and grammar, or by intellectual disability, global developmental delay, Autism Spectrum Disorder, or another mental or neurologic disorder.

The new delineations are based primarily on some significant conceptual changes regarding autism as a condition. First, there have been many studies that present strong evidence for a primarily genetic component, yet if environmental interactions (even if they are based on genetic susceptibility) cannot be entirely ruled out, there is an indication of the need for both aspects to be considered in the diagnosis. Second, autism is to be regarded as a lifelong disorder emphasizing differences in appearances of children, importance of early diagnosis, and the likely need for sustained lifelong support, paying little clinical legitimacy to the notion of recovery (even in the case of vast improvement). Third, the significance and centrality of social interaction and social communication across the spectrum has been emphasized. Fourth, the use of the term Autism Spectrum Disorder was likely chosen due to the commonality of its colloquial though somewhat meaningful use in the field, a potential attempt to give true meaning to a vaguely defined yet pervasive and functional term. Furthermore, it was decided that the use of the term "pervasive" to describe the condition was a misnomer, as symptoms of ASD appear to be best understood specifically as they connect to social-communicative areas and restricted/repetitive behaviors particularly. The elimination of Asperger's Disorder specifically was justified as being due to the difference in such cases as originally presented by Asperger himself, as well as the aforementioned inconsistencies in conceptualizing Asperger's Disorder. Additionally, data indicate clearly that there is a disproportionate representation between a diagnosis of Asperger's Disorder among white individuals from middle-class or affluent families and a diagnosis of PDD-NOS among minority individuals from more socioeconomically challenged families. Finally, in the context of a "spectral" diagnosis, consideration is allowed for individual specificity and diagnostic variability, mostly through the strong suggestion for diagnosticians to provide supplemental narratives of the individual being diagnosed. Such factors described should include, but are not limited to, severity of ASD symptoms, patterns of onset and clinical course of action, potential etiological factors, cognitive abilities, associated conditions (such as Fragile X, Down's Syndrome, Tourette's Syndrome, etc.), and any other relevant features apparent to the diagnostician. [34]

As many instances of significant change do, the diagnostic changes in the DSM-5 were not accepted ubiquitously by the greater field, and many well-known and qualified clinicians adamantly question, if not fervently oppose the changes. Among the most significant of the issues, there is deep concern that the new diagnostic criteria could:

> substantially alter the composition of the autism spectrum. Revised criteria improve specificity but exclude a substantial portion of cognitively able individuals and those with ASDs other than autistic disorder. A more stringent diagnostic rubric holds significant public health ramifications regarding service eligibility and compatibility of historical and future research. [35]

Additional concerns about the restructuring of the diagnosis, which are alluded to in the above quote, have to do with the stringency of the new rubric. Some clinicians believe that while specificity may be gained, sensitivity is sacrificed. [36] That is, the condition may be better defined using a single diagnostic category, but the rigidness with which it is defined may serve to exclude some individuals from the diagnosis, yielding a withdrawal or refusal of services by school districts.

One of the most significant protests to the new classification system is in the realm of the newly created *Social Pragmatic Communication Disorder*. The common objection in this case is twofold. First, it is qualitatively unclear as to how this disorder is truly different from Pervasive Developmental Disorder-Not Otherwise Specified, which was, itself, likely functioning as a "catch-all" diagnosis for those who did not meet DSM-IV-TR criteria for the other two subtypes within PDD, in that "SCD is largely consistent with a

DSM-IV-TR conceptualization of PDD-NOS . . ."[37] Second, and perhaps most importantly, as a brand new diagnostic label, it is unclear as to whether SCD is, indeed, legitimate in and of itself. This is a puzzling development, as the unclear distinction of Asperger's Disorder appeared to be one of the initial impetuses of the convening of the DSM-5 workgroup. It appears that the same unclear distinction exists with the inclusion of SCD. As Ozonoff suggests:

> [inclusion of SCD seems] logically and internally inconsistent for the DSM-5, so pioneering in its dimensional approach, to introduce a *separate category* [italics in original] that is so qualitatively similar to another condition.[38]

Finally, a wide range of clinicians question the timing of the change, disbelieving that a long enough duration did, indeed, exist to confidently illegitimate the behavioral phenotype structure of the DSM-IV-TR. Barely a 30-year history existed using a behavioral phenotype framework, and a smaller window existed if one differentiates between the editions of the DSMs that changed the nomenclature as well as the criteria of the phenotypes in some significant, if not fundamental ways. As such, it is possible that research conducted after the DSM-5 is incomparable to the research conducted before it, potentially rendering past studies conducted within the older frameworks obsolete. This can be daunting for a young but fruitful field, and add inconsistency and complication to an already poorly understood and ill-defined condition.

Complicating the matter further, what accompanies a perspective of diagnostic focus is also a preoccupation within the concept of normality. That is, the pervasive belief that if something is diagnosable in that it differs from the typical experience of development or ability, then there must be a corresponding notion of normality, or what the typical experience is (or at least *should* be). As proposed by Douglas Baynton, the concept of the "normal" in the 20th century was an outgrowth of the concept of the "natural," which took strong hold in the 19th century. The most important social contribution to the metamorphosis of this concept was the change of societal focus from "God and faith" to "science and reason." Whereas a society centered on God could likely accept differences, even severe ones, as simply part of "God's plan" with those who are different remaining "God's children," these faith-based explanations were regarded as inadequate from a scientific and reason-based perspective. The shift toward reason, then, gave way to the concept of normal and its opposite (and enemy) the abnormal or, "defective," the clear framework for the medical model of mental disorder diagnostics. As Thomson suggests:

[the normate is] the constructed identity of those who, by way of bodily configurations and cultural capital they assume, can step into a position of authority and wield the power it grants to them. [39]

Combined with a capitalist "gain-based" idea of progression, especially in
the area of economics as well as notions of "social evolution," a systematic
means of identifying, sorting, and addressing the problem of disorder became
necessary, leading to the medical model of disabilities and the field of psychiatry.

The tendency for society to view disability as a whole from the medical
model perspective is particularly pernicious with specific regard to educational practices. From the perspective of the medical model, disabilities are
organic in nature, existing within the individual regardless of setting or environmental circumstance. As a result, the occurrence of disability or disorder
invariably leads to the necessity of treatment and rehabilitation, therefore
increasing the individual's chances of becoming normal, or as close to normal as possible. This progression is deemed socially desirable as "normal"
people only (or at least those that are not so abnormal as to be excluded) can
be fully functional and valuable in society, especially capitalistically, so
abnormality should be regarded as a detractor from progression and, thus, be
abated through corrective, restorative, or rehabilitative practices. Therefore,
from the medical model perspective, there is an axiomatic view of what is
right (normal) and what is wrong (abnormal).

While the medical model may be very much in line with capitalistic and
outcomes-based thinking, it fails entirely to regard the influence of either
environmental or social factors on an individual's experience. As such, the
only way for society to address disability or disorder is to correct it or
remediate it, with failure to do so resulting only in institutional exclusion of
the individual of some sort or another, not amelioration of the societal element that prevents such accessibility. This deficiency makes clear way for
the perspective of disability and disorder of any kind, including Autism
Spectrum Disorder, to be considered from a socially constructed perspective.

AUTISM SPECTRUM DISORDERS AS A SOCIAL CONSTRUCT

Despite the ostensible improvement within the context of the field of psychiatric diagnosis, the perspective of deficiency and abnormality is maintained
and pervaded by its function. That is, the context of diagnosis is framed in a
context of deficiency in particular areas, mandating that individuals "fail" to
develop and behave "normally" in order to qualify for a diagnosis. This
practice validates the dominance of the medical model.

There is, however, an alternative means of viewing Autism Spectrum
Disorder (with full understanding that by retaining the nomenclature in terms

of its "disorder," continued credence is paid to the medical model; however, an argument for a change in nomenclature is beyond the scope of this particular treatise). By viewing ASD as a social construct rather than a psychiatric disorder, society (and, ipso facto, schools) will be better able to justly handle the different needs and requirements of individuals with Autism Spectrum Disorder.[40]

Social constructionism, or the process by which phenomena begin to be viewed not as factual and invariable occurrences but as protean issues within a social domain, is based on the following tenets:[41]

1. A critical stance is used for "taken-for-granted" means of "seeing the world" challenging the notion that a view is based on natural perception or unbiased, objective observation, which cautions us to be ever-suspicious of assumptions.
2. Historical and cultural specificity are considered; all ways of understanding are culturally and historically relevant, whether the "knower" is conscious of this or not.
3. Knowledge is sustained by social processes; people construct knowledge and perception of reality between one another; it is propagated strongly through the use of language.
4. Knowledge and social action are mutual processes; how one person (or groups of people) view the world is deeply connected to social behavior.

Essentially, the concept of social constructionism opposes the notion that knowledge is a direct result of the perception of reality, but rather that the people within a culture (or sub-culture) construct the meanings of reality amongst and between one another through their interactions. Grinker's aforementioned point regarding the lack of labels for ASD in some cultures and the unwillingness to pathologize the condition despite its recognition in others is demonstrative of how the concept of social constructionism is directly applicable to the notion of ASD. As such, the perspective of social constructionism is predominantly "anti-essentialist." That is, there can be no essential, universal reality, but only one that is constructed through social processes, interactions, and language, resulting more likely in various experiential *realities*. Therefore, to facilitate a process of social constructionism is to reject dogmas of any kind. As posited by Gergen, who suggested that all knowledge is historically and culturally specific:

> An analysis of theory and research in social psychology reveals that while methods of research are scientific in character, theories of social behavior are primarily reflections of contemporary history. The dissemination of psychological knowledge modifies the patterns of behavior upon which the knowl-

edge is based. It does so because of the prescriptive bias of psychological theorizing, the liberating effects of knowledge, and the resistance based on common values of freedom and individuality. In addition, theoretical premises are based primarily on acquired dispositions. As the culture changes, such dispositions are altered, and the premises are often invalidated.[42]

It is from this perspective that the understanding of the authoritative and eliminative role that behavioral psychology played historically becomes essential. As social science relies almost entirely on language and its description of social processes (even when communicating quantitative aspects), the dominance attained by behaviorism is directly attributable to the medicalized and behavioristic tendencies of the educational field throughout the 20th and into the 21st century; because schools are directly connected to society (if not the beginnings of them, *a la* Dewey), it appears to be obvious as to why ASD is persistently seen as a disorder rather than a social construct in Western societies. As Gergen explains further:

social psychology is primarily an historical inquiry. Unlike the natural sciences, it deals with facts that are largely nonrepeatable and which fluctuate markedly over time. Principles of human interaction cannot readily be developed over time because the facts on which they are based do not generally remain stable. Knowledge cannot accumulate in the usual scientific sense because such knowledge does not generally transcend its historical boundaries.[43]

This clearly represents an entirely antithetical notion to that of the behavioral perspective, which posits, more confidently than perhaps any other branch of social science that its tenets represent fact and are, as some claim, irrefutable as demonstrated by "evidence." However, this cannot be true, as Gergen reveals quite convincingly, rather that behaviorism has the advantage of being the dominant voice in social science as well as in education, allowing its points to be heard more clearly and audibly, and implemented almost universally, if not thoughtlessly, though not as a result of its "factual basis," but as a result of its position of authority and rhetorical dominance. Resultantly, refutations or critiques of this narrative are less public and more suppressed, creating a significant gap between rhetoric and true evidence-basis. This can be counteracted by a means of recognizing that the best option in social science:

is to maintain as much sensitivity as possible to our biases and to communicate them as openly as possible. Value commitments may be unavoidable, but we can avoid masquerading them as objective reflections of truth.[44]

While social constructionism provides a very viable framework within which social constructs can be formed, it does not fully explain the process by which such constructs take root and actually influence social practices.

Though initially proposed in the context of race, the theory of racial formation as delineated by Omi and Winant can also be (and has been) applied to other forms of social constructions. As Omi and Winant explain, "[r]ace was thought of as a biological concept, yet its precise definition was the subject of debates which . . . continue to rage today."[45] This description bears quite an identical commonality with what has been discussed about Autism Spectrum Disorder thus far, with a new "age" of vastly different means of definition quite recently proffered. Omi and Winant describe that the term "racial formation" is used "to refer to the process by which social, economic, and political forces determine the content and importance of racial categories, and by which they are in turn shaped by racial meanings."[46] While undoubtedly there are different types of political forces at work in the formation of ASDs and the meanings may have somewhat different outcomes, the analogy remains strong as it denotes the role that authoritative and hegemonic forces play in the delineation of meanings and social outcomes for individuals who fail to meet the standards of the "norm," which is clear in the case of disability (and disorder).

It is therefore the main contention of this chapter that the conception of Autism Spectrum Disorder is by no means a clearly delineated and definable condition, but rather is only purported to be by an authoritative, politically driven, and hegemonic force that is omnipresent in the fields of social and medical science, particularly that of psychiatry, psychology, and education. This contention is not entirely unprecedented, and has been espoused by an emerging number of writers and philosophers, among which Majia Nadesen is arguably the best known (though a book by Eyal et al., 2013, has recently contributed similar ideas, the perspective put forth is quite different from other socially constructed philosophies), and Alicia Broderick. Nadesen, both a parent of a child with ASD and a social scientist and intellectual, begins her basis of argument around the notion that parents and teachers are most often directed toward explanations of autism written from the biological and neurological perspective as such diagnoses are given by doctors. This treatise adds the claim that, as a result of pervasive authority (not necessarily in terms of actual expertise but rather in terms of policy making) in the field, they are also directed toward primarily behavioral approaches. These trends are cooperative and mutually beneficial, as behavioral approaches make strong use of the medical model's distinction between normal and abnormal (this argument will be discussed in detail later in the treatise). On the contrary, however, Nadesen suggests that autism should be regarded as a socially constructed concept (and likely not even a "disorder"), as she explains:

> autism, or more specifically, the *idea* [italics in original] of autism is fundamentally *socially constructed* [italics in original] . . . [this] is not to necessarily

reject a biological basis for conditions or symptoms that come to be labeled as "autistic." Rather, I use the phrase "socially constructed" to point to the social conditions of a possibility for naming of autism as a distinct disorder and to the social conditions of possibility for our methods of interpreting the disorders, representing it, remediating it, and even performing it.[47]

Therefore, from the perspective of this treatise, the medical model of viewing autism is overtly rejected in favor of viewing it as a social construct. That is, not something that is organically sourced and, therefore, organically responsible for deficits, burdens, and challenges. Rather, the concept of autism is protean in and of itself, changing not only based on increased understanding of the "condition" itself or outplay of it, but ever changing roles of individuals who are different from the "normal" in society. Because autism is not viewed as a condition to be treated, but rather a social construct that is part of a person needing to become as functional and contributive to the society as everyone else, the perspective of using and applying single-mode "treatment" methodologies to "train" or "change" individuals, namely Applied Behavior Analysis, is devalued as a legitimate perspective, as is the notion of "treatment" altogether. Rather, the argument is made that individuals with autism, as should all individuals, be regarded holistically, as being dynamic and possessing needs and displaying aspects of living, some of which are directly related to a set of traits they possess as a result of a condition, some of which are not, but none of which should be distinguished or "treated" as a "deficiency." Because American (and arguably other Western-type) society highly values the dichotomy between normal and abnormal, our schools have functioned primarily as a grounds for separating the normal from the abnormal, and assimilating those who could be "normalized" while excluding those who could not be "normalized." Applied Behavior Analysis is fundamentally based on this system of normalization and assimilation.

The remainder of the work will focus on investigating the ways in which the tenets and practices of behavior analysis and its respective interventional approaches function as hegemonic and hyper-authoritative, as well as dismissive of individuality and ignorant of a holistic approach toward individuals. It is not, by any means, an attempt to devalue the approach as a whole, as there is an integral contribution that the process of Applied Behavior Analysis makes to a holistic educational approach of individuals with diverse needs. It will, however, proffer an outright rejection of the notion that behavior analytic approaches are superior to other approaches and should, therefore, play the most central role, if not the singular role, in the education of individuals with autism.

NOTES

1. Canguilhem G (1994) *A Vital Rationalist: Selected Writings from Georges Canguilhem.* New York: Zone Books, 42.

2. Barend Verhoeff, "Autism in Flux," *History of Psychiatry,* 24(4), 2013, 446.

3. Roy Richard Grinker, *Unstrange Minds,* 2008.

4. Ibid.

5. Darold Treffert, "The Savant Syndrome: An Extraordinary Condition. A Synopsis: Past, Present, Future." *Philosophical Transactions of the Royal Society: Biological Sciences.* May 2009, v. 364, 1522, 1351–57.

6. Leo Kanner, "Autistic Distrubances of Affective Content." In *The Nervous Child,* 41.

7. Majia Nadesen, *Constructing Autism: Unraveling the Truth and Understanding the Social,* 2008.

8. Kanner, 1943, 242.

9. Ibid., 242–48.

10. Lorna Wing, "Asperger's Syndrome: A Clinical Account," *Psychological Medicine,* 11 (1), 1981, 115–29.

11. James Ladell Sanders, "Qualitative or Quantitative Differences Between Asperger's Disorder and Autism? Historical Differences." *Journal of Autism and Developmental Disorders,* 2009, 19, 1560–67.

12. Hans Asperger, "Problems of Infantile Autism." *Communication,* 1979, 13: 45–52, 48

13. Sanders, 2009.

14. Kathrin Hippler and Christian Kliepera, "A Retrospective Analysis of the Clinical Case Records of Autistic Psychopaths Diagnosed by Hans Asperger and His Team at the University Children's Hospital, Vienna," *Philosophical Transactions of the Royal Society of London* (2003), v. 358, 291–301.

15. Jeffrey P. Baker, "Autism in 1959: Joey the Mechanical Boy," *Pediatrics,* 159 (6), 2010, 1101.

16. Kanner, 1973, as cited by Grinker, 2007, 72.

17. Baker, 1973.

18. http://www.autism.com/ari/newsletter/203/page1.pdf.

19. Bruno Bettelheim, "Joey: A Mechanical Boy," http://www.weber.edu/wsuimages/psychology/FacultySites/Horvat/Joey.PDF.

20. James D. Herbert et al. "Separating Fact from Fiction in the Etiology and Treatment of Autism: A Scientific Review of the Evidence." From http://integrativehealthconnection.com/wp-content/uploads/2011/11/Etiology-And-Treatment-Of-Autism1.pdf.

21. Gary B. Mesibov and Victoria Shea, "The TEACCH Program in the Era of Evidence-Based Practice." *Journal of Autism and Developmental Disorders.* From http://www.interactingwithautism.com/pdf/treating/184.TEACCH%20program%20in%20the%20era%20of%20evidenced%20based.pdf.

22. Grinker, 2008.

23. Ibid., 103.

24. Ibid.

25. Ibid.

26. Verhoeff, 2013.

27. Nadesen, 2008.

28. Lorna Wing, et al. (2011). "Autism Spectrum Disorders in the DSM-V: Better or Worse than the DSM-IV?" *Research in Developmental Disabilities,* 32, 768–73.

29. Rutter and Schopler, 1992, 476, as cited by Verhoeff.

30. Tantam, 1988, as cited by Leekam, 2000. (Susan Leekam et al., "Comparison of ICD-10 and Gillberg's Criteria for Asperger Syndrome" *Autism,* 4(1), 11–28.

31. Szatmari et al., 1989, as cited by Leekam, 2000.

32. Gillberg et al., 1993, as cited by Leekam, 2000.

33. Catherine Lord et al. "A Multi-Site Study of the Clinical Diagnosis of Different Autism Spectrum Disorders," *Archives of General Psychiatry,* 2012, 69(3): 306–13.

34. Walter E. Kaufman (n.d), "The New Diagnostic Criteria for Autism Spectrum Disorders." From http://www.autismconsortium.org/symposiumfiles/WalterKaufmannAC2012Symposium.pdf.

35. J.C. McPortland et al. (2012). "Sensitivity and Specificity of Proposed DSM-5 Diagnostic Criteria for Autism Spectrum Disorder." *Journal of the American Academy of Child and Adolescent Psychiatry*, 368.

36. Kauffman, n.d.

37. McPortland, 370.

38. Ozonoff, 2012, as cited by Verhoeff.

39. Rosemary Garland Thomson, *Extraordinary Bodies: Figuring Physical Disability in American Culture and Literature*. New York: Columbia University Press (1997), 8.

40. This argument can be made for all "disorders" and "disabilities," but will be kept in the context of ASD for the purpose of this treatise.

41. Vivien Burr, *Social Constructionism*. New York: Routledge, 2003.

42. K.J. Gergen. "Social Psychology as History."*Journal of Personality and Social Psychology*, 26(2), 309.

43. Ibid., 310.

44. Ibid., 312

45. Michael Omi and Howard Winant, *Racial Formations in the United States*, 1994, 11.

46. Ibid., 12.

47. Majia Nadesen, *Constructing Autism: Unraveling the 'Truth' and Understanding the Social*. New York: Psychology Press, 2005.

Chapter Four

Evidence-Based Practices and Their Use in Educational Interventions

The use of evidence-based practices in the context of educational interventions is one that requires a careful analysis of both history and conceptualization in order to be fully understood in terms of its intended use and purpose as well as its widespread misapplication and misunderstanding. While many of the ideas in social science are elusive, evidence-based practice presents a unique challenge in terms of its definition, conceptualization, and application mainly as a result from its origination in the medical sciences, an area that is dually influenced by both the natural and social sciences, suffusing then to the area of psychology and eventually into the field of education primarily through legislative and policy making activity. The difficulty with which practitioners and researchers have dealt with satisfactorily capturing and implementing a well-structured means of evidence-based practice has been significant, though its use as a definitive evaluative standard for educational interventions, despite its lack of a solid conceptualization, remains dubiously intact. Ultimately, the result of this difficulty is a haphazard and self-serving application of the concept yielding bold claims to be allowed for some methodologies while no claims have been allowed for others. While the putative purpose of evidence-based practice in education, and specifically special education, is to enhance the scientific validity of human service practices acting as a means of both consumer and practitioner protection, what has happened, in reality, is a re-politicization and a struggle for dominance that involves science far less than it does territoriality and rhetoric, namely in the form of bold and largely unfounded claims. In the field of Autism Spectrum Disorder this is most characteristic by the field of Applied Behavior Analysis.

This chapter will address the history and development of the concept of evidence-based practices from its origination in the field of medicine, through its re-application in psychology and its ultimate adaptation for educational intervention. Focusing on both the legislative and scientific influences for such applications, the argument will be made that the concept of evidence-based practices was prematurely applied to educational interventions, and the consequence has been its misuse by applying it as rhetorical power to prematurely establish and maintain supremacy of the behavior analytic approach over other equally as valid and promising methodologies. Furthermore, this chapter will examine means of evaluating evidence-basis for educational interventions in terms of their strengths and weaknesses, specifically pinpointing problems with the method of evidence-basis employed by the field of Applied Behavior Analysis methodologically, as well as in terms of interpretation of findings and application to the field. Finally, a new, more comprehensive definition will be proffered for the term *evidence-based practices* that will be more applicable, amenable, and appropriate for the various methods necessitated in effectively implementing comprehensive educational interventions for individuals with ASD specifically.

LEGISLATION AND THE STRUGGLE FOR DEFINITION

The concept of evidence-based practices (EBPs) in education is typically regarded as an adaptation of evidence-based medicine, which originated in the field of epidemiology. According to the main tenets of epidemiology, the purpose of evidence-based medicine (and, *ipso facto*, evidence-based practices in any human service field that has adopted some form of it as a standard) is to narrow the distance between clinical practice and public health using research conducted in related fields and clinical expertise to inform such clinical practices. As a result, the practice of human services can be treated as both an art and a science, capitalizing on the expertise and experience of clinicians as well as the rigor and control of scientific investigation. According to Sackett and colleagues:

> Evidence-based medicine is the conscientious, explicit, and judicious use of current best evidence in making decisions about the care of individual patients. The practice of evidence based medicine means integrating individual clinical expertise with the best available external clinical evidence from systematic research. By individual clinical expertise we mean the proficiency and judgment that individual clinicians acquire through clinical experience and clinical practice. Increased expertise is reflected in many ways, but especially in more effective and efficient diagnosis and in the more thoughtful identification and compassionate use of individual patients' predicaments, rights, and preferences in making clinical decisions about their care. By best available external clinical evidence we mean clinically relevant research, often from the basic

sciences of medicine, but especially from patient centered clinical research into the accuracy and precision of diagnostic tests (including the clinical examination), the power of prognostic markers, and the efficacy and safety of therapeutic, rehabilitative, and preventive regimens. [1]

Sackett offers the field a comprehensive and well-defined conceptualization of the multiple components of medicine and medical services, and how it is optimized by aligning itself with both the individualized needs and experiences of the patient while still retaining the rigor and strength of scientific investigation and empirical evidence. What happens to the definition as it moves to the social sciences and, ultimately, the field of education is curious, losing quite a bit of specificity upon its adoption by the American Psychological Association (APA) as well as its incorporation into the legislation (though not under the moniker of "evidence-based practices") in both the Elementary and Secondary Education Act (known also, temporarily, as No Child Left Behind) and the Individuals with Disabilities Education Improvement Act (the most current iteration of IDEA reauthorized in 2004). According to the APA, evidence-based practice is defined as, "the integration of the best available research with clinical expertise in the context of patient characteristics, culture and preferences."[2]

Curiously, the specificity of the definition between that of Sackett in 1996 and that of the APA in 2006 was significantly diminished. While the APA definition retains the general spirit of Sackett's definition, it lacks almost entirely any operational descriptions about how evidence basis should, or even could be evaluated. That is, which specific client characteristics are deemed important, and on a similar note, how the very subjective and protean concepts of culture and preferences are defined is entirely absent. In this case, it appears that it is not only clinical expertise that takes focus, in that each clinician has almost complete latitude in determining not only what treatment to use, but whether such treatment can be deemed as being evidence-based. The urgency of this significant loss in specificity of such a critical definition is in the field of education's tendency to follow developments in psychology. There are many examples demonstrating the indelible if not causal link between movements in psychology corresponding with movements in education, with that of behaviorism as a prime example. That noted, it is likely that the policymakers responsible for establishing a notion of evidence-based practice in education, though interestingly not under that specific term, looked to and relied heavily upon the vague definition offered by the APA more so than that offered by Sackett in the original conceptualization.

The Elementary and Secondary Education Act (ESEA) references a guideline that is clearly demonstrative of a form of implementing evidence-based practices with regard to educational interventions in that, methods, be they curricular, instructional, or otherwise be informed by:

> research that involves the application of rigorous, systematic and objective procedures to obtain a reliable and valid knowledge relevant to education activities and programs.[3]

Similarly, the Individuals with Disabilities Education Improvement Act (IDEIA) posits a similar statement regarding the use of interventional methodologies for students with special needs specifically in that the use of such methods must provide:

> A statement of the special education and related services and supplementary aids and services, based on peer-reviewed research to the extent practicable, to be provided to the child.

What remains ever curious about this second adaptation is the elimination entirely of the role of clinical expertise (or the expertise of the teacher) and the respective roles of culture and preference. It seems that the definitions in both instances of educational legislation now rely entirely on purportedly rigorous peer-reviewed research methods to be deemed as evidence-based practices, creating urgency in the field not to spend time truly vetting such methods, but rather to place their efforts in publishing about their methods in peer-reviewed journals. This transformation is dubious when relating back to Sackett's original definition closely. In Sackett's definition, there seemed to be a clear delineation of the equality of each of the components in evidence-based medicine, while in the delineation in the educational law, there is a clear elimination of those other, more "subjective"(or expertise-based) components while retaining the supposedly "objective" facet of peer-reviewed research. The problem lies in the research process, especially in a social science that is action-based and concept-based, as education and teaching inarguably are. Specifically, peer-reviewed research refers to a process of ensuring rigor of methodology and sensibility and context of claims; it does not, however, put forth any type of guideline as to what types of research apply to evidence-based practices in education. Therefore, the field was left to work out on its own what would be deemed as sufficient evidence basis and what would not. It is this opportunity that was clearly seized by the behaviorist faction in the field of education, specifically in the realm of Autism Spectrum Disorders, and the point of genesis for what would become a nearly imperious reign of behavioral perspectives, practices, and policies. If the standard of evidence-basis is the existence of peer-reviewed research available, then the means by which achievement of evidence-basis was to be claimed was by a grand-scale effort toward publication, forcing the consumer to value quantity over quality.

As is often the case in educational reform, especially such reform that is directly tied to legislation, there is financial benefit provided to those programs that find ways to exemplify such new and promising practices. In August of 2002, in order to stimulate progress toward the implementation of evidence-based practices (at least in its vague form delineated in the legislation) the United States Department of Education established a grant pool of $18.5 million to be overseen by the *What Works Clearinghouse* (WWC), an initiative of the Institute for Education Sciences. The WWC identifies itself as:

> a resource for informed education decision making . . . the WWC identifies studies that provide credible and reliable evidence of the effectiveness of a given practice, program, or policy . . . and disseminates summary information and reports on the WWC website.[4]

As part of the initiative, the WWC developed the *Design and Implementation Assessment Device*, a tool for identifying evidence-based practices. The instrument itself, however, has been the subject of much controversy due to its perceived emphasis and value (if not over-emphasis and over-value) on the use of randomized clinical trials (RCTs), which are generally seen as the "gold standard" in research practices. This is particularly problematic for educational researchers, however, especially those in the specific field of researching interventions for individuals with exceptionalities for a variety of reasons to be discussed in further detail later in the chapter.

From this dubious rollout of vague legislation and policy making and questionable practices in vetting educational interventions, there were a few significant voices who attempted to share their expertise with the field in order to concretize an elusive concept and, at least potentially, transform it into a useful practice. Bryan Cook and Sara Cothren Cook, both respected members of the Council for Exceptional Children's Division for Research, continue to be strong voices in favor of the adoption of evidence-based practices in educational interventions, but also warn the field of likely consequences from careless and hapless attempts of its application. Submitting that evidence-based practices are, ultimately, entirely necessary in ensuring, protecting, and preserving high quality and ethical treatment and service provision for all students, Cook and Cook are careful to admonish that "EBPs are not self-implementing mechanisms that will be embraced and utilized automatically."[5] Therefore, in order for teachers to be convinced to abandon the field's long-standing traditional means of simply "believing" in methodologies without the support of evidence, the field must make a concerted effort to be clear about what EBPs actually are and how evidence-basis can be accurately determined. Based on this premise Cook and Cook propose four main tenets upon which EBPs should be defined. First, research design is of utmost importance when it comes to establishing an intervention's evidence-basis. Second, the quality of research studies is imperative, and must be held in line with quality indicators, or those characteristics that are possessed by well-designed studies. Third, the quantity of research studies that support a given intervention may be used as supportive of its evidence-basis (a point which is qualified later in this treatise). The final indicator is magnitude of effect, which indicates how robust the findings of studies supporting an intervention are.

According to Gresham, to view evidence-based practices as a whole is largely inutile, and will do little, if anything, to clarify which practices in education are apt to be effective and which are not. Furthermore, if evidence-based practices are to be understood and applied at all in education, educationists of all types (teachers, parents, students, administrators, school psychologists, among others) must become better versed in the concepts of experimentation and research, and be able to view educational interventions in terms of changes in dependent variables (or the variables that are targeted to be measured such as behavior, academic achievement, performance, etc.) and independent variables, or systematic and well-controlled interventions that can be seen as clearly attributable to such changes. The means to do this effectively and accurately, claims Gresham, is not in the broad concept of evidence-based practices, but in the more localized concept of treatment integrity. Treatment integrity is typically viewed as having three dimensions. *Treatment adherence* refers to the degree to which an intervention is implemented as planned or intended by the designers of the intervention. *Interventionist competence* refers to the skill and experience in implementing a particular treatment. *Treatment differentiation* is the extent to which interventions differ on critical dimensions, either as a result of the practitioner, the individual, or the environment in which the intervention is being implemented.[6]

While Gresham's clarification on these three dimensions is important in its own right, what remains even more important is the refocusing of the concept of evidence-basis equally on rigor to the design of the approach as well as the experience of the interventionist. By removing both aspects from the legislative definitions, the drafters of the legislation effectively posited the idea that all children and all teachers are identical, and that any differences between them, if at all genuine, should have no effect on teaching methodologies so long as the peer-reviewed research supports those methodologies. The consequences of such framing are becoming quite apparent now in the context of recent developments and federal initiatives, the most obvious being *Race to the Top* and the adoption of the *Common Core State Standards* which call for, among other things, a vast standardization of practices, content, and formalized evaluations for all children and teachers nationwide regardless of individual differences including culture, value, environmental importance, or learning specifications (such as giftedness or disability). Secondly, Gresham retains the importance of both quantitative and qualitative values in evaluation of any kind. Specifically, treatment adherence is more amenable to a quantitative dimension as it can be measured in terms of the number of critical treatment components retained in the application, while therapist competence is more likely a conceptualization of the qualitative type, though that is not to say there are no means of quantifying, at least in estimations, some of the aspects of therapist competence. Treatment differentiation represents theoretical differences between interventionists as well as treatments, and can be captured by both quantitative and qualitative measures.

Kazdin further clarifies the specific workings of how such evidence-based practices can be applied in a more workable fashion, mainly through the use of two concepts: mediators and mechanisms. A *mediator* is a construct that demonstrates an important and noticeable statistical relation between an intervention and an outcome (or, as Gresham frames, an independent and a dependent variable). Mediators, however, may not explain the process through which this change comes about. Therefore, with mediators, no causation can be claimed, only the existence of a change in an outcome during the time frame that the intervention was implemented. If such a process is to be gauged, interventionists must focus on *mechanisms*, which are more specific and can reflect the actual processes, or individual steps, through which an intervention follows to produce the change. The goal, then, of any intervention evaluation would be to achieve a means of attaining an explanation at the mechanism level, but this is difficult to do as it requires vast control and significantly accurate measurement abilities, both of which are difficult, if even truly possible to attain in classroom and even clinical educational settings. What is the more likely outcome is mediation with the identification of *moderators*, or some characteristic that appears to influence the direction or magnitude of the relationship between the intervention and the outcome.[7]

Mediation is not, in itself, a static concept, however, as Kazdin defines seven components of mediation within which an interventionist can frame findings, allowing for a more detailed and workable sense of effectiveness. The components are as follows:

1. Strong association—connection between the intervention and the hypothesized change
2. Specificity—that a particular, specific aspect of the therapy or the foundation itself accounts for it, not multiple potential factors
3. Consistency—replication of findings across studies and well-documented sessions
4. Experimental manipulation—if an effect can be shown through experimentation it strengthens the mediator

5. Timeline—interventions and effects must be linearly associated and accounted for specifically
6. Gradient—showing that greater "doses" are associated with greater change
7. Plausibility—how such findings correlate or integrate with current knowledge or findings[8]

THE PROBLEM OF PARADIGMS

The notion of paradigms in the natural and social sciences is a well-accepted concept in both its existence and its indefatigable influence on the way that problems and questions are approached and investigated. Strangely, however, it has been a distinct challenge to accurately and consistently define what paradigms are. Even Thomas Kuhn, to whom the development of the concept of paradigm is largely attributed, is thought to have defined the term in up to twenty-one different ways.[9] How a concept can be so elusive to capture while maintaining such a distinct influence on the practices of a field can be a formidable challenge to address, but one that must be present in any work that intends to handle methodological applications of theories. While this work will not attempt to argue a definition for paradigms as a concept, it will submit that Guba's (1990) suggestion of how they may be addressed is a useful framework. According to this framework, paradigms must be conceptualized based on three concepts: ontology, epistemology, and methodology. *Ontology* seeks to understand the nature of the knowable or, in other terms, the nature of reality. That is, are there universal truths that exist and are attainable to the investigator or the knower (often referred to as "capital T" truths), universal truths that exist but are only attainable to the investigator or knower through their own perceptions (often referred to as "little T" truths), or the existence of many truths, all of which are simultaneously possible and knowable, if not created directly by the investigator or the knower? *Epistemology* seeks to understand the relationship between the investigator or the knower and the known, or at least knowable. That is, can the investigator or knower affect or even create a truth or a reality, or is it existent in its form regardless of whether it is sought or known by anyone? Finally, *methodology* aims to understand how such questions should be approached and, ultimately, investigated to determine an answer. That is, in what way should the investigator or knower go about determining truths? According to Guba, the answers to these specific questions are what differentiate one paradigm from another, and these differentiations have a vast influence on the types of questions, answers, or natures of truths each paradigm proposes, how these questions are investigated, as well as how such truths are ultimately applied to their respective fields.

Guba suggests that there are four main paradigms that can apply to social sciences including education: positivist, post-positivist, critical theorist, and constructivist. Each paradigm bears its own unique combination of ontology, epistemology, and methodology which distinguishes it as a paradigm in and of itself, but more importantly, the types of questions asked and the way in which those answers, or attained "truths" are investigated and conceptualized will result in a vastly different application in professional practice, affecting the outplay of relationships between human beings and, in many ways, crafting and influencing the nature of a culture.

Positivism. According to Guba, positivism is the predominant paradigm within the sciences, and one which is directly related to the vast influence that behaviorism had on the social sciences. Ontologically, Guba characterizes positivism as being "realist." That is, positivists believe that there is a single reality that exists, and it is one that is driven by "immutable natural law and mechanisms."[10] The ability to understand these laws must be approached through a means that is free of both context and time, and can be universally generalized. Many of these concepts take on the form of cause and effect dichotomies. Epistemologically, Guba contends that positivism adopts a dualist/objectivist perspective. From this vantage it is not only possible, but necessary for the knower to adopt a distant and non-interactive posture to the sought truth, forcing the knower to systematically eliminate values, opinions, expectations, and other potentially biasing and confounding variables which are apt to influence the outcome of an investigation. Methodologically, positivism adopts an experimental and manipulative approach to investigation in which the questions and/or hypotheses are stated in advance, known as *a priori*, and are then subjected to empirical tests carried out under carefully controlled conditions, the results of which will either support or negate them. Accordingly, most positivist investigations are predominantly, if not entirely quantitative, as number-based findings are seen as being less influenced by human biases and therefore more trustworthy and reliable.

While many would submit relatively easily to the notion that the positivist perspective is, in large part, synonymous with the scientific perspective, this submission may be premature and made without sufficient analysis. Undoubtedly, this hackneyed submission is evidence in and of itself of the pervasive influence that the positivist paradigm has had on scientific investigation, even in the layperson's perception. However, the reality that the positivistic perspective relates can be significantly problematic. First to accept that there exist universal truths regardless of the position of the knower is to ignore, almost entirely, the deep influence that culture can have (culture being a concept whose comprehensive definition far exceeds the scope of this discussion, but one that is regarded as so complex and based on so many factors, physical, mental, metaphysical, and otherwise, that it cannot be dismissed). Second, it is not likely that knowers, even under the most carefully controlled circumstances, can possibly contrive a situation pure enough to observe a truth in its purest form. Third, and finally, it is entirely impossible for human beings to eliminate personal biases sufficiently enough to conduct and relate only facts and truths. The very attempt to know a truth is, in itself, a value judgment in that those questions must be weighed against one another to create a prioritization of which "truths" are sought first, and which "truths" are sought later. Therefore, the questions themselves are ultimately value judgments and, resultantly, biases.

Postpositivism. Postpositivism is a variation of positivism, but one that Guba characterizes as accepting some of the weaknesses that positivism presents and attempting to address them in a way that will make such an approach more utile. Ontologically, Guba suggests that postpositivism adopts a "critical realist" perspective. From this vantage, the truth that reality exists and is controlled by immutable laws is upheld, but it is submitted that such a truth can never be fully apprehended by a human knower. Therefore, knowers can only attain an incomplete and inferential understanding of "truth." Epistemologically, postpositivists are "modified objectivist," which still holds objectivism as a regulatory ideal, but one that can only be partially attained. As such, critique and approval by external evaluators such as the "critical tradition" and the "critical community" are most important to the acceptance and propagation of those "truths" that are apprehended. Finally, the methodology of postpositivists is characterized as being "modified experimental and manipulative." Similarly to the modification of the epistemology, postpositivists believe that questions should be investigated and addressed in as pure and unbiased a way as possible, but believe that this can be done only through a process of critical multiplism. That is, many approaches can and should be used to investigate truths, not only quantitative analyses. Among such other options are qualitative approaches and discovery-based methods, both of which can address variables that do not necessarily have to be framed *a priori*, but may be found and developed throughout an investigative process.

Postpositivism addresses many of the challenges created by positivism both methodologically and practically. Submitting to the notion that positivism calls for perfect conditions for investigation, postpositivism proposes that since these conditions are impossible to attain, there must be methods devised to address whatever imperfections exist in the research setting, such as critical multiplism. There remains, still, a particular problem with the postpositivist approach. Mainly, it ultimately accepts the positivist approach of "capital T" truth as correct, but places the flaw in the concept on human capability. That is, the positivist perspective that reality is set and generalizable is an accurate depiction, but humans are incapable of attaining such truth so it must adjust its own methods, resulting only in an approximated and imperfect attainment of "Truth." The shortfall in this way of thinking will be addressed in greater detail in the imminent discussion of both critical theory and, most completely, constructivist theory.

Critical Theory. While Guba's characterization of critical theory is, in many ways, incomplete and oversimplified, it will serve as complete enough for this particular discussion, especially in the avenue it creates to expound on the constructivist contentions with positivist-based approaches (including those of postpositivist thinking). Ontologically, Guba suggests that critical theory is comparable to postpostivist theory in its critical realism. The main differences lie, rather, in the epistemological and the methodological approaches. Epistemologically, critical theory is regarded as "subjectivist." That is, there is not only a direct connection between the knower and what is to be known, but that the knower can have a direct influence on what is to be known. This is a significant diversion from the positivist-based approaches in that truths are guided by not only natural, but immutable laws; that is, human inquiry and human influence serve only exploratory purposes since it cannot affect the truth itself. Critical theory not only maintains an opposition to this notion, suggesting that truth can actually be directly manipulated by human values. This is epitomized in the critical theorist methodology, termed as a dialogic/transformative method, which seeks to eliminate false consciousness thus facilitating transformation.

Critical theory puts forth the first formidable opposition to positivist-based theories by outlining and addressing the relationship between the knower and the known (or potentially known). If the knower cannot affect the known in any way, then there would be no means for change. However, there are countless examples of how not only discovery of certain truths (a postpositivist process), but the influence of one's perception over a truth has been a catalyst for change (for example, many states' legitimization of same-sex marriages requiring a redefinition of marriage itself). Such processes demonstrate that truths are, indeed, not immutable by nature, but are changed based on human interaction alone. From this perspective, there is vastly more room for qualitative inquiries and such inquiries do not necessarily have to yield similar results to be deemed acceptable or truthful.

Constructivism. Constructivism as a paradigm puts up the most formidable offense to positivism and, in many ways, postpositivism and critical theory as well. While the framework for addressing the positions of each paradigm will be maintained in terms of ontology, epistemology, and methodology, it is important to address the idea, propagated by Guba and supported by others, that constructivism dissolves the necessity for the dichotomous distinction between ontology and epistemology by suggesting that it is the observer (or the knower) that *literally* creates realities, not just affects or manipulates them, as conceptualized by critical theory. The issue becomes clear when one tries to superimpose the triadic positions onto constructivism. Ontologically, one may try to reduce the approach into a "relativist" perspective. Relativism suggests that realities exist only in the form of multiple mental constructions which are based in local and specific social experiences of the person who holds them. As such, epistemologically, there is a subjectivist relationship. That is, the inquirer and the inquired (or the knower and the known) are "fused" into a single entity (termed by Guba as "monistic"). Therefore, the findings that an investigator gathers are literally their own creation resulting from an interaction, or a combination, of the ontological and epistemological processes. This is a resultant of a hermeneutic and dialectic process, in which individual constructions are elicited, compared, and contrasted with the purpose of generating constructions upon which there can be substantial consensus.

While the constructive approach is deemed by many as "far-reaching" and even outright rejected by some, especially in the positivistic realms, a truly intellectual analysis will undoubtedly reveal the true feasibility of such an approach; shedding one's allegiance to a positivistic approach, even if a tacit one, however, is a necessity in order to do so. Even those who are traditionally seen as positivistic, such as John Dewey, can be just as easily analyzed in constructivist terms as it was the way in which the individual interacted with a stimulus combined with his or her prior knowledge or experience which created that individual's learning, or in Dewey's nomenclature, a "warranted assertion."[11] What constructivism allows for, if not requires is the existence, acceptance, valuation, and use of a variety of experiences and realities even under the same conditions. Ultimately, constructivist approaches eliminate the necessity for a concept of normality, laying the groundwork for a truly diverse and ever-diversifying culture that maintains the value of individuality and difference. Valle and King identify the issues of positivism astutely:

> What is unknown or unusual to us will be explained or accounted for by natural sciences in general (e.g., physical, chemistry, and biology) and by the methods they employ in particular. This natural scientific approach makes a number of assumptions, the three most crucial . . . being that: (a) the phenomenon under the study . . . must be observable . . . ; (b) the phenomenon must be measurable . . . ; and (c) the phenomenon must be such that it is possible for more than one observer to agree on its existence and characteristics.[12]

Further expounded by Giorgi:

> The priority is given to the measurement perspective, and, in order for something to be measured, only its tangible aspects can be apprehended, and thus the indices itself of a phenomenon become more important than that phenomenon [itself].[13]

Constructivism, then, rejects three main aspects of positivism in place of three distinct values. First, constructivism values qualitative research over quantitative research. Second, constructivism values relevance over rigor as the criterion for quality. Third, constructivism values grounded theory (theories which are "led to") rather than *a priori* theory (theories that are "sought after"), thus eliminating the need for causal relationships of observable variables and replacing them with propositional, tacit, and expansionist (as opposed to reductionist) approaches.

THE STRUGGLE FOR APPLICATION OF EBP IN EDUCATION

While the discussion of defining evidence-based practices in general continues, the field of education, specifically, has been equally as engaged in attempting to determine how this concept could and, more importantly, should, relate to its own practices. The struggle has been no different than that of other fields, with proponents of various types of research methodologies vying for inclusion, or even supremacy, as a valid means of meeting the relatively vague mandates of the concept. The case is clear, however, that some modes of evidencing effectiveness for educational interventions have garnered more positive attention, rightfully deserved or not, and have thus been popularly deemed more evidence-based than others. It is important, however, that popular acceptance or consensus within the field as a whole not be confused with actual validation of practices. In many ways to the contrary, this sense of popular validation can be seen as detrimental to such validation, as its general "acceptance" has, in many instances translated into haphazard or compromised practice and overstated application serving the function of merely rhetorically validating practices without rigorous supporting evidence.

The first issue that garners attention in addressing how EBP is handled in educational interventions is determining which methodologies of inquiry, data collection, and data analysis would be apt to satisfy the mandates of evidence-basis. This is a question with no simple answer, and one that is in no way devoid of paradigmatic influences, ideological and philosophical belief, and notions of methodological supremacy as well as inferiority. The complex question remains: should there be a single "gold standard" for validating educational methodologies (or, in some cases, a single methodology within a subfield), or is it more prudent, ethical, and responsible for the field to embrace multiple methods of research and investigation?[14] In an attempt to answer this question as it relates specifically to the field known as special education, or those educational interventions intended to target the individualized needs of students that have documented exceptionalities or significant learning challenges, the Council for Exceptional Children's Division of Research assembled a task force to address the issue. The charge of this task force was to investigate both the current state of research as it applies in special education as well as proffer recommendations as to what types of research methodologies may be used to investigate and, ultimately claim evidence basis in terms of quality indicators. As a result of the study, the task force indicated that there were four main types of research that were employed in the study of special education practices: (1) experimental/quasi-experimental group designs; (2) correlational designs; (3) single-subject designs; and (4) qualitative designs.[15]

Experimental Group Design. Experimental group design, also known as a randomized clinical trial in some cases, is regarded as the strongest methodology in any form of scientific research. Deemed the only design that could even potentially claim causality (though only after adequate replication and double-blind procedures have been satisfactorily implemented), experimental group designs are based on comparison between two or more groups differing on a single key variable, with other potential interfering variables, called confounds, accounted and controlled for by the research and analytic design itself. The experimental group receives some form of treatment (in the case of educational interventions, it could be a particular curriculum, a particular behavioral intervention, or the like) while the control group does not receive the treatment being investigated. Based on the results or the differences the investigators determine by the outcomes measured, a conclusion is suggested.

There are a few key components that make experimental designs particularly strong, so long as the methodologies are applied correctly and consistently. First, the random assignment of individuals to groups can control for selection bias. If an investigator creates groups consciously or purposefully, it can result in a comparison that is biased or entirely invalid because the grouping may have been intentionally created in order to demonstrate the desired result. This intentionality threatens, if not entirely invalidates the strength of the study. Second, there is a clear cut difference between the two groups. With a well-defined treatment, the investigator can say with much more confidence that the difference in outcomes was a result of the intervention itself, not some other extraneous factor, as such factors would likely have been naturally controlled for through the random assignment process. Third, with replication, or repeated implementations of the same study resulting in similar or identical outcomes, the studies can be used to infer causality. That is, the field can begin to trust the notion that the intervention *causes* the outcome, not just indicates that there is an association between the two.

There are, however, significant challenges to the implementation of experimental group design, especially in educational contexts. First, to be able to truly randomize individuals in an educational context is difficult. For example, if the purpose of a study is to investigate specific characteristics of individuals, such as autistic traits, hyperactivity, or the like, randomly assigning groups can be challenging, if not entirely impossible, since those qualifying characteristics cannot be activated and deactivated at will. Second, there is an ethicality issue when it comes to the random assignment to treatment groups. That is, even if an intervention is thought to be even potentially beneficial, it challenges researchers' ethical behavior to knowingly not provide the intervention to a group of individuals for a certain period of time for the sake of scientific investigation. Conversely, if there is a potential for a deleterious effect of an intervention, prolonged exposure of any time frame can be regarded as unethical. In either case, though there are examples of successful experimental studies in education, the random application of interventions to individuals with special needs can be distinctly challenging to ethical practice.

Quasi-Experimental Group Design. Quasi-experimental group design is a construct of the social science field that is designed to address the challenges of pure experimental design while still being able to investigate, though with less certainty, the potential causality between variables. While the basic structure of quasi-experimental group design is the same as experimental group design, the major difference lies in the intentional non-random group assignment. That is, groups are intentionally comprised of individuals with particular qualifying characteristics that can be systematically observed and potentially controlled for in *post hoc* analyses, or those statistical processes that can be employed after data are already collected and observations are made. For example, if an investigator is interested in comparing the difference of a behavioral intervention for students with non-compliant behavior with and without a diagnosis of *Autism Spectrum Disorder*, the investigator can intentionally set up two groups: one with non-compliant behavior and the *presence* of ASD, and one with non-compliant behavior and *nopresence of* ASD. The results for this study can provide information about how such an intervention may affect individuals differing on a particular variable specifically (e.g., ASD or non-ASD), but is not as strong as a random assignment, as the groups were consciously constructed and may retain certain confounding variables threatening the validity of the findings.

Correlational Designs. Correlational designs are methodologies that employ primarily descriptive and predictive investigation of a generally large sample of individuals in the absence of any sort of grouping. In other words, large samples are used, but they are regarded as one large group without the need for comparison rather than two or more groups that are compared to one another on some variable(s). For the purposes of this discussion, correlational research can be divided into two categories: simple and complex. Simple correlational studies often use the statistical analysis of Pearson correlations, which categorize the strength of the relationship between variables (usually in dyads) as small, medium, or large. Complex correlational studies are able to enhance these correlations in terms of their predictive value and statistical strength. Using statistical analyses such as regressions and analyses of variance (of which there are multiple models), investigators can determine with a certain testable degree of confidence the predictive association between variables, resulting not only in a ranking system of most predictive to least predictive, but in a way that accounts for a specific percentage of outcome variance. For example, researchers may be interested in determining the role that a variety of factors play in an individual's adaptability score. Using a score as a dependent variable (e.g., a Vineland score), variables such as parental involvement, number of hours of intervention outside of school, type of diagnosis, and teacher experience could be both ranked in predictive value, as well as be shown to account for a particular percentage of variance in the Vineland score. Correlational analyses have some distinct strengths in the field of educational research. First, these types of analyses can often be designed and implemented with little environmental control or manipulation necessary. That is, with experimental and quasi-experimental analyses, much effort needs to be put into controlling for various aspects of the environment in order to minimize the potential of confounding variables. With correlational designs, however, naturalistic environments are often sufficient enough, or even desirable for collecting data. Second, correlational designs do not necessitate specific interventions.Therefore, the challenges involving both group formation and the ethicality of implementing interventions between groups is eliminated. Finally, the methods by which correlations, simple or complex, are employed are relatively simple and, therefore, practicable even in a busy and less controlled classroom environment.

Though correlational analyses can be very useful, they must also be kept in context as they, too, have distinct weaknesses to their utility. First, investigators, as well as those reading and applying the findings of investigations, must take care to not overstate the interpretation of a correlation, be it descriptive or predictive. That is, correlations cannot be used to suggest causation to any degree. Second, the way in which correlations are investigated, especially using methodologies within regression analysis, are very sensitive to investigator control. More specifically, small but significant choices such as the order in which variables are entered into a regression equation, the way in which variable values are calculated, and the type of regression analysis used (i.e., stepwise or hierarchical) can yield significantly different results, deeming correlation values very sensitive and potentially inaccurate. Therefore, correlation analyses should be regarded only as investigational procedures, informing further and more rigorous methods of analysis.

Single-Subject Designs. Single-subject designs are commonly used in educational research contexts, especially those that are action-based. While garnering much attention in educational research circles and in some facets of psychological research, the design and analytical processes involved with single-subject designs are particularly controversial, being exclusively implemented by some and overtly refuted by others. There are certain keystones to single subject design that make the design distinct from other research designs. First and foremost, single-subject designs intentionally avoid making between-subject comparisons. That is, participants in a single-subject study are never compared to one another, but rather compared to themselves only in the context of the dependent variable before the implementation of the independent variable known as a baseline and during/after the implementation of the independent variable (in most cases, some sort of intervention or, perhaps, condition). Secondly, and somewhat indicative of a potential misnomer, single-subject designs do not include, necessarily, only one subject (as do case studies, which represent an entirely different methodological approach, but are often erroneously regarded as synonymous). Rather, single-subject designs seek only to compare single individuals. That is, a comparison is made within one single subject. Finally, in most cases, results in the context of interpreting relationships between dependent and independent variables are analyzed using visual inspection, with little, if any mathematical analysis. It is important to note that not all single-subject designs are equally regarded in terms of value, nor are they regarded as equal even amongst supporters and practitioners of the methodology. While the purpose of experimental and quasi-experimental group designs is to gauge causation using statistical analyses of significance, the goal of single-subject research is to demonstrate a functional relationship. A functional relationship is any systematic change in the targeted direction as a result of the intervention and/or manipulation of an independent variable.[16] As such, there are only some single-subject designs that are seen as being able to truly demonstrate a functional relationship, with the most common ones being a withdrawal design (known also as an ABAB design), a multiple-baseline design, and, in some cases, a modified reversal design (known also as BAB). If the design demonstrates a functional relationship, it is concluded that the effect was likely caused by the independent variable. Because a low number of participants are used in typical single-subject design studies, multiple studies showing the functional relationship are necessary.

While single-subject designs are widely accepted, supported, and deemed capable of vetting instructional methodologies as evidence-based, there are a number of notable concerns and potential weaknesses. While these concerns will be discussed in much greater detail in a later chapter, a brief survey of them will be laid out presently. First, it must be explicitly stated that the distinctly low number of participants in each study is of particular concern. Despite the lack of between-subject analysis, even a series of several single-subject designs only barely meet the minimum number of participants deemed necessary by the standards of group design statistics. Furthermore, unlike in the statistical processes of group design, there are no equivalents in single-subject design to evaluate power analysis, or any other means of determining whether or not the total number of participants was, indeed, enough to validate any claims. This weakness alone is a distinct threat to its acceptability as a stand-alone means of gauging the evidence-basis of an educational intervention. Second, and similarly, there is a nearly entirely absent mathematical basis to single-subject design. While some studies will use simple descriptive calculations such as means, medians, and modes, these are not, by any means, sophisticated enough to imply causation, if even to truly imply effect of any kind. It is important to note that there are mathematical procedures that have been created and suggested for use in single-subject design, but have not achieved widely regarded validity by any means. Furthermore, reliance on visual inspection analyses to make the boldness of claims that are made in single-subject designs is dubious, at best. Finally, the rigor with which results and designs are reported in the literature is distinctly lacking.

Qualitative Research Designs. Perhaps the most misunderstood and controversial of all research designs, qualitative research designs have been held to the highest level of scrutiny and, in some cases, complete disregard in terms of validity. However, many in the field of education have fervently and effectively made the case for the legitimacy of qualitative designs, especially in the context of educational interventions. According to Brantlinger and her colleagues, among the most vocal proponents of the use of qualitative methods in educational research, qualitative research can be defined as "a systematic approach to understanding qualities, or the essential nature, of a phenomenon with a particular context."[17] As such, Brantlinger insists that qualitative designs, when implemented with care and rigor do, indeed, produce empirical results that can inform knowledge, demonstrate evidence of support, and can contribute to the field in an articulate and utile fashion equal to that of quantitative studies. The following list represents the generally accepted branches of qualitative research:[18]

1. *Case study*—exploration of a bounded system (group, individual, setting, event, phenomenon, process) which can include autobiography and biography.
2. *Collective case study*—a study that takes place in multiple sites or includes personalized stories of several similar or distinctive individuals.
3. *Ethnography*—description and interpretation of a cultural or social group or system which will typically include observations, interviews, and document analysis.
4. *Action research*—researcher brings ideas for practice to fieldwork to have an impact on the setting/participants while collecting data.

5. *Collaborative action research*—researcher and practitioner share ideas about how to change practice and work together to modify a situation as well as collect information for a study.
6. *Grounded theory*—research done to generate or discover a general theory or abstract analytical hunch based on study of phenomena in a particular situation (or multiple situations).
7. *Phenomenology*—studies the meanings people make of their lived experiences.
8. *Symbolic interactionism*—studies interpretive processes used by persons dealing with material and social situations.
9. *Narrative research*—collection of personal narratives which are based on the recognition that people are storytellers who lead storied lives.
10. *Life/Oral history*—extensive interviews with individuals to collect first person narratives about their lives or events in which they participated.
11. *Quasi-life/oral history*—encouraging participants to recall and reflect on earlier as well as current meaningful occurrences in their lives.
12. *Interpretive research*—used synonymously with "qualitative work" and/or to refer to research framed within certain theories (e.g., critical, feminist, disability study, critical race).
13. *Content analysis*—close inspection of text(s) to understand themes or perspectives (may also refer to the process of analysis within other methodologies of qualitative research).
14. *Conversational analysis*—studying interactional situations, structure of talk, and communicative exchanges including the recording of facial expressions, gestures, speed or hesitancy of speech, and tone of voice.
15. *Discourse analysis*—deconstructs common sense textual meanings which identifies meanings that undergird normative ways of conceptualizing and discussing phenomena.
16. *Ideological critique*—discourse analysis that assumes political meanings (such as power disparities) or ideologies are embedded in and infused through all discourses, institutions, and social practices.

Data collected from qualitative studies can lead to a deep and broad understanding of particular aspects of individuals' life experiences, including those experiences in the classroom. By focusing on these experiences, many of which are either difficult to measure quantitatively, or for which quantitative measure would detract from the detail or deeper meanings, the qualitative researcher gives a direct voice to those who are involved in a study, rather than describing or measuring on their behalf, as is the case in many "objective" quantitative designs.

However, no fair analysis could forego a critique of qualitative research methodologies either. First and foremost, the employment of subjectivity is an ever-present threat to its validity. That is, while qualitative analysis can give voice and attention to variables ignored by or inutile to quantitative analyses, it can also leave ample room for the effect of researcher bias, especially in the realm of interpretation, if not properly controlled for or bracketed in the description of findings. Secondly, ecological assessments, as qualitative studies are, may lack any level of control over the environment, having no means of minimizing or accounting for reactivity or interaction effects. Finally, without more rigidly defined variables, reports of qualitative results can be both precarious and ill-constructed, leaving more potential vagueness and inutility in practical environments.

Establishing the types of research designs and methodologies is in no way the end of the discussion as there are still many questions to be addressed in determining how these methodologies are to apply in educational settings. Many would presume that the most relevant discussion would center on which methodology is best; that is, which could give the most convincing information about causality (which methods cause the best outcomes). This question, however, is not most important and, in many ways, actually de-tracts and distracts from productive discussions in EBP. The main issue consists of a series of questions, each of which will be addressed individual-ly.

What type(s) of variable(s) is/are the researcher seeking to investigate? From a positivistic perspective, that is, one that seeks to define variables stringently and make distinct causal, or at least explanatory connections be-tween variables (most likely a dependent and independent variable), this answer appears to be relatively clear. That is, the types of variables investi-gated are those that can lead to causal conclusions. However, this perspective alone can be vastly limiting to the depth and breadth of types of information that are truly available in educational investigations. It is in the context of this facet of the discussion that the value of qualitative means of investiga-tion becomes clear. While positivistic perspectives will choose and define only those variables that can be explanatory or linked, as closely as possible, to causation, constructive approaches are far more comfortable either choos-ing variables that may be, at best, descriptive or, in other cases, not predeter-mine any variables at all, allowing for a truly *emic*, or "inside" perspective gleaned simply by observing and "becoming" one of the individuals, groups, or cultures being investigated. As Brantlinger makes clear, not all empirical information is causal or explanatory, but can very well be descriptive and deepening in terms of cultural understanding and interpersonal relationships at the individual and group levels. As depicted earlier by Lincoln, qualitative studies are not only an alternative to quantitative-based studies, but can, in many ways, be seen as more valuable as they value far less the *a priori* reductionist cause-effect dichotomy in favor of the grounded expansionist discovery of tacit and propositional phenomena within an environmental context.[19]

What type(s) of relationships(s) is/are the researcher looking to evaluate? Similarly to the first question, it is often assumed that the most valuable question in educational research is evaluating causal effects. In an overly positivistic and, more specifically, behavioristic perspective, focusing on outcomes alone is sensible as causality is valued highest. However, with a broadened perspective and a more inclusive research approach, there are other relationships between different types of variables that are equally as valuable, especially if investigators are interested in the process of learning and the building of interpersonal relationships of classroom communities as opposed to simply evaluating "what works" in increasing behaviors, however they be measured, as opposed to "what doesn't." According to the National Academy of Sciences, three overall types of research are applied in typical educational investigations: descriptive (what is happening?), causal (is there a systematic effect?), and process or mechanism (why or how is it happening?).

In what setting(s) is/are the researcher looking to conduct the investigation? While settings between types of research may not vary greatly, the feasibility of the application of results may. In positivistic realms, a necessity of applying research findings is replication of the study conditions and clear definitions by which variables can be observed (in terms of the dependent variable) and manipulated (in terms of the independent variable). Without near-perfect replication of such conditions, the results of the study are ill-applied, distinctly limiting the actual utility of such results. Therefore, while these methods are often seen as most reliable in terms of conditional control and definition of variables, they are actually the most challenging to replicate in applied settings. Even for research conducted in well-controlled classroom settings, these studies are often overseen and assisted by highly trained researchers as well as research assistants who are often trained themselves in research methodology and intervention-specific practices.[20] Qualitative research, on the other hand, depends far less on controlled environments and making causal connections than it does on gathering information from various aspects of the natural setting with less attention to causal relationships than on interpersonal connections between community members. In these cases, control over conditions of the classroom is actually undesirable as it would disrupt the naturalistic environment in which relationships can be built.

For what further purpose(s) is/are the investigator looking to conduct the investigation? This question reveals another clear difference between the positivistic perspective with that of the critical theorist and constructivist. From the positivistic perspective, the most well-founded means of support is replication. That is, how many studies across how many participants can be conducted that produce the same or at least similar results. Based on replication, support for the approach is garnered and evidence-basis is strengthened. Again, from an outcomes-based perspective, this type of support is sensible. However, from the constructivist perspective, replication of similar results is of far less importance, as the difference between environments, classrooms, students, and respective findings are as important as similarities. The reason for this lack of importance is due to the *purpose* of the investigations. Constructivist research endeavors do not necessarily value, at least initially, how commonality can be supported between subjects (or before, during, and after interventions, as is the case in single-subject designs) in the way that positivistic approaches do. Rather, constructivist approaches are comfortable investigating how relationships unfold over time, whether they align with theory (especially predetermined theory), and value descriptions of differences and similarities.

What methodology of research is best suited to meet the needs and purposes of the investigation? Once the above questions are answered appropriately, the investigator can then determine what type of methodology will best meet the research needs. It is imperative, however, that researchers pose questions and choose investigative methodologies not due to pressures of legislation or paradigm and what they believe to be the "standard" in popular practice, but rather how the entire process of understanding can be best understood. The process of determining such questions and their subsequent answers should be embarked upon without sensitivity to time (in terms of finding results quickly to facilitate timely publication), pressures of legislative descriptions of "evidence-basis," or pressures of determining causality. Rather, educational investigations should be well-planned, steeped in philosophy, history, and theory equally as much as in causality, and framed in terms of what aspects of the overall question are necessary to investigate and in what ways.

THE REFOCUSING OF EVIDENCE-BASED PRACTICE

While there is little argument that employing a valid measure of evidence-basis is not only productive to the field, but ensures the use of high-quality and ethical interventional approaches, there are significant errors that can be attributed to evidence-based practices, especially in the way that is employed by the field of behavior analysis. Some of these deficiencies are being addressed by the field as a whole, while some are clearly not.

The first issue is that, in many discussions of EBPs, there is a dichotomous view; that is, an approach is either evidence-based or not. This dichotomous approach is vastly dangerous as well as counterproductive as it eliminates the possibility of emerging evidence. If an approach is deemed "not evidence-based" then it is likely to be abandoned entirely on those grounds alone. This leaves only one option: continuing to garner evidence for approaches that have already been deemed evidence-based. However, an approach which has not sufficiently achieved the rank of "evidence-based" may not have done so for a variety of reasons. First, it is possible that the approach is quite new, and there has not yet been enough opportunity for its theory and practice to develop sufficiently enough for evidence-basis. Second, it is possible that the way in which such approaches are to be studied have not yet been perfected, or even established at all. As aforementioned, in a field that is preoccupied with positivistic frameworks, approaches that look more deeply into variables and concepts that are not as easily defined operationally are often prematurely dismissed. Third, but in no way final, the venues for such research to be disseminated are, in many ways, limited due to the established predominance of positivism. That is, many dominant peer-reviewed journals may be less open to, if not entirely dismissive of publishing research evaluating less established approaches or research endeavors using less traditional methodologies, while those journals that are willing to do so risk being less accepted or lowly regarded by scientific communities based on their unorthodoxy. It must be clearly stated, however, that this lack of acceptance is not necessarily based on a lack of rigor or a lack of investigative skill and legitimacy of the researcher, but rather exclusion based on perceived supremacy and cultural control of one approach.

The issue of the dichotomous perception of EBP has been addressed by Odom and his colleagues.[21] According to Odom, there are three potential categories for evidence basis: well-established evidence, emerging and effective practices, and probably efficacious. While imperfect, this conceptualization clearly allows practices that are garnering more support for various reasons a platform upon which to continue its research and maintain its rightful place in the discussion within the field. The Council for Exceptional Children has proposed another continuum of definitions for evidence-basis which may be more utile than that of Odom's. According to CEC, *Evidence-based practices* can be defined as those practices for which original data have been collected to determine the effectiveness of the practice for students with exceptionalities. These interventions have been vetted by rigorous research designs and general acceptance by the scientific community through various peer review processes. *Promising practices* refer to those interventions that have been developed based on theory or research, but for which an insufficient amount of original empirical support currently exists. This does not mean that there is no support, but rather there is not yet enough support or the support garnered was not collected through the use of a strong research design. Finally, *emerging practices* are practices which are not strongly based on data or theory (or at least are not yet), but rather have been developed less systematically and for which there may be anecdotal support, but lacking any systematic or legitimate support. What is important about these distinctions is the possibility of motility. That is, a practice can begin by being placed in "emerging practices" but through increased attention and systematic investigation (quantitative or qualitative) can, at some point, be considered "promising" or "evidence-based."

Ultimately, what is necessary for the field of education if EBPs are to be truly used to its potential benefit is to refocus its centricity from an overtly positivist perspective to that of a constructivist perspective. From the positivist perspective, the field allows itself to value only outcomes and quantities. That is, until you can "show" a cause and effect, the educational practices are deemed invalid. This puts an undue pressure on practitioners to use the same principles repeatedly simply because it is more amenable to *showing* results, not necessarily because it is actually helpful or productive for the individual. Rather, if the field were to refocus its value on the discovery and theory building process rather than entirely on outcome output, the value of individualization could be maintained, and little, if any effort, would need to be spent on "proving" what works quantitatively, but rather building a future society of self-aware and empowered citizens who are entitled to be who they are, not what their outcomes are measured as. It is this grounded theory and discovery-based process that can validate the focus on a comprehensive educational practice for individuals with ASD.

NOTES

1. D. L. Sackett, W. M. C. Rosenberg, J. A. M. Gray, R. B. Haynes, W. S. Richardson. 1996. "Evidence Based Medicine: What it is and what it isn't." *British Medical Journal* 312: 71–2 [3].

2. American Psychological Association, "Evidence-Based Practice in Psychology." Retrieved on October 23, 2013 from http://www.apa.org/practice/resources/evidence/evidence-based-statement.pdf.

3. Elementary and Secondary Education Act [34 CFR 300.35] [20 U.S.C. 1411(e) (2) (C) (xi)] [sec. 9101(37)].

4. http://ies.ed.gov/ncee/wwc/aboutus.aspx.

5. Bryan Cook and Sara Cothren Cook, CEC Division for Research, 2011, 2.

6. Frank M. Gresham, "Evolution of the Treatment Integrity Concept: Current Status and Future Directions." School Psychology Review (2009) 38:4, 533–40.

7. A. Kazdin, "Mediators and Mechanisms of Change in Psychotherapy Research."*Annual Review of Clinical Psychology*, 3, 1–27.

8. Ibid.

9. Egon Guba, *The Paradigm Dialog*, 1990.

10. Ibid., 20.

11. John Dewey, *Logic: The Theory of Inquiry*, New York: Henry Holt and Company, 1938.

12. Lincoln in Guba, 1990, 69.

13. Ibid., 70.

14. Samuel L. Odom et al. (2005). "Research in Special Education: Scientific Methods and Evidence-Based Practices" *Exceptional Children*, 71, 137–48.

15. Ibid.

16. Alberto and Troutman, 2012.

17. Ellen Brantlinger et al. (2005). "Qualitative Studies in Special Education." *Exceptional Children*, 71(2), 195–207.

18. Ibid.

19. Lincoln in Guba, 1990.

20. Cecil R. Reynolds and Sally E. Shaywitz. "Response to Intervention: Ready or Not? Or, From Wait-to-Fail to Watch-Them-Fail," *School Psychology Quarterly*, 2009, 24, 130.

21. Sam Odom et al. "Evidence-Based Practices for Young Children with Autism: Contributions for Single-Subject Design Research." *Focus on Autism and Other Developmental Disabilities*, 2003 18(3), 166–75.

Chapter Five

Establishing the Connection between ASD and Behaviorism

This chapter will explore the origins of the seemingly deep and ostensibly "natural" connection between behavior analytic approaches and Autism Spectrum Disorder. Beginning with the initial instances of what would become the field of Applied Behavior Analysis for individuals with severe intellectual disabilities and autistic tendencies (as the diagnosis was not yet officially available), the chapter will attempt to trace the connection to the current trends in equating ABA with autism treatment. This chapter will reveal that the perspective of behaviorism was not only utilized to potentially "treat" individuals with ASD, but was also proposed, at least initially, as a potential means of etiological explanation. Through the increased availability of behavior analytic approaches as well as the deepening connection between positivism and education, it will be demonstrated that ABA was the most likely candidate to gain widespread acceptance for a number of important social, political, and methodological reasons. Considering its close characterization with the legislative language of IDEA as well as the formidable effort of the field to publish and publicize, the very quality indicator dictated by the federal educational legislation, a veritable public relations campaign was waged on both parents and school systems alike resulting in a deep and seemingly indelible connection between ABA and ASD.

There were, however, consequences of this campaign that affected many aspects of the quality of education and services provided for individuals with ASD, both external and internal to the practice of ABA. Internally, because the method was garnering so much attention, the demand for the availability of services made way for a multitude of practitioners with questionable skills and qualifications to provide ill-structured and, in many cases, vastly diluted and misdirected variations of it, violating the very important standard of treatment integrity. Externally, the overexposure that ABA achieved in the field muted, if not silenced, many other distinctly promising educational approaches, serving eventually to systematically exclude these approaches from the literature and the discourse in order to maintain its own supremacy. These issues will be handled deeply throughout the remainder of the treatise.

THE BEGINNINGS OF BEHAVIOR ANALYTIC APPROACHES FOR HUMAN BEINGS

Behaviorism, at least in the context of what would most aptly be regarded as Watsonian behaviorism, had indeed established a well-respected canon of empirical literature by the 1960s, but the vast majority of the findings and the supposed empirical underpinnings of the theory were based in manipulation and observation of animal behavior, primarily mice, pigeons, and cats. Though widely accepted by many as a valid explanation for the learning process in humans as well, this acceptance remained largely a "leap of faith" as there had been no substantial research or empirical evidence that these principles could or would be transferrable to human behavior. On a wide scale of understanding human behavior this gap in research was important, but in the narrowed context of the field of intellectual and developmental disabilities, and what would become Autism Spectrum Disorder, this disparity was especially important. While the means of identifying individuals with intellectual disabilities and autistic tendencies was in practice, largely for exclusionary purposes such as institutionalization or hospitalization which, in many cases, were facilitated under the auspice of treatment, there was little evidence documented about what, if any, treatment or educational approaches were being used successfully or unsuccessfully with such individuals.

Likely one of the first researchers to investigate the potential application of behaviorist principles to human beings with intellectual disabilities and autistic tendencies (or at least the first to publish the account) was Charles B. Ferster, who began to publish the results of his work in the very early 1960s. Ferster, however, used his results not only to indicate a potential treatment for children with autistic tendencies, but also as a potential etiological explanation for the occurrence of the autistic tendencies, namely from the vantage of parental causation, an unusually comparable explanation to that of Bettelheim's, which is often vehemently opposed in the contemporary behavioral community. Ferster explains the initial connection between the general principles of behaviorism and his particular interest in its application to children with autistic tendencies:

> I should like to analyze how the basic variables determining the child's behavior might operate to produce the particular kinds of behavioral deficits seen in

the autistic child. To analyze the autistic child's behavioral deficits, I shall proceed from the general principles of behavior, derived from a variety of species, which describe the kinds of factors that alter the frequency of any arbitrary act. The general principles of behavior applied to the specific situations presumably present during the child's developmental period will lead to hypotheses as to specific factors in the autistic child's home life which could produce the severe changes in frequency as well as in the form of his behavior.[1]

This approach was new in terms of both treatment and etiological explanation. While it is Kanner who is actually credited with the initial notion of parental causation, these types of explanations remained largely psychoanalytic in context, and therefore not likely demonstrable, at least in the behavioral or positivistic sense of demonstrability. Ferster's approach, however, presumed to be able to not only operationally identify how such autistic tendencies could be *changed* using the principles of reinforcement, as many, if not most contemporary approaches do as well, but also demonstrate how they were ultimately *caused* by behavioral functionality, specifically sourced from the parent-child dynamic.

Ferster's descriptions of the "autistic child" bore little difference from previous clinical descriptions; however, the reach of the behavioral explanation appeared to be entirely novel in terms of not only human behavior in general, but what was regarded as aberrant human behavior. As he suggests:

> Although the autistic child may have a narrower range of performances than the normal child, the major difference between them is in the relative frequencies of the various kinds of performances . . . the autistic child spends large amounts of time sitting or standing quietly. Performances which have only simple and slight effects on the child's environment occur frequently and make up a large percentage of the entire repertoire. . . . Autistic children almost always have an inadequately developed speech repertoire . . . [e]ven when large numbers of words are emitted, the speech is not normal in the sense that it is not maintained by its effect on a social environment . . . it is usually in the form of a *mand* [italics in original]. . . . The main variable is usually the level of deprivation of the speaker. It lacks the sensitive interchange between the speaker and listener characteristic of much human verbal behavior. . . . In the case of the autistic child, it frequency affects the listener (parent), who escapes from the aversive stimulus by presenting a reinforcing stimulus relevant to the child's mand . . ."[2]

Ferster clearly indicates that though the behavior of the individual is most influenced by environmental stimuli, as is the case in all humans, such behavior is at least maintained by the parents' reinforcement of it from a seemingly entirely escape-maintained fashion. As such, Ferster asserts that the main motivation of the autistic child is to communicate a demand in such a way that gains him or her access while simultaneously causing the listener to escape the situation by providing such access. This can be seen as almost two levels of complementary reinforcement on the "autistic child's" side and one on the listener: the child gains the desired outcome and avoids further contact with the parent while the parent avoids an aversive outcome of what Ferster calls "atavistic," or aggressive and destructive behaviors such as aggression, tantrums, or self-injury. These patterns continue to embed themselves in the "home life," creating and maintaining the function and utility of the autistic behavior.

Ferster deepens his assertion of the pivotal role of the parents in the creation and maintenance of autistic behavior based mainly on non-existent or insufficient (leading to intermittent) reinforcement. As such, Ferster offers three distinct factors in parental behavior that contribute to the process. The first is explained in terms of "general disruption of the parental repertoire," by which he suggests that any means of disruption of routine that the child causes will have a direct effect on the frequency that the parent reinforces the child. He uses the example of a "depressed parent," who, by emotional state alone, would likely reinforce the child less frequently, potentially maintaining and exacerbating aberrant behavior. This leads to the second factor, which Ferster suggests is the "prepotency of other performances," or the nonexistence, or insufficiency, of reinforcement of non-aberrant behaviors. The third factor is related to the first two as a likely result. Ferster suggests that since the child becomes largely intolerable, interrupting the parental repertoire and demanding attention almost entirely with aberrant behavior, the child itself essentially becomes an aversive stimulus, creating a largely escape-maintained behavior pattern for the parent (which, as mentioned before, may work also as an access and escape-maintained dual function for the individual, ultimately reinforcing "atavistic" behavior).

To this point, however, Ferster has addressed only the resultant behavior, yielding one to wonder whether he actually purports a behavioral "cause" of autistic tendencies or simply maintenance of pre-existing tendencies by environmental consequences. Indeed, Ferster does offer such an explanation, leading one to believe, at least in the absence of any other indications, that "autistic tendencies" (or, perhaps autism itself) has an entirely behavioral etiology stemming from the parent(s). As he suggests:

> The development of the atavistic behavior in the child by the parent is necessarily a very gradual program in which the beginning steps involve small magnitudes of behavior such as whining, whimpering, and crying. As the parent adapts to these or becomes indifferent to them because of the prepotence of other kinds of activity, then progressively larger orders of magnitude become reinforced. The large-magnitude tantrum may be approximated or "shaped" by gradual differential reinforcement. . . . The sensitivity of the parent to aversive control by the child will depend on the general condition of the parental repertoire. . . . The same factors in the parental repertoire that tend

to produce nonreinforcement of the child's behavior—general disruption of the parent or other behaviors prepotent over the child—correspondingly produce reinforcement of the large-order-of-magnitude tantrums. The parent whose total repertoire is severely enough disrupted to interfere with the normal reinforcement of the child's behavior will also react only to tantrums that are of a large order of magnitude aversiveness. . . . Only between the ages of 1 1/2 to 4 years does the parent have sufficient control of the child to weaken his performance to the degree seen in infantile autism. This is a critical period in the child's development during which his behavior is especially susceptible to extinction[3]

Ferster also proposed that behavioral principles were the means of addressing the autistic behavior as well. In his report of one of the earlier clinical studies that investigated the potential effect of the application of behavioral principles with individuals characterized as autistic, Ferster relates some early success in using a mechanism that provided intermittent reinforcement. Ferster describes the study:

The children operated the reinforcing devices in the room either by pressing a key or depositing a coin. The key was a telephone-type lever switch, mounted in a translucent plastic panel which could be lighted from behind [which emitted] an audible click whenever the switch was sufficiently depressed.[4]

Under intermittent circumstances, the mechanisms would release reinforcers such as food, candy, toys, and "trinkets" based on performance of the action. This methodology was clearly an extension of the types of experimentation used by both Thorndike and Skinner with cats, pigeons, and rats, respectively. Determined as successful by Ferster based on his findings, he suggested four main conclusions indicating ways in which the behavioral perspective can be directly applied to an individual with autistic characteristics:[5]

1. Reinforcement: The frequency with which the subjects responded was increased by using reinforcers such as food, music, candy, etc.
2. Schedule of reinforcement: Both the fixed-ratio and variable-interval schedules of reinforcement produced their normal and characteristic effects on the child's performance. The accidental reinforcement of responses during the periods of interval reinforcement and the loss of this "superstitious behavior" under fixed-ratio reinforcement demonstrated another aspect of normal behavior.
3. Stimulus control: New stimuli, if present when a response would produce reinforcement and absent when it went unreinforced came to control whether or not the child performed.
4. Conditioned and generalized reinforcer: The delivery of a coin was a conditioned reinforcer in maintaining the performance recorded, and

the coin was also used to actuate a wide variety of reinforcers in the manner of a generalized reinforcer.

Donald Baer, Montrose Wolf, and Todd Risley were highly noted early researchers who were instrumental in expanding the purview of behavioral explanations to human beings during the 1960s through multiple publications of research findings, primarily using case studies and early examples of what would develop into single-subject research designs. The behavior analytic methodology begins to gain significant momentum in the realm of human learning, however, through a 1965 publication by Birnbrauer and colleagues which, in many ways, lays the groundwork for the soon deeply regarded relationship between the behavioral process and human learning by connecting the behavioral process directly with the acquisition of both functional and academic skills. As stated:

> Instruction, whether aimed at developing academic skills in retarded children, increasing general knowledge in normal children; or advancing mathematical sophistication in gifted youngsters, may be conceived of as a process in which a teacher systematically and effectively arranges and rearranges the environment to bring about desired behavioral changes. Teaching on this basis, in whole or part, has been called programmed instruction. In its most promising form, programmed instruction is a budding technology based upon an experimental analysis of behavior.[6]

This was one of the first indications in which the concept of replacing behaviors was used synonymously with learning itself and applied not to just one individual, but suggested as a practice that can be generally applied in a classroom for all types of individuals or in instructional practices *en masse*. Furthermore, it expanded the utility of behavior analytic approaches to both functional and academic areas. Historically, this was an important publication as it was during this time of American history that schools were becoming vastly populated with the children and young adults born during the "baby boom." As such, classrooms were growing in numbers as were students presenting various challenges. Such a systematic and seemingly ubiquitous approach would likely hold great appeal for schools and educational personnel dealing with increasingly larger numbers of consumers. Hence, a new market for behavioral approaches was born, and it was one that provided an opportunity for mass application.

In the specific field of teaching "retarded" children, Birnbrauer et al.'s paper was equally as influential. As stated by the authors:

> Specifically the objectives of the investigation were: (1) to develop a motivational system for effectively strengthening academic and appropriate classroom conduct; (2) to develop programmed procedures which aim to strengthen

cooperative and industrious behaviors in young, retarded "educable" children who previously have shown little or no academic progress, and whose reactions to previous educational experience often range from apathy to rebellion, and (3) to develop programmed instructional materials (*including teacher manuals*) [italics added] for reading, writing, arithmetic . . . and other correlated practical subjects.[7]

While the aforementioned efforts undoubtedly set the stage for what would become the deep connection between ASD and behavior analytic approaches, it is likely that the deepest and most indelible means of connection were solidified through the work of O. Ivar Lovaas, founder of the Young Autism Project at the University of California, Los Angeles. Up until this point, while there was a growing canon of literature reporting on effective uses of behavioral approaches for individuals with autistic tendencies, there were no indications, as yet, on how well these approaches held up over time, which is a crucial component to anything that could be considered a viable and effective therapeutic approach. Early publications by Lovaas and his colleagues from the early 1970s were instrumental in the direct application of behavioral therapy to children with autistic tendencies (again, autism in any form was not yet established as a diagnostic category, yet widely used within the field of psychiatry and clinical psychology as a characteristic descriptor). Lovaas' 1973 report in the *Journal of Applied Behavior Analysis* was significantly influential. According to Lovaas et al.:

> The primary purpose of the present paper is to present some measures of generalization and follow-up data on 20 children that we have treated with behavior therapy during the last [seven year period]. We hope to provide the reader with an approximation of changes one might expect to see in autistic children undergoing behavior therapy. However, it is also our belief that the results presented here probably underestimate the benefits of such therapy for autistic children because the results were influenced by our extensive efforts at measurement and replication as well as therapy.[8]

In the context of this report, Lovaas and colleagues indicated that notable changes in behavior were observed in all individuals, though to varying degrees, including decrease of certain inappropriate behaviors such as echolalia and self-stimulation along with a respective increase in appropriate behavior such as appropriate speech, appropriate play, social non-verbal behaviors, increases in spontaneous use of language, and increases in a particular measure of IQ as well as "social quotients." This paper distinctly furthered the field of behavior analysis as it was, at least until that time, reflective of the largest sample of individuals accounted for within a single study. The study also introduced what would become a familiar cautionary tale of behavioral approaches; that is, in order for generalization of the behaviors to be maintained, generalization of the environmental consequences must also be maintained. As Lovaas and colleagues explain:

> It is implied in the above discussion that we view the problem of maintaining the treatment gains (generalization over time) as a special case of stimulus generalization. When the child stayed home with his parents who had learned our techniques he did not regress . . . because the environments before and after discharge were similar. . . . However, the child who was discharged to a state hospital entered a new environment that did not possess (or did not program) effective reinforcers. Remember that the children had not "lost" the behaviors we had given them (some "progressive disease" had not rotted their brains), they simply did not perform, they were unmotivated, unless we re-exposed them to the treatment contingencies. [9]

This statement suggests an early indication of some very important issues to come that will work both for and against the legitimacy of behavior analysis as a viable therapeutic approach, namely, the necessity of maintaining more deliberate and simulated, if not artificial, environments in order to attain generalization once the formal therapy has ended, or at least to achieve any form of lasting effect of what had occurred in the clinical environment. Lovaas' early study indicated that maintenance of such an environment was essential to the lasting effect of behavioral therapy, and studies continue to address this major challenge in behavioral therapy even in the context of the most current research.

Lovaas cemented his influence and the connection between ASD and behavior analysis roughly fifteen years later in 1987 with a paper that, though heavily critiqued by many, would serve, undeniably, as a watershed moment for this now seemingly indelible relationship between ASD and behavior analysis. This paper was to be historic for many reasons, some positive for the field of behavior analysis and some quite deleterious. In either case, however, it remains remarkably controversial. As Lovaas states:

> This article reports the results of intensive behavioral treatment for young autistic children. Pretreatment measures revealed no significant differences between the intensively treated experimental group and the minimally treated control group. At follow-up, experimental group subjects did significantly better than control group subjects. For example, 47% of the experimental group achieved normal intellectual and educational functioning in contrast to only 2% of the control group subjects. [10]

This study laid the groundwork for many issues that the field of behaviorism would soon face. In terms of the advantageous, Lovaas' results, if indeed accurate, indicated that there was, quite clearly, a means of a successful therapeutic approach to ameliorating the challenges of individuals with autism. Furthermore, it contributed a positive social message that there should be legitimate interest in serving individuals with autism and intellectual disabilities in a therapeutic and educational environment as opposed to a non-rehabilitative institutional approach. Both of these points were to benefit the field as a whole, not only that of behavior analysis.

There were, however, also detrimental effects to Lovaas' study in the context of both behavior analysis as a potential model for therapeutic treatment as well as the way in which the behavioral model would come to view autism as a condition. The use of Lovaas' word "recovered" has become very important in discussions of not just Lovaas' study, but the overstatement of the proponents of behavioral treatment in general. It is clear that Lovaas posits that "recovery" is synonymous with the achievement of "normal functioning" on IQ tests, reinforcing the connection between the medical rehabilitative model and behavior analysis, an association that will become deep-seated and significantly important in later arguments. From this perspective, the goal of "therapy" is to make a child "more normal," which is stated in behavioral literature under many types of terms including "increasing appropriate behavior" as well as "reducing or replacing inappropriate behavior." Many studies since Lovaas', including current projects, continue the standard of gaining "normal" functioning as analogous to recovery (though it is important to note that the field of behavior analysis has been careful with the term "recovery" any longer, replacing it with notions such as "normal intellectual" or "normal behavioral" functioning). Because no other approach had thus far claimed to achieve "recovery" for autistic children, a de-contextualized reading of Lovaas' study would certainly be likely to translate into legitimate grounds for supremacy of the behavioral approach as well as popular acceptance.

Many in the field responded to Lovaas' claims with much suspicion, if not overt incredulity. Perhaps one of the most vocal opponents was Eric Schopler, who wrote the journal:

> I was dismayed to read your uncritical reporting of Ivar Lovaas's dramatic claims to have made normal or almost cured half of the children he treated with intensive behavior modification. His cure rate for autism, greater than any other claimed in recent history, has resulted in exaggerated and misleading media coverage. The source of this misunderstanding can readily be traced to . . . methodological error in the Lovaas (1987) study. They include Lovaas's biased selection of children and his inappropriate outcome criteria. The cumulative effects of these errors is to leave his claim of a 45% cure rate without supporting evidence. [11]

The critiques of the Lovaas (1987) study remain intact, with many questioning multiple methodological applications of the approach including the legitimacy of the "prorated mental age," which is a measure Lovaas invented for the sake of this study, the actual level of severity or even existence of true "autism" in the subject selection, and the inability of any other research endeavors to replicate his findings in any comparable fashion. [12,13] This study, despite its largely unfounded claims, has also had significant impact on both case law findings and educational policy and legislation, leading to vast conflicts regarding the role that IDEA should play in providing such services to individuals with ASD and what the individual agencies' responsibility in replicating the conditions described in the Lovaas study is, as well as others. [14]

Behavior analytic approaches appeared to be becoming a mainstay in therapeutic options for people with intellectual disabilities in large part due to Lovaas' 1987 report, increasing the opportunity for treatment options for individuals with autistic tendencies, especially those in clinical, institutional, or hospital settings. Beginning in the latter part of the 1970s through the 1980s there was a distinct surge in the publication of research studies in which challenging behaviors of individuals with autistic tendencies or one form or another of the Pervasive Developmental Disorders under which the types of autism were categorized (diagnosable from 1980 onward) were reported to have been reduced and even eliminated using behavior analytic approaches. These findings were also analyzed more systematically due to the developing modality of single-subject research design. These were prime circumstances for the behavior analytic model to gain deep alignment with the rehabilitation focused medical model and the increasing responsibility of the relatively new field of child psychiatry's role in treatment interventions for children with autism. It was also during this time that the positivistic tenets of observability, measurability, and parsimony of behavior analytic intervention were solidified as foundational to the approach. According to Holburn:

> In the 1970s it was popular among behavior modifiers to ignore feelings and other mental states. One motto was "if you can't observe it, it doesn't exist," and reliable observation required consensual agreement. We proudly emphasized experimental control and carefully measured one or two target behaviors, usually as a function of a single variable intervention like time-out or positive reinforcement, or more complex treatment packages like overcorrection. Another motto was "the simpler the better," because simpler techniques were easier to describe. [15]

Another function of the systematizing of behavior analytic approaches was the development of a distinct vernacular, but one that was increasingly esoteric and therefore less useful in the greater field. As Holburn states, "[w]e used a technical language that made sense to us, although it sounded like a foreign language to many parents and staff, and sometimes even to other treatment professionals." [16] This development allowed the field, at least internally, to legitimize itself as a scientific discipline replete with its own language system and methodology.

Despite its gain in applicability, however, there were substantial challenges to the approach that were developing, some of which would come to test the very legitimacy of behavior analysis for some time. Though the field itself was rapidly systematizing and touting its own advances as scientific, there was an increasing concern about the utility of behavior analytic approaches outside of the very deliberate and well-controlled clinical and in many cases, institutional environment, which was far easier to manipulate than that of the natural environment outside of the therapeutic setting. This challenge was often equally as present in the therapeutic environment itself. As Holburn further relates, "for many of us, our methods rarely produced durable gains in the residential environment because the interventions were usually superimposed briefly on the naturally occurring contingencies that generated and maintained the problem behavior . . ."[17] As further related by Bradley (1994), "[t]he practice of behavior analysis became an end in itself, bound by rigid regimens and incapable of responding to root causes."[18] The point made by Lovaas (1987) that denigrated the "hospital setting" which was unable to "reproduce" the therapeutic environment, essentially intended by Lovaas to ingratiate the strength of behavior analytic approaches, was now revealing itself to be one of its deepest problems. That is, in isolated clinical conditions when there are enough trained staff members available to consistently keep the simulated therapeutic environment intact and a sufficient schedule and availability of reinforcement, behavior analytic approaches can work. Without such mechanisms in place, however, generalization simply fails, rendering the previous gains somewhat useless therapeutically. The true social importance and greater social consequences of the behavior analytic approach were very much in question, and the indications did not seem to be positive.

Adding significantly to the growing mistrust in behavior analytic approach was the growing attention around the use of aversive consequences such as electric shock, loud noise, ammonia caplets, among other deleterious stimuli. These approaches were regarded as overly mechanistic and disregarding of individual feelings, not to mention the serious questions the methods raised about ethical treatment of clearly vulnerable people. Put by Gaylord and Ross, the use of aversive stimuli "drew a humanistic response of disdain."[19]

It is clear that though there were significant gains in the area of applying behavior analytic principles to interventions for individuals with autism (either before or after the diagnosis was legitimized), there were some significant downfalls experienced by the field that have continued to warrant close attention. The timeframe that led up to 1990, when the *Individuals with Disabilities Education Act* as it is currently framed solidified many of the "benefits" that would be used to bolster the legitimacy of behavior analytic approaches, soon became most widely known as Applied Behavior Analysis both formally and informally. The following section will deal with the developments from 1990 onward in order to contextualize the "law of the land" with "the state of the art."

CONTEMPORARY APPLICATIONS AND THE GROWING CLAIMS OF ABA SUPREMACY

Since the year 1990, which was significant in the greater field of special education due to the reauthorization and renaming of the *Education for All Handicapped Children Education Act* (known initially as PL 94-142) to the *Individuals with Disabilities Education Act* (IDEA), the marking of "contemporary" will be considered as those happenings from 1990 onward. While the struggles of all involved agencies to provide appropriate and acceptable educational services to individuals with a variety of disabilities continued both before and after this putative watershed moment for the field of special education, the provisions that were again guaranteed and would purportedly be overseen more stringently would directly affect the types of educational services available to individuals with ASD in particular both within and outside of the school and classroom environment. While there are myriad examples of individual schools and classrooms within schools that have been established to serve the needs of individuals with ASD, some of which were (and are) entirely behavioral in nature and others that were (and are) not, it is prudent to say that it was during this contemporary period that the specific field of Applied Behavior Analysis, especially those factions which were closely associated with ASD, would begin to vociferously claim their supremacy and entitlement to the imprimatur of "most" or even "only" evidence-based approach.

A significant development in this area was the establishment of the Behavior Analyst Certification Board (BACB), which was officially founded in 1998. In order to streamline individual states' efforts to credential professionals who sought to be practitioners of behavior analytic interventions for children, such as those in Florida, New York, Pennsylvania, and Oklahoma, the BACB subsumed these individual entities and became the sole "credentialing" organization for the practice of behavior analysis. Though experiencing multiple revisions in credentialing requirements and specific titles of such credentials (and likely to continue to do so), the BACB claims to provide what is seen as the terminal credential in behavior analysis, the Board Certified Behavior Analyst.[20] While the vast majority of states do not recognize the attainment of such a credential as licensure and distinctly limit the privileges that such a credential can grant, it is fair to say that the BACB has been successful in furthering the notion that behavior analytic approaches, especially for ASD, are to be seen as the main, if not sole method worthy of the term evidence basis. While officially unrelated despite the clear dominance of BCBAs on the Board of Directors, Advisory Board, and Committees, the Association for Science in Autism Treatment (ASAT) furthers similar claims.[21]

While ASAT is, by all accounts, somewhat of a significant presence in the field of education in ASD, the BACB is by far more prominent as a result of their influence in practice and credentialing issues. The mission of the BACB is:[22]

> to develop, promote, and implement, and international certification program for behavior analyst practitioners. The BACB has established uniform content, standards, and criteria for the credentialing process that are designed to meet:
>
> 1. The legal standards established through state, federal, and case law;
> 2. The accepted standards for national certification programs; and
> 3. The "best practice" and ethical standards of the behavior analysis profession.

At this level of discussion, it appears that the BACB situates itself in the context of a guidance-based organization with direct interests across the field of health and behavioral sciences. However, a closer look at the contents of the available BACB materials shows a clear and concerning preponderance of information regarding practices for individuals with ASD specifically. Interestingly, there are no other specific disability classifications targeted with separate documentation and policy guidance by the BACB, despite their initial claim of "enhancing the development, abilities, and choices of children and adults with different kinds of disabilities . . ."[23] If the BACB is truly making the claim that behavior analytic approaches are universally regarded as best practice, it is curious as to why the only targeted disability with official documentation is ASD.

According to the *Behavior Analyst Certification Board Health Plan Coverage of Applied Behavior Analysis Treatment for Autism Spectrum Disorder*, a guidance document released by the BACB in anticipation of the growing availability of health plan coverage for ABA services, Autism Spectrum Disorder is defined as a disorder:

> characterized by varying degrees of difficulty in social interaction and verbal and nonverbal communication, and the presence of repetitive behavior and restricted interests. This means that no two individuals with an ASD diagnosis are the same with respect to how the disorder manifests. However, the severity of the disorder is a reality for all individuals with this diagnosis and their families. Because of the nature of the disability, people with ASD will often

not achieve the ability to function independently without appropriate medical-
ly necessary treatment.[24]

There are a number of interesting and curious aspects of this definition. First,
there is no reference to the DSM characterizations specifically, which is seen
as the authoritative delineation by which ASD is to be diagnosed by those
qualified to do so, despite the similar organization of the characteristics
described in the first sentence. This is of note because BCBAs cannot, by
such credential alone, diagnose ASD. Therefore, to propose a definition that
does not reference the DSM at all is unusual, if not misleading. Secondly, the
focus appears to center around the notion of functionality, specifically dysfunction that will affect both the individual with ASD and his or her family.
Thirdly and perhaps most dubious, is the conclusion which denotes "medi-
cally necessary treatment." Since behavior analysis is not, by any means, a
medical treatment nor are BCBAs necessarily medical doctors or other such
medical professionals, it is of particular interest, if not suspicious, as to why
it would be characterized as such. Perhaps the most obvious reason, however,
is to continue to solidify the alignment between behavior analytic approaches
and the medical-rehabilitation model, a clear attempt to enhance its self-
proclaimed scientific credibility even more so by association.

If to this end it remains questionable whether the BACB is, actually,
promulgating the supremacy of the behavior analytic approach for individuals with ASD, the document's very characterization of ABA clearly takes
this stance:

> ABA is the design, implementation, and evaluation of environmental modifi-
> cations to produce socially significant improvement in human behavior. ABA
> includes the use of direct observation, measurement, and functional analysis of
> the relations between environment and behavior. ABA uses changes in envi-
> ronmental events, including antecedent stimuli and consequences, to produce
> practical and significant changes in behavior. These relevant environmental
> events are usually identified through a variety of specialized assessment meth-
> ods. ABA is based on the fact than an individual's behavior is determined by
> past and current environmental events in conjunction with organic variables
> such as their genetic endowment and ongoing physiological variables. ABA
> focuses on treating behavioral difficulties by changing the individual's envi-
> ronment rather than focusing on variables that are, at least presently, beyond
> our direct access. The successful remediation of core deficits of ASD, and the
> development or restoration of abilities, documented in hundreds of peer-re-
> viewed studies published over the past 50 years has made ABA the standard of
> care for the treatment of ASD.[25]

This definition and its conclusive linkage between ABA and its supremacy in
the treatment of ASD as the "standard of care" solidify many significant
aspects of the behavior analytic approach. The first is the clear indication that

despite the undeniable existence of "ongoing physiological variables" these variables remain secondary to the more accessible ones, such as overt behaviors and their respective environmental stimuli. Second is the notion that ASD is invariably seen as a deficit-based condition with an indication of abnormality or, perhaps, sub-normality. Aligned with the medical rehabilitative perspective, ABA can provide remediation for these behaviors potentially leading to *restoration* (a careful replacement of the controversial term "recovery"), presumably of normal functionality. This distinction is interesting as the BACB definition of ASD specifies that no two individuals with ASD are alike; however, it appears that a counter-claim of a single approach (or at least, a single theory of learning) can feasibly remediate, if not restore (or recover), this vast multitude of "realities." Finally, by claiming that there are "hundreds of peer-reviewed studies" that substantiate the claim that ABA is the "standard of care" the BACB attempts to clinch its claim of ABA's scientific legitimacy. These points, though mentioned only briefly in this section, will be handled and critiqued in-depth in the next chapter.

The question of comprehensive models (not to be confused with comprehensive ABA treatments as defined by the BACB) is another area of unilateral conclusiveness from the standpoint of the BACB. According to the BACB:

> Findings from several studies show that an eclectic model, where ABA is combined with other forms of treatment, is less effective than ABA alone. Therefore, treatment plans which involve a mixture of methods, especially those which lack proven effectiveness, should be considered with caution and, if approved, should be monitored carefully. If there are treatment protocols that are not aligned with the ABA treatment approach, these differences must be resolved in order to deliver anticipated benefits to the client. [26]

While a deep analysis and critique of these claims also will be proffered in the next chapter, some basic points would benefit from being elucidated immediately. First is the use of the term "eclectic," which, in and of itself connotes a haphazard conglomeration of approaches which are, presumably, lacking in "proven effectiveness." However, no further definition of "eclectic" is provided by the BACB. Second, while the document suggests findings from "several studies," the reference page lists only one (note: the strength of this study will be discussed in detail in the next chapter), and the sole study referenced is a comparative study in only the loosest of terms. Finally, a clear presumption is made that there is a notion of "guarantee," if not "anticipation" of benefit to the client from ABA approaches.

Arguably, the most important notion to consider in the matter of examining the field of behavior analysis beyond simply the current methodological states of the research in and of itself are the bold, if not unethical, claims that are consistently made by proponents of the exclusivity and supremacy of the behavior analytic approach, examples of which can be found over several years of literature publication. A sample of these claims is found below:

> The treatment of individuals with autism is associated with fad, controversial, unsupported, disproven, and unvalidated treatments. Eclecticism is not the best approach for treating and educating children and adolescents who have autism. Applied Behavior Analysis (ABA) uses methods derived from scientifically established principles of behavior and incorporates all of the factors identified by the US National Research Council as characteristic of effective interventions in educational and treatment programs for children who have autism. ABA is a primary method of treating aberrant behavior in individuals with autism. The only interventions that have been shown to produce comprehensive, lasting results in autism have been based on the principles of ABA. [27]

Additionally:

> Among the numerous treatments available for helping to educate people with autism, applied behavior analysis (ABA) is the best empirically evaluated. . . . In fact, ABA has been recognized by the surgeon general of the United States as the treatment of choice for autism in his mental health report for children: "Thirty years of research demonstrated the efficacy of applied behavioral methods in reducing inappropriate behavior and in increasing communication, learning, and appropriate social behavior." [28]

Finally:

> It is now widely acknowledged that, to date, the forms of treatment enjoying the broadest empirical validation for effectiveness with individuals with autism are those treatments based upon a behavioral model. These treatments all have as their foundation the systematic application of the psychological principles of learning to human behavior. This form of treatment is derived from the experimental analysis of behavior, which is a science dedicated to understanding the laws by which environmental events determine behavior. [29]

These statements, which are but a sample of those found in the literature and various other media of behavior analysis, are used to caution consumers and practitioners that any methodology which is not based in or derived from behavior analytic principles are not, and cannot, be scientifically valid, and are therefore not only inutile, but detrimental to the well-being of individuals with ASD. While deep and direct criticism of such claims will be delineated in the following chapter, it is important to notice that these claims are based not nearly as much in science as they are in rhetoric *about* the science. Duly important is that it appears, with little if any exception, that behavior analysis is the only field that both claims superiority and overtly promotes exclusivity in approach at risk of detriment to the consumer, a vastly questionable ethical practice. The potential ramifications that claims such as these can have on the state of a field that should be steeped in education and enhancement of quality of life can be extremely deleterious and serve only as a form of self-preservation for the field itself. As the next chapter will delineate, the effects of these claims are not only methodological, but have clear and concerning consequences on the social treatment of individuals with ASD.

NOTES

1. Charles B. Ferster. (1961). "Positive Reinforcement and Behavioral Deficits of Autistic Children." *Child Development*, 32, 437.
2. Ibid., 439.
3. Ibid., 446–47, 453.
4. Charles B. Ferster. (1961). "The Development of Performances in Autistic Children in an Automatically Controlled Environment." *Journal of Chronic Diseases*, 13, 313.
5. Ibid., 341.
6. J.S. Birnbauer et al. (1965). "Programmed Instruction in the Classroom." In L.P. Ullmann and L. Krasner (Ed.), *Case Studies in Behavior Modification* (358–63). New York: Holt, Rinehart & Winston, 358.
7. Ibid.
8. O. Ivar Lovaas et al. (1973). "Some Generalization and Follow-up Measures on Autistic Children in Behavior Therapy." *Journal of Applied Behavior Analysis*, 6 (3), 131–66.
9. Ibid., 162.
10. O. Ivar Lovaas. (1987). "Behavioral Treatment and Normal Educational and Intellectual Functioning in Autistic Young Children." *Journal of Consulting and Clinical Psychology*, 55(1), 3.
11. Eric Schopler from http://www.autismwebsite.com/arri/v013/page6.pdf.
12. Patricia Howling et al. (2009). "Systematic Review of Early Intensive Behavioral Intervention for Children with Autism." *American Journal on Intellectual and Developmental Disabilities* 114(1), January 2009, 23–41.
13. Frank Gresham et al. (1999). "A Selective Review of Treatments for Children with Autism: Description and Methodological Considerations." *School Psychology Review* 28(4), 559–75.
14. Catherine Nelson and Dixie Snow Huefner. "Young Children with Autism: Judicial Responses to the Lovaas and Discrete Trial Training Debates." *Journal of Early Intervention*, 2003, 26(1), 1–19.
15. Steve Holburn. "A Renaissance in Residential Behavior Analysis? A Historical Perspective and a Better Way to Help People with Challenging Behavior." *Behavior Analyst* 1997, 20, 64–65.
16. Ibid., 65.
17. Ibid., 65.
18. Bradley, 1994, as cited by Holburn, 65.
19. Gaylord-Ross, 1990, as cited by Holburn, 66.
20. www.bacb.com.
21. http://www.asatonline.org/.
22. www.bacb.com.
23. www.bacb.com/index.php?page=2.
24. Behavior Analyst Certification Board, Health Plan Coverage of Applied Behavior Analysis Treatment for Autism Spectrum Disorder, 2012, 4.
25. Ibid, 4.
26. Ibid, 18.
27. Richard M. Foxx. "Applied Behavior Analysis Treatment of Autism: The State of the Art." *Child and Adolescent Psychiatric Clinics of North America*, 17(4), 2008, 821.

28. Beth Rosenwasser and Saul Axelrod. "The Contributions of Applied Behavior Analysis to the Education of People with Autism." *Behavior Modification*, 25(5) 2001, 671.

29. Laura Schreibman. "Intensive Behavioral/Psychoeducational Treatments for Autism: Research Needs and Future Directions." *Journal of Autism and Developmental Disorders*, 2000 30, 373.

Chapter Six

The Betrayal of Behavior Analysis for Autism Spectrum Disorder

The claims of either supremacy or, in more extreme cases, exclusivity that proponents of the field of Applied Behavior Analysis (ABA) regularly state was adequately delineated in the previous chapter. The rhetoric in ABA employs many strategies, the principal one being the putatively irrefutable fifty-odd year legacy of "evidence-basis" in order to continue to propagate and maintain these claims. This campaign has garnered much success, and it is reasonable to say that ABA has attained dominance in both the theoretical and methodological discourse in the education of individuals with ASD in the early childhood, school-age, and post-school realms. This is, however, a dire problem for multiple reasons. One of the main issues with the unfortunate attainment of hegemony is the monopoly that the field of ABA has gained over the value system in both conceptualizing and applying educational practices in ASD. The success of this approach can be explained in simple terms: American educational inquiry (as well as other individualistic and capitalistic countries and cultures), is guided primarily by pragmatism and positivism, concepts that have equal influence in policymaking. As Sailor and colleagues explain:

> if evidence generated in accordance with only one epistemology is allowable for informing professional practice, while evidence generated from another standpoint is not, then policy moves to restrict not only what can be known, but also what can be done with presumed knowledge . . . within a pragmatic tradition, a question for research often implies function.[1]

This is precisely the condition in the current climate of the vastly behaviorally influenced field of educating individuals with ASD. As Barry Prizant explains, "[a] subgroup of professionals in applied behavior analysis has espoused an 'ABA' only approach for children with ASD, and makes recommendations conveying this restricting message to families and agencies serving children."[2] This is a claim that is propagated by both the Behavior Analysis Certification Board (BACB) and the Association for Science in Autism Treatment (ASAT). The consequences of these unfounded claims are multifaceted and will be discussed with great detail in this chapter. Among these problems, however, one of the most dire is that such claims can have a direct result in limiting options for education and treatment for families and individuals as they are being actively convinced that there is little, if any need to look beyond ABA and, in many ways, that they would be acting deleteriously for their children by even potentially considering other methodological approaches.

The irresponsibility of such claims is not touted only by those outside of the field of ABA. The late Ted Carr and colleagues demonstrate the ubiquity of this concern in the December 2008 issue of the *Autism Advocate*, which was devoted to the topic of ABA, by purporting, "the idea that there is a best treatment for autism is counterproductive and misleading."[3] Effectively, supremacist promulgations serve only to stymie progress and maintain authoritative control of a field. As Prizant wisely suggests:

> When the message "ABA is the only way" is conveyed in print, at conferences, and in educational/treatment programs, especially to parents of young children, it violates the primary goal of family-centered practice, which is to support parents in making the most informed decisions for their child and family through increasing knowledge and understanding of the variety of treatment options available. To be clear, principles and practices in applied behavior analysis have long made contributions to intervention and educational programming for children with ASD; however, the notion that it is not possible to have quality programs unless they are ABA programs is not supported by current research and practice. Specifically, there is no credible research that supports these claims, and there is a great deal of emerging evidence to the contrary. Furthermore, when such claims are used to steer families *exclusively* [italics in original] toward ABA practice, and away from other considerations, it is a disservice to children with ASD and their families when the result is limitations in parent input and choice about treatment options.[4]

This chapter will address how the field of behavior analysis betrays both the spirit and fundamental underpinnings of education in the following ways: (1) the field of behavior analysis, as a whole, submits unfounded and vastly overstated claims of methodological and evidentiary superiority; (2) the practice of behavior analysis violates social justice by focusing on assimilation, recovery, and maintaining ableist perspectives; and (3) behavior analysis sacrifices a holistic and humanistic approach to individuals with ASD for a self-serving, minimizing, reductionist, positivistic, and quantitative approach.

METHODOLOGICAL CONCERNS IN BEHAVIOR ANALYSIS

As delineated clearly in chapter 5, it is the field of behavior analysis alone that submits claims of superiority in the treatment of individuals with ASD, urging agencies and parents to adopt an "ABA only" approach on the sole grounds of "scientific evidence." However, the definition of "scientific evidence," or "evidence-based practice" espoused, applied, and propagated by the field of behavior analysis warrants close scrutiny. With such scrutiny, it is clearly revealed that the studies cited to support these claims as peremptory significantly lack evidence that methodologies falling under the realm of behavior analysis (which, in itself, lacks a solid definition) are, indeed, superior. The two most significant issues in the context of claiming supremacy lie in methodological considerations of single-subject design, the research methodology widely applied as a means for vetting the effectiveness of behavior analytic interventions, and the generalization of behavior analytic treatment outcomes.

UNFOUNDED AND OVERSTATED CLAIMS OF
EVIDENTIARY SUPERIORITY

As delineated in chapter 4, single-subject designs are a type of research methodology in which a small number of participants are examined using a "within-subjects" mode of analysis, comparing individual changes in behavior before a particular intervention is implemented (baseline phase) and during/after an intervention is in practice (treatment phase, maintenance phase, and generalization phases). This type of research, though inarguably valuable in many ways, distinctly lacks key quality indicators of valid research findings to be deemed legitimate enough to make claims of causation (couched in the alternative term "functional relationship" by behavior analysts), if even correlation. The first serious consideration when taking the findings of single-subject designs into account is the lack of information regarding *treatment integrity*, known also as *fidelity of implementation*. Treatment integrity, universally regarded as an important marker of reliability, can be defined as "the degree to which an independent variable is implemented as intended"[5] as expounded in chapter 4. That is, unless the accuracy and orthodoxy with which an intervention is used is assessed in some fashion (generally using a quantitative type of measure), a field (or even a single researcher) cannot claim, with any confidence, that the "concept" or "practice" being implemented is indeed comparable across studies, much less practical applications that are guided by the research. What makes this particularly troublesome in the field of behavior analysis is that, according to multiple studies, only 18 to 30 percent of studies in the *Journal of Applied Behavior Analysis*, the field's flagship journal, reported any measures of such integrity data, yielding the vast majority of such studies comparability and, therefore, claims of effectiveness as a "practice" largely, if not entirely unsubstantiated.[6] While it is imperative to note that more current articles are beginning to include measures of treatment integrity, the measures are, themselves, still nascent and in need of validation. Furthermore, it is important to note that in direct observation methodology such as that employed in single-subject research, the concept of reactivity among study participants is a distinct threat to both legitimacy of findings and treatment integrity, as treatments may need to be adapted for individuals in order to effect any change in behavior. Any modification to the treatment protocol as intended, however, can be deemed a threat to treatment integrity and, therefore, detract from the reliability and, therefore, generalizability of the findings. However, the failure to adapt approaches and methodologies to individualized needs is a disservice to the participant (or, ultimately, student), landing the researcher and/or practitioner in a precarious ethical dilemma. Additionally, treatment integrity of a particular practice may, itself, degenerate as different models, styles, and variations develop between practitioners making the very declaration of a "unified practice" a categorical unlikelihood, if not impossibility.

Another fundamental hallmark of single-subject research methodology is the use of visual means of data analysis to determine intervention results. Visual analysis refers to the practice of visually inspecting trend lines (ascending trends, or data that increase; descending trends, or data that decrease; variable trends, or data that both increase and decrease unpredictably; and stable trends, or data that neither increase nor decrease markedly) with very little, if any use of additional mathematical or statistical analysis. Such mathematical practices are generally limited to means or percentages (despite the effort of some behavior analysts to contribute more statistically oriented practices which are rarely employed).[7] The practice of visual analysis has been the principal practice of data analysis in the field since its development during the 1970s and continues as the principal means today. Initially the use of visual analysis was presented as a strong indicator of change, as it was expected to be sensitive only to large changes in behavior. Therefore, effects of independent variables were intended to be proclaimed only when such changes were large enough to be detectable visually, yielding a significant advantage over statistical analyses in the area of Type II errors, or missing an existing effect. While visual analyses can give some initial impressions about general trends of data and individual responsiveness to an independent variable, it is important to note that visual analyses alone cannot possibly enable researchers to posit reliable quantitative data from individual studies, especially in comparison to one another. Current research suggests, however, that as the popularity and availability of single-subject research design grows, the political and professional need for publication has resulted in an inflation of Type I errors, or claiming an effect of the independent variable when no effect indeed exists, with dependence on visual analysis being a very possible explanation for the error itself.[8] This can be a distinct warning that claims of supremacy are vastly premature, especially if they are being made based on an increasing amount of Type I errors. To complicate these matters more, Type I errors can be inflated even greater in interventions that use existing responses to guide intervention changes. That is, if an individual response is deemed as indicative of a change and a decision is made about the implementation of that respective intervention, both the condition for the change and the change itself can continue a cycle of Type I errors, resulting in continuous erroneous reports of positive findings.

The commonality of such errors is not the only issue that threatens the legitimacy of visual analysis, however. Research indicates clearly that analysts with greater experience in visual analysis appeared to be more conservative, utilizing stricter criteria when assessing data from a graph than those with less experience, indicating that whether or not an effect is deemed based on visual analysis is not an objective matter, but subjectively influenced. This finding can pose a significant threat to the validity of single-subject research in that research findings in general do not indicate the experience level of the principal assessor nor do they relate any methodological control for such factors. Additionally, low intra-judge ratings are reported, raising questions about even individual trends in consistency of analysis. This is also problematic as it cannot be addressed by interobserver agreement, which judges the consistency with which the response is observed *between* observers, not a legitimization of the interpretation of effect of the independent variable for a single observer or an overall analysis.[9] The concept of the questionable reliability of visual analyses is not new, with critiques and admonitions appearing from within the field of behavior analysis as early as the late 1970s.[10] Little of note has been done, however, save for some increased usage of basic descriptive statistics like means, medians, and modes, to enhance this lack of quantitative foundation. This is a rather significant problem for a research methodology claiming to be based on quantitative data analysis while, rather, it appears to actually rely only on quantitative data collection and visually qualitative data analysis.

The second methodological flaw in the claims of supremacy by the field of behavior analysis is the over-reliance on generally weak comparative studies and quantitatively few meta-analyses to support claims of strong evidence-basis. As demonstrated in the *Guidelines* document published by the BACB, the claim that interventions utilizing principles of ABA alone were demonstrated to be more effective than eclectic treatments, deeming ABA the "standard of care" in ASD were based on a questionably designed comparative analysis (again, as only one citation was provided despite the claim of "many" studies, one can only evaluate the statement based on the identified article). Statements such as this appear to suggest that the BACB supports the notion that behavior analytic approaches alone are the most effective means of intervention. This does not seem to be uncommon in the field of behavior analysis. It is essential, then, to question whether the quality of such studies is even capable of vetting such claims of supremacy. As is the case in many such analyses, conflicting information is found, leading the true scientist to have to cede caution to the conservative interpretation of "insufficient evidence" of supremacy or even noted effectiveness.[11, 12] For example, the BACB *Guidelines* document cites a study by Howard and colleagues (2005) as basis for the claim that eclectic models are empirically shown to be less effective than pure ABA models.[13] However, close examination of this particular study reveals multiple methodological flaws that severely limit, if not entirely disqualify, the findings of the paper. While the authors offered a smattering of generic limitations such as non-random group assignments, non-blind data analysts and data collectors, and the use of group mean scores, a relatively basic and somewhat careless comparison, there are indeed far more serious methodological flaws that threaten the overall validity of the study altogether. The first flaw is found with respect to the grouping of subjects beyond its non-random assignment. The treatment that would ultimately be deemed most effective, the Intensive Behavior Analytic Treatment (IBT) was comprised of 29 participants, nearly double the amount of the other two comparison groups made up of 16 participants each. It is important to note that the study delineated three distinct groups, not an IBT group and a combination of the other two groups, which would have yielded a more comparable subject distribution. Furthermore, there was a considerable inequity in both ethnic and diagnostic distribution between the groups, with 10 to 25 percent more white students in the IBT group, and 10 to 30 percent more children diagnosed with autism in the IBT group. The flaws extend beyond distribution inequalities, however, and become more alarming when instructional practices are considered. The IBT group received 35 to 40 hours of 1:1 therapy per week across multiple settings using discrete trial, incidental teaching, and "other" non-specified treatments with the availability of treatment manuals as well as consultation assistance provided by individuals with master's degrees and/or board certification in behavior analysis. However, the AP and GP groups received 25 to 30 and 15 hours of instruction per week, respectively, in a 1:1 or 1:2 and a 1:6 ratio, respectively, receiving the opportunity for guidance from a consultant with one to two years of graduate work without Master's degrees or board certification in behavior analysis. Further, proving similar to most other behavior analytic research reports, measures of treatment integrity for any of the groups were not reported and, therefore, cannot be considered as being a factor, deeming the very methodologies used as unreliable.

Analytically, there are substantial flaws with the Howard et al. study as well. First and foremost, in terms of operationalization, a foundation of behavior analytic research, the operational definition designated for each treatment group was quite vague. The IBT group was said to have received discrete trial instruction, incidental teaching, and "other" non-specified behavior analytic treatment approaches for which there were manuals, none of which were defined outside of the context of such "manuals." The remaining groups were defined in an equally nebulous fashion, with the second group characterized by methods of PECS, DTT, TEACCH, SIT, "circle time," and music, and the third group characterized by general education programming marked by "developmentally appropriate activities." While the researchers are careful to indicate the lack of specificity for the third group as beyond their control, there is no explanation regarding the vagueness of the approaches over which they had more direct influence, nor is there present any attempt to strengthen to descriptions or definitions of the non-IBT groups. Further, it is unclear as to why more detailed descriptions of at least the qualitative type could not be supplied by the researchers to provide a clearer means of the less defined approaches. Secondly, the focus of the analysis appeared to be performance on a battery of tests as opposed to engagement in operationally defined behaviors. Behavior analytic research holds observable and measurable criteria as a foundational tenet, promulgating that, as a rule, such dependent variables are the only type which can garner evidence of progress. Why then, would a comparison study be different? Furthermore, the main statistical process utilized was a regression analysis, though one which was not specified as stepwise or hierarchical, a significant factor in the outcome of such a procedure. Regression analyses represent a statistical process that is most vulnerable to product manipulation, as they are extremely sensitive to processes as simple as order of variable entry into the regression equation. Not only was such an analysis used as the main modality of comparison, but they were further de-contextualized in the absence of *post hoc* tests, which would have demonstrated better control over variables, especially when there were such obvious disparities in group demographics. A further in-depth analysis of the Howard et al. article, which includes responses to counter-critiques from within the field of behavior analysis, was also put forth by Schoenberger.[14]

In addition to the general weakness of such comparative studies, meta-analyses are also often used to lend credence to the supremacy of behavior analytic interventions. What makes the use of meta-analyses particularly problematic is the very essential question of inclusion criteria. Which studies are included, why they are included, as well as which studies are excluded, and why they are excluded can make the difference between conflicting findings. There are no concrete rules, however, that dictate these decisions, leaving the experimenter up to his or her own application of personal philosophy and/or theory. Ultimately, such stylistic considerations can be construed as little other than potential method biases which invariably lead to measurement error, thus threatening the validity of the conclusions that are drawn between measures.[15] Therefore, reliance on meta-analyses at all to demonstrate supremacy or exclusivity is a dangerous, if not an entirely unfounded strategy.

Despite these methodological weaknesses, however, it remains important to keep such considerations in context. As mentioned previously, these data do not indicate ineffectiveness of behavior analytic approaches by any means, nor should such issues act as an impetus to focus less or dismiss or discontinue research involving behavior analytic practices. In fact, quite the contrary will be argued in the following chapter. However, these findings should be used to reject the notion that behavioral methodologies should be deemed superior to the effect that other approaches should neither be implemented nor further studied, as the field's most prominent advocacy organization, the BACB, very clearly suggests. As Herbert and colleagues explain:

> Taken together, the literature on ABA programs for autism clearly suggests that such interventions are promising. Methodological weaknesses of the existing studies, however, severely limit the conclusions that can be drawn about their efficacy. Of particular note is the fact that no study to date has utilized a true experimental design, in which subjects were randomly assigned to treatment conditions. This fact limits the inferences that can be drawn about the effects of the programs studies. Moreover, these concerns are compounded by the pretreatment differences between experimental control conditions in each of the studies reviewed. Other methodological concerns include questions about the representativeness of the samples of autistic children, unknown fidelity to treatment procedures, limited outcome data for most studies, and problems inherent in relying on IQ scores and school placement as primary measures of autistic symptoms and functioning . . . the available research on these programs is more akin to program evaluations than to traditional studies of treatment efficacy or effectiveness.[16]

Considering the statements claiming supremacy of ABA outlined in chapter 4, especially those submitted by Schreibman who references experimental qualities of behavior analytic research, Herbert's criticisms are well-founded and applicable to claims of superiority and exclusivity.

Given these methodological considerations, it is functionally impossible to ignore the notion that Applied Behavior Analysis in itself lacks a solid definition, yielding an imprecise, and perhaps even nonexistent, true conceptualization. As Schreibman herself posits, "[t]echnically, applied behavioral analysis is not a treatment for autism, it is a research methodology."[17] In other terms, ABA can be regarded as a learning theory, a categorical term that encapsulates multiple methodological practices, or a means of referring to any use of environmental consequences to change overt behavior. Given this protean and inconsistent conceptualization, to claim it whole enough to even be an entity for supremacy is flawed.

PROBLEMS WITH GENERALIZATION OF TREATMENT OUTCOMES IN BEHAVIOR ANALYSIS

In addition to the methodological concerns regarding the claims of supremacy raised by the field of behavior analysis, there is also a significant challenge to the efficacy of such interventions in terms of their generalizability. While it is clearly irrefutable that the field of behavior analysis maintains significant territory in the educational approaches for individuals with ASD, the same can no longer be said about its influence in the treatment of individuals with schizophrenia, as well as other disorders previously thought to be behaviorally controlled, representing a significant historical change. The trends observed regarding the previous role of behavior analysis in the treatment of schizophrenia may act as somewhat of a portent to what appears to be happening currently in the context of educating individuals with ASD.

In the field of psychiatry, specifically the branch that deals directly with schizophrenia, a fervent debate continues between the roles that psychopharmacology has played, and continues to play, in the treatment of schizophrenia as compared to that of behavior analytic interventions. According to Wyatt and Midkiff, the "rise of biological causation theory . . . has come about as a direct result of the powerful influences of organized psychiatry and the pharmaceutical industry."[18] While there is no doubt that the pharmaceutical industry's lobby plays a significant and direct role in medical practice as well as public policy, the notion that it, in itself, was entirely causal of the replacement does not seem prudent. In response, many representatives of the supposed "biological causation" approach claim that the interest of both parties came about as a direct result of the failure of behavioral interventions alone to effectively treat the enigmatic condition of schizophrenia. Instead, the position of the behaviorists can be regarded as such:

> Although traditional accounts of these [schizophrenic type] behaviors posit that they are symptoms of an underlying disorder, behavior analysts view these behaviors as a class of operants influenced by environmental contingencies . . . being *responsible for maintaining* [italics in original] under natural conditions prior to treatment is utterly different than being *capable of influencing the behavior* [italics in original] during treatment. The rhetorically swift move from "may be maintained by" to "or at least are sensitive to" is in fact a scientifically major move between a theoretically strong etiological or maintenance *explanatory* [italics in original] claim to a much weaker claim about being able to have an effect on a symptom. This sort of equivocation on what

one is claiming obscures the structure of the argument and makes it easy to avoid paying the falsificationist piper.[19]

This idea represents how the claims of behavior analysts are inconsistent, vacillating between authoritative claims of causation and subtler claims of influence. In any case, it all appears to be an attempt to maintain what little relevant voice is still maintained by behavior analysis in the field of schizophrenia. What the field of behavior analysis appears to continue to do is display an unclear and inconsistent response to advances in the greater field of science either by nominally aligning themselves with such developments (e.g., the relatively new field of behavioral psychopharmacology) or by systematically ignoring their existence along with foundational discoveries (such as neuro-emotional networks in the brain that give much credence to relationship-based theories of ASD and processing networks in the brain that proffer evidence for sensory-based approaches). What remains is a political and social attempt to maintain what was once the authoritative, if not definitive, voice in Western psychology and, for a time, medicine. This voice grew exponentially weaker in the clinical settings of schizophrenia with the increasing availability as well as effectiveness of psychopharmacological treatments. But why did the efforts of behavior analytic interventions fail in schizophrenia so distinctly? According to Wakefield, the clear answer was the lack of generalizability:

> token economies were eclipsed because research failed to demonstrate adequate generalization to natural environments to make them a viable treatment given deinstitutionalization. Indeed, behavioral researchers—not armchair critics or outsiders . . . have been saying that generalization is the key test of success and that the results have been disappointing. For example . . . the generalization of treatment effects to stimulus conditions in which token reinforcement is not given might be expected to be the *raison d'etre* of token economies. An examination of the literature leads to a different conclusion. There are numerous reports of token programs showing behavior change only while contingent token reinforcement is being delivered. Generally, removal of token reinforcement results in decrements in desirable responses and a return to baseline or near-baseline levels of performance.[20]

Ultimately, the failure of behavioral interventions to facilitate meaningful behavioral and functional changes in the natural environment coupled with the promise and increasing success of psychopharmacological treatments to do so can be viewed as a more apt explanation for the "eclipse" of behavioral intervention, as opposed to some conspiratorially orchestrated coup of corporate interest and political lobbying. If an intervention is only effective under particular conditions which are not naturalistic and require manipulation of the environment, the treatment cannot, therefore, qualify as effective since simulated conditions, if not entire environments, are needed for the effects of the treatment to be maintained outside of the treatment setting and, therefore, cannot withstand generalization to the natural environment.

While some researchers and practitioners in the field accepted these emerging scientific revelations and attempted to integrate the core findings of behavior analysis through the pioneering of newer, more legitimate hybrids such as cognitive-behavioral therapy, many gripped their field's tenets even more tightly, unwilling to "go quietly" leading to a need for a new domain in which theoretical and clinical dominance could be gained. Ideally it would be a domain for which there has been no real biological or psychopharmacological advancement; a field that remained devoid of not only promising treatments, but any real answers at all. This field was Autism Spectrum Disorders.

However, the challenge of generalization remains applicable for ASD, with many theorists continuing to regard generalization not as an operant response in and of itself, but as a passive phenomenon that comes as a result of any behavior change process. As noted by Stokes and Baer as far back as the late 1970s:

> Generalization has been and doubtless will remain a fundamental concern of applied behavior analysis. A therapeutic behavioral change, to be effective, often (not always) must occur over time, persons, and settings, and the effects of the change sometimes should spread to a variety of related behaviors. Even though the literature shows many instances of generalization, it is still frequently observed that when a change in behavior is accomplished through experimental contingencies, then that change is manifest where and when those contingencies operate, and is often seen only in transitory forms in other places and other times. . . . The frequent need for generalization of therapeutic behavior change is widely accepted, but it is not always realized that generalization does not automatically occur simply because a behavior change is accomplished. Thus, the need actively to *program* [italics in original] generalization, rather than passively to expect it as an outcome of certain training procedures, is a point requiring both emphasis and effective techniques. That such exhortations have often been made has not always ensured that researchers in the field have taken serious note of and, therefore, proceeded to analyze adequately the generalization issues of vital concern to their programs.[21]

This concern continued through the 1980s with an article by Steven Hayes and colleagues, the former a well-respected and widely published behavior analyst who expressed deep concern that research efforts in Applied Behavior Analysis were becoming purely technical without adequately addressing and testing the principles of behavior analysis or maintaining the importance of socially significant behaviors and conceptual questions. That is, behavior analysis had become far too demonstrative of the principles "at work" rather than conceptually, as social science is designed to be, testing the validity and suitability of theories. This resulted in a massive quantitative increase in the publication of behavior analytic studies, but threatens its true qualitative contribution to the field of social science. As Hayes suggests:

> the term "analytic" means the clear demonstration of an effect: "An experimenter has achieved an analysis of a behavior when he can exercise control over it" (Baer et al., 1968).[22] The importance of component analyses, parametric analyses, and other more sophisticated analytic attempts are often to be found less in "control" (in an immediately applied sense) and more in "understanding" (in a scientific sense). One may easily control, say, aggressive behavior through the use of punishment without having contributed significantly to the understanding of aggression.[23]

One such area Hayes cited specifically was that of generalization, which he believed to have lost much meaning as well as importance in application. As Hayes suggests:

> It is also noteworthy that the large majority of generalization research has been concerned with generalization across settings and with maintenance, with relatively little attention given to response generalization or generalization across persons. Some clinical populations, such as autistic and retarded children, display behavioral deficits (and excesses) which are so extensive that one behavior at a time applications of behavior modification have not proven very fruitful. For such populations it would seem that we *must* [italics in original] investigate strategies that produce multiple or widespread behavior change—that is, a technology for promoting response generalization.[24]

As such, the importance of generalization research and the notion that the field has become cure-based is an indication that, even amongst the most contributive to the field of behavior analysis, there is much to be concerned about in terms of the true value and bold claims of behavior analysis. Hayes indicates a similar concern:

> Once one has adopted the view that the immediate and primary aim of applied behavior analysis is client cure, it follows that there is less need for component and parametric analyses. If one has an effective treatment program, the pressure to refine it may be quite low, and one need only compare it to others periodically. It is interesting to note that, although Baer et al. clearly expected more complicated analyses to be done as applied behavior analysis matured, the exact opposite has occurred.[25]

This remains as true today as it was when Hayes originally wrote this article in 1980.

The message that the disparagement of behavior analytic approaches is not the intention of this argument warrants reassertion at this time, and it will be reasserted repeatedly to maintain this idea throughout the work. Rather, the purpose of this treatise is to refute the notion that behavior analytic interventions can and should be viewed as superior to other treatment modalities, including a more comprehensive methodology. The fact that research has repeatedly failed to demonstrate that generalizability of behavioral effects achieved in a well-controlled therapeutic environment with the availability of consistent and contrived reinforcement can be maintained under naturally occurring conditions is a foundational failure of the approach. Therefore, this situation alone demands a reconsideration of how such an inability can be addressed. Since the field of behavior analysis itself has not offered any more credible and evidence-based alternatives, the field is obligated to continue to search for such effective interventions elsewhere despite the vociferous claims of supremacy.

PROBLEMS WITH THE CHARACTERIZATION OF ABA AS "SCIENTIFIC"

In many ways the field of behavior analysis shrouds itself with a rhetorical superimposition of "science." Notions of "scientific teaching" abound in the literature describing approaches for treating behaviors and conditions, especially in the context of ASD. Claims of "scientific evidence" based on the "scientific method" of investigating connections, if not causations, between independent and dependent variables overwhelm journals, mostly those created for the specific mission of ABA to be fulfilled (such as the *Journal of Applied Behavior Analysis*, the *Journal of the Experimental Analysis of Behavior* and, in many respects, ASD focused journals such as *Focus on Autism and Other Developmental Disorders*, among others). However, these claims of "scientific basis" appear, with some closer observation, to be more in line with rhetorical claims than true demonstration legitimized outside of its own self-serving modalities. As such, the concept of "science" appears to serve more of a functional role in behavior analysis rather than an evaluative or standardizing one. That is, the increased association between "science" and "behavior analysis" acts as a rhetorical tactic to increase the association between "medicine" (what many in the public realm view as being synonymous with science) and behavior analysis. The analysis offered by the language used in the BACB *Guidelines* document (see previous chapter) reveals this to be a very deliberate association, but for what real purpose and to what end? It is suggested that the purpose is quite clear and quite simple: for the field of ABA to harness the power of suggestion and association in order to propagate its own cause. By defining itself as "evidence-based" it meets, part and parcel, the requirements indicated by the two main pieces of legislation governing education: the Elementary and Secondary Education Act (formerly known as No Child Left Behind) and the Individuals with Disabilities Education Act (known also as the Individuals with Disabilities Education

Improvement Act, its 2004 reauthorization). This alignment would allow both an authoritative claim as well as a "pre-approved" means of acceptability by schools desperate to simply remain in compliance with the ever complicating laws and methods of oversight, especially those precarious and potentially litigious situations involving individuals with disabilities.

However, does behavior analysis really meet the requirements to be characterized as scientific, or is it more aligned with the notion of "scientism"? Scientism implies:

> an exaggerated kind of deference toward science, an excessive readiness to accept as authoritative any claim made by the sciences, and to dismiss every kind of criticism of science or its practitioners as anti-scientific prejudice. [26]

Furthermore, scientism claims unequivocally that the "empirical-analytical method of science evolved from a synthesis between formal methods of reasoning and empiricist methods of data collection."[27] Methods based in scientism, then, instead of working toward socially relevant and reasonable application of such science, effectively create what Heinz and Lyytinen call a "data monster" without relevance or context to the real issue.[28] The purpose, therefore, of scientism becomes less about finding relevant information to affect a pertinent social issue and more about obeying the rules of its own methodology regardless of the value that other methods and means of investigation may provide. As such:

> The danger of scientism when applied to the resolution of practical problems lies in a narrowing of problem perception to those aspects which are "researchable" by given scientistic methods. What is not researchable is by definition not publishable and therefore not fundable. By a conceptual sleight, all relevant practical problems on which good types of scientistic evidence cannot be brought to bear (but could at least be examined, say, from a phenomenological perspective) are defined to be illegitimate as far as science is concerned. [29]

This scientistic viewpoint of behavior analysis can be traced directly back to Skinner (and, in many ways even to Watson's later writings). Skinner did not submit that any language, including scientific language, was capable of being essentially descriptive of private phenomena.[30] As Skinner states:

> The ultimate criterion for the goodness of a concept is not whether two people are brought into agreement but whether the scientist who uses the concept can operate successfully upon his material. [31]

The scientistic allegiance of the field of behavior analysis in ASD is clearly demonstrated in the contents of the BACB task list for interventionists working individuals with ASD.[32] While many of the tasks are irrelevant to the present discussion, reflecting general best practices rather than those specific to behavior analysis, there are some specific tasks that warrant closer examination. Of course, how each individual behavior analyst addresses the tasks in his or her own practice is impossible to predict and would be unfair to presume. It is, however, reasonable to use the *Guidelines* document as general litmus to how such issues are suggested to be addressed by the presumed oversight organization of behavior analysis. The first questionable task indicates, "Explain myths, fads, and controversies to consumers and the public" (A-3). Indeed, this is an important discussion, but in what ways are these "myths, fads, and controversies" defined? Though the task list does not provide a definition, it would be reasonable to suspect, based on the clear language of the *Guidelines*, that anything falling out of the realm of what could be considered ABA practice (and, therefore, by the Board's own account, not evidence-based) could, and likely should qualify as a "myth, fad, or controversy." While cloaked in terms of a public service, the authoritative means by which these views, clearly based only on interpretation, could be misused as authoritative propaganda is concerning. Indeed, if one were to observe the replacement of behavior analytic practice by psychopharmacological practice in schizophrenia, this context could undoubtedly characterize the behavior analytic treatment as a fad, since it did not last and was, ultimately, shown to fail the most important clinical test of generalizability. Furthermore, many of the "research" endeavors propagated by behavior analysts, especially that of Lovaas' 1987 report would fit such criteria as well. Additionally, the task "Research the relevance, reliability, validity, and proper use of various assessment instruments" (C-1) warrants some investigation as to its function for the behavior analyst. If a behavior analyst were to do this according to a complete review of the literature, a necessary inclusion would be the findings of Gresham, amongst others, indicating the vastly underreported reliability measures involving treatment integrity; perhaps the most important measure for a treatment-based approach to attain. However, this issue is addressed nowhere in any of the publicly available BACB documents, despite its inclusion in multiple issues of the *Journal of Applied Behavior Analysis*. Most concerning, however, are the respective tasks "Research best scientific evidence regarding validity and necessity of medical and 'biomedical' tests, limitations of inferences that can be drawn from them" (C-4) and the entire section (G) involving "non-behavior analytic intervention." In the context of these tasks, the BACB calls for the behavior analyst to be critical of relevant approaches; certainly a vital component of a comprehensive, exhaustive, and unbiased analysis. However, the tasks involving such critical research, especially involving limitations, are directed exclusively at "non-behavior analytic" interventions. At no point does the task list indicate a critical analysis or a debriefing of any potential limitations or hazardous by-products of behavioral intervention. This omission would lead the consumer and/or public, then, to believe that there are none, as the hazards of the others were clearly revealed. This, of course, is entirely untrue and a staunchly unethical suggestion, even if only an omission. The hazards of behavior analytic interventions are multitudinous and include, but are in no way limited to, the lack of generalizability in natural settings, prompt dependency, disregard of private events including emotional states, hyper-focused attention on external reinforcement, the role of food in intervention leading to potential health problems such as obesity and diabetes, among others, all of which are unequivocally indicated in the extant literature. This point is put clearly by Wakefield:

> [Pseudoscience] includes not taking into account the entire gamut of evidence bearing on an issue, insisting on the existence of as-yet-unconfirmed causal processes that fit one's theory but have no *prima facie* plausibility, citing politics of other unscientific considerations in defending one's own position, invoking various methodological factors such as parsimony rather than addressing the evidence, abandoning parity of reasoning in assessing rival theories, using verbal gymnastics to preserve the semblance of cherished principles semantically even where the substance has been disconfirmed, simply not allowing disconfirmation or accepting reasonable plausibility arguments, and so on.[33]

This is not to posit, by any means, that behavior analysis is, indeed, a pseudoscience; nor does it suggest it is in danger of becoming one. It is to posit, however, that if the incredulity of any other potential intervention or idea that is "non-behavioral" persists, especially in the area of neuroscience, the field increasingly runs the risk of edging itself out of relevance and becoming an archaic form of thought and a largely isolated faction of professionals as a result of its own behavior. The evidence to contradict the supremacy of behavior analysis is simply far too clear. Furthermore the evidence to support supposedly rivaling, though not incompatible theories and methodologies will be shown, in the next chapter, to be equally as possessive of such evidence, as well as being as promising pending future research endeavors.

THEORETICAL AND PHILOSOPHICAL CONSIDERATIONS

Behavior Analytic Interventions Focus Disproportionately on Extrinsic Motivation

The issue of motivation is a key foundation in behavior analytic interventions, though the means by which it is conceptualized by behavior analysts may be highly limited and vastly oversimplified. While behavior analytic interventions focus disproportionately, if not entirely, on extrinsic motivation, it virtually ignores the significance and, in some cases, even the very existence of intrinsic motivation, a highly studied and empirically verified phenomenon, with the most significant contributions credited to the work of Deci and Ryan. In order to begin to censure the way in which behavior analytic approaches minimize the significance of intrinsic motivation, a deeper study of what motivation is and how extrinsic and intrinsic motivation are defined and conceptualized is necessary.

By definition, to be *motivated* means to "be moved" by something; this means that an individual who has no inclination to act would be characterized as unmotivated, whereas an individual who does have an inclination to act and does, indeed act would be deemed motivated. The most common and basic distinction between types of motivation is extrinsic motivation, which is characterized by acting in order to attain a separable outcome, and intrinsic motivation, which is characterized by acting because it is inherently interesting or enjoyable.[34] However, motivation is by no means truly dichotomous.

Though extrinsic motivation has been demonstrated to be powerful, undoubtedly serving as an impetus for action in some cases, it has also been characterized as "pale and impoverished" in many of its states. As such, though it may inarguably move individuals to act in one way or another, dependence on extrinsic motivation alone can also result in acting with resentment, guilt, negligence, resistance, or disinterest because one is only externally catalyzed to engage in the action, as opposed to being internally and, therefore, more genuinely inclined to act.[35] According to Deci and Ryan:

> Extrinsic motivation is a construct that pertains whenever an activity is done in order to attain some separable outcome. Extrinsic motivation thus contrasts with intrinsic motivation, which refers to doing an activity simply for the enjoyment of the activity itself, rather than its instrumental value.[36]

Because extrinsic motivation appears to initiate *compliance* out of functional benefit or obligation more than *acting* out of interest or enjoyment, maintaining behavior through external reinforcement requires a relatively constant availability of some external resource. Intrinsic motivation, on the other hand, is defined as:

> The doing of an activity for its inherent satisfactions rather than for some separable consequence. When intrinsically motivated a person is moved to act for the fun or challenge entailed rather than because of external prods, pressures, or rewards.[37]

More specifically, two forces exist within intrinsic motivation: internalization and integration. *Internalization* is the process of taking in a value or regulation. *Integration* is the process by which individuals more fully transform the regulation into their own will so that it will emanate from their sense of self.[38]

How then, does the difference in motivational types play out in classrooms and learning-based activities? According to Deci and Ryan, this is a significant question that requires particularly close attention. Research shows that it is through intrinsic motivation that an individual's sense of competence is enhanced only if they feel a simultaneous sense of autonomy, in that the locus of control is internal rather than external. So the reward or the functionality of the behavior is not, in itself, likely to be motivating enough in terms of gaining competence, or anything beyond mere compliance; only behaviors that are both intrinsically motivated and self-determined are. As such, a multitude of studies that are classroom-based indicate that intrinsic motivation is maintained best in environments that support student autonomy as opposed to teacher control. Students who feel they are under control as opposed to intrinsically motivated have been shown to lose initiative as well as learn less competently.[39]

This is not a concept that has been ignored by behaviorists, however. Many behaviorists, beginning with Skinner, have addressed intrinsic motivation as a difficult, if not impossible, concept to observe and measure, relegating it as ill-indicative of scientific worth due to lack of operational definition and, therefore, evidence.[40] As such, it was deemed functionally irrelevant to motivation, leaving external motivation as the only relevant process in behavioral motivation due to its observable and measurable accessibility. Theories regarding and responses to intrinsic motivation in the behavior analytic community spanned from total dismissal due to lack of "observable evidence," to alternative accounts or explanations, such as intrinsic motivation being a mistaken concept for what was really response variability occurring after reinforcer termination, as well as explaining the continuance of such behaviors based on cultural values that are subject to continuous, though tacit praise and other social consequences acting as reinforcement, a prime example of what many behaviorists refer to as "explanatory fictions." Theorists outside of behavior analysis, however, dispute this claim and are quite willing to accept the legitimacy of and evidence for intrinsic motivation, indicating that behaviorists were focusing on the action of the reward itself, rather than the process of innate psychological needs such as competence, autonomy, and relatedness, as well as overall satisfaction. Indeed, these latter nonbehavioral theorists did not deny the existence or the function of extrinsic motivation, but rather took issue with regarding it as the main, if not only, relevant motivating force and, in many cases, even sought to identify some of its detriments to human behavior and intentionality.

Research from multiple studies, however, which have explored the relationship between external rewards and intrinsic motivation appear to report findings that are strong and consistent: Persistent use of external rewards primarily have a negative effect on intrinsic motivation for genuinely interesting tasks. That is, even when there is no external reward present, individuals who are under the influence of consistent external reward show progressively less interest in tasks that were, previously, intrinsically motivating. As such, these findings also provide little support for behavioral theories of motivation, despite the bold claims of the behavioral community.

Behaviorism Threatens Social Justice through Focusing on Assimilation, Ableism, and Normality

With the behavior analytic perspective hinging on replacing socially inappropriate behavior with socially appropriate behavior, a general theme in behavior analytic interventions is a tacit acceptance of the normal/abnormal dichotomy. From this perspective, the overarching cultural function of ableism is permitted to not only propagate in the general classrooms, but also permeate throughout the classrooms for children with ASD, which are often self-contained and that are designed to be, among other things, socially safer and more educationally amenable environments for such less corrigible individuals. Coupling this notion with aforementioned ideas of failure to achieve generalization, either in any natural environment or even a somewhat more inclusive simulated environment, the underlying notions of behaviorism maintain separatism for those who cannot be "appropriate" and assimilation only for those who can be "appropriate," at least to culturally and socially acceptable standards. This notion is instated even more deeply in the sense that a multitude of behavior analytic studies supposedly demonstrating effectiveness, beginning with that of Lovaas (1987) and continuing in the current literature will use the litmus of "normal functioning," mainly in terms of Intelligence Quotient tests and other standardized means of "normality" to claim the respective interventions' ultimate effectiveness.[41] There is no greater portrayal of ableism than advertising the success of intervention in terms of how "normal" it makes the recipient. Below is a sample of such claims taken from the behavior analytic literature:

- There is little doubt that early intervention based on the principles and practices of Applied Behavior Analysis can produce large, comprehensive, lasting, and meaningful improvements in many important domains for a large proportion of children with autism. For some, those improvements can amount to achievement of completely normal intellectual, social academic, communicative, and adaptive functioning.[42]
- We also now know that applying effective [behavior analytic] interventions when children are very young (e.g., under the age of 3–4 years) has the potential for achieving substantial and widespread gains and even normal function in a certain number of these youngsters.[43]

- During the past 15 years research has begun to demonstrate that significant proportions of children with autism or PDD who participate in early intensive intervention based on the principles of applied behavior analysis (ABA) achieve normal or near-normal functioning . . . [44]
- Findings demonstrated that many children with autism could make dramatic improvement, even achieve "normalcy."[45]

Even those studies and rhetorical pieces in the literature that do not claim, outright, that behavior analytic intervention can result in recovery, the implicit focus on "social appropriateness" maintains the dichotomy of the normal versus abnormal, with success deemed as getting as close to normal as possible. However, the term (or at least the concept of) recovery remains a rhetorical device in behavior analytic writing, and one that seemingly violates one of its foundational rules: operationalization. Beginning with Lovaas and continuing with the current writings that indicate recovery or at least progress toward "normality," there is a blatant lack of operationalization beyond the most commonly used indication of a standardized test score; an unusual choice for behavioral research as such a quotient is almost entirely based in cognitive notions of assessment as opposed to behavioral. As Broderick notes:

> Given the epistemological (positivist), methodological (quantitative, experimental, treatment-effect design), and theoretical (operant behaviorism) grounding of Lovaas's research [as well as others], it seems unlikely that a behavioral researcher would fail to provide an operational definition for such a provocative description of an outcome. This omission suggests that perhaps the power of the term recovery lies in its rhetorical, rather than its operational, use. . . . People who read (and perhaps, more importantly, who read *about*) [italics in original] this study hear, "nearly half of all children who participated in this protocol have recovered" or "nearly half of all children who participated in this protocol are *normal* now." [italics in original] And the implicit rhetorical "therefore" of these findings is, "and if your [autistic/disabled/abnormal] child participates in an identical intervention protocol, he or she has nearly a 1 in 2 chance of being *normal* again. [italics in original] [46]

One of the earlier instances of this powerful rhetoric of recovery aligned with behavior analytic interventions is found in *Let Me Hear Your Voice* by Catherine Maurice (a pseudonym), one of the earliest examples and most widely read personal accounts of a family (namely, a mother) dealing with autism and the promise of behavior analytic intervention. This account brandished the two most important perceptual elements of legitimacy of an intervention: a personal endorsement from a parent who "understands" further legitimized by a (supposed) extensive body of supporting scientific literature. Maurice, herself, constructed a view of ABA as based in "reason" and "science" as opposed to "emotion" and "faith," allowing her to make more prudent clinical decisions despite her highly emotional parental perspective. This is to proffer the idea that emotional input into clinical decision making is not only distracting, but destructive: a message that behavior analysis has long embodied. This clinical superiority serves an imperative function, as it allows the field to maintain its position of authority without losing the client's perception of "care." That is, clear-minded, objective, and clinical practitioners who can "help" desperate parents make reasonable decisions that are unfettered by their fragile emotional states. By constructing this mutually exclusive binary option: (a) hopelessness without intervention or, worse, false hope with "pseudoscientific" or "antiscientific" intervention; or (b) recovery (or at least progress toward normality) with behavior analytic intervention, the field creates a platform for the parent to feel as if they are being negligent, if not abusive if they do not err on the "logical" side of choosing a "proven" scientific intervention as opposed to an "unproven" fad.[47] Danforth's observation about the modern culturally positivistic perspective is of particular appropriateness in this situation:

> From this [modernist] perspective, hope lies in the gradual, scientific production of improved approximations of "truth" and the development of intervention technologies, practices, programs, and instruments "that work" according to the truth-clarifying research. . . . Postmodernists find the historical myth of scientific progress to be a socially constructed story of uncertain truth value . . . postmodern scholars critique the sociopolitical effects of that narrative.[48]

Indeed, there is a body of research that suggests the connotation of "normality" achieved through early intensive behavioral intervention was a strong theme and contributor to dissatisfaction amongst parents of children with ASD.[49]

But if one intervention is to provide for hope, there must be a reason to think that the opposite will be of dire consequences. This is achieved by the over-reliance of the behavioral perspective on deficit-based diagnostic criteria, such as that of the Diagnostic and Statistical Manual (at least through DSM-IV-TR), highlighting what the individual cannot, will not, and will likely never do without effective intervention. The choice then is either "proven" intervention or a catastrophic life of tragedy and misfortune. As Broderick suggests:

> In the context of the ongoing reproduction of ABA discourse of the first element of this conceptual dichotomy—the representation of autism as inherently tragic, catastrophic, and hopeless—the concept of hope for recovery stands in stark contrast to this dominant picture of hopelessness and despair and is presented as the only hopeful vision available, or at least, as the only

real hope [italics added]. Recovery thus becomes almost synonymous with hope itself—in the apparent absence of other visions of hope, hope for recovery may be welcomed by those who insist on embracing hopeful visions of futures for young children labeled with autism in spite of the dire prognoses traditionally offered. [50]

For an approach that is overtly dismissive of emotions in intervention, the emotional state of the family clearly plays a pivotal role in its rhetoric for acceptance, if not dominance.

Also implicit in the position of behavior analytic interventions is the hyper-importance of outcome as opposed to process. With outcome as the single focus, the role of operationalization becomes not only easier to apply, but necessary in demonstration of the claims. When parents can "see" their children approaching "normal" they also believe they can "see" the effectiveness of the intervention. The ability of behavior analysis to purportedly quantify many of its outcomes and superimpose such progress on the powerful visual representation of graphs also helps the function and effectiveness of the rhetoric quite a bit. However, just because one pays no attention (nor measurement) to a simultaneously occurring process does not mean that such processes are not occurring, nor does it mean such processes are not affecting the individual. Perhaps, though the process of behavior analytic interventions yields observable outcomes that resemble behavior that is more closely approximated to "normal," therefore resulting in the children's increased opportunity for inclusion (at least by the largely practiced ableist perspective), the message of the process may also be a relentless mantra of "you are not normal enough" or "you are not good enough as you are" or "you will only be better once you are normal." It would not be fair to assume that this is not true simply because the individuals cannot, or do not, indicate this themselves. This message is related by Kephart:

> What, in the end, are you fighting for: Normal? Is normal possible? Can it be defined? Is it best achieved by holding up in the offices of therapists, in special classrooms, in isolated exercises, in simulating living, while everyday "normal" happens casually on the other side of the wall? And is normal superior to what the child inherently is, to what he aspires to, fights to become, every second of his day? Normal in terms of what, and by what sacrifice? [51]

The preoccupation with normality, then, simply appeases the socially unjust mechanisms of ableist school cultures. Ableism can be defined as:

> The devaluation of disability [that] results in societal attitudes that uncritically assert that it is better for a child to walk than roll, speak than sign, read print than read Braille, spell independently than use a spell-check, and hang out with nondisabled kids as opposed to other disabled kids, etc. In short, in the

eyes of many educators and society, it is preferable for disabled students to do things in the same manner as nondisabled kids. [52]

Another more politically based definition of ableism is conjectured by Rauscher and McClintock as:

> A pervasive system of discrimination and exclusion that oppresses people who have mental, emotional, and physical disabilities. . . . Deeply rooted beliefs about health, productivity, beauty, and the value of human life, perpetuated by the public and private media, combine to create an environment that is often hostile to those whose physical, mental, cognitive, and sensory abilities . . . fall out of the scope of what is currently defined as socially acceptable. [53]

The consequences of abelism can be seen pervasively throughout the topography of the typical public school. The most common way that ableism is demonstrated in schools is through the notion that exceptionality is, by nature, based in organic deficits that are to be remediated. Once sufficiently remediated with the resulting behavior of the child deemed "socially acceptable" or "academically capable," then and only then can these individuals begin to become more "integrated" into the mainstream school culture. While it is in no way contended that behavior analysts themselves are acting deliberately to fulfill and propagate an "ableist" culture with intentionally "ableistic goals" in mind, it is necessary to emphasize that the very behavior analytic practices as applied to individuals with Autism Spectrum Disorder are based upon ableistic principles, and therefore lead to outcomes that maintain ableistic outcomes. Behavior analytic approaches hinge on this very notion of social improvement to the end of normality, and maintain the notion of inclusivity as being a privilege that is to be earned through assimilation rather than a right that is to be unconditionally provided.

Behavior Analysis Sacrifices a Holistic and Humanistic Approach to Education

While debates over the best, most humanistic, or most effective means of educating any type of students will (and should) ever remain a fervent one, there has been a clear message in the field of special education from its very inception, if not even earlier before its formal establishment: all individuals are individuals, and should be treated as such. This notion is virtually axiomatic, though it is entirely compromised with even a slight notion that a single-mode approach, even one that can possess some systematic variation, could be considered as best or most effective. By reducing the phenomenology of ASD to that of a behavioral disorder, and the remediation to this fundamental condition of ASD as behavioral intervention, behavior analytic approaches neglect the idea, now widely demonstrated by research, that ASD

is a multi-faceted and complexly structured condition which cannot be exclusively characterized in terms of deficiencies. By denying or even ignoring
this complexity as well as the general complexity of the human experience as
a whole, the field of behavior analysis transcends from simply engaging in
minimization to a potentially unethical practice of denying the reality of the
human condition in a variety of forms: emotional, experiential, sensorial, and
behavioral, among others.

Since language and its use is the key to social constructions as well as
legislation and public policy, the language used by the field of behavior
analysis has played a pivotal role in propagating what is, essentially, a mini-
malist perspective to that of a positivistic scientific perspective. By maintaining that ASD is a disorder (as opposed to a social construct or even human
condition) that needs to be remediated (as opposed to adapted to and/or
accepted), the field of behavior analysis also maintains its similar philosophy
to the medical rehabilitative model, the dominant cultural model not only in
Western medicine, but in Western educational settings as well. Proffering
explanations for ASD in the dominant language of "causation" and material-
ism and offering treatment in terms of observable outcomes is far more
compatible with the current focus of both educational legislation and policymaking, despite its true legitimacy in addressing the experience of the human
being. As Rogers explains:

> A critical discourse analyst's goal is to study the relationships between lan-
> guage form and function and explain why and how certain patterns are privi-
> leged over others. In the sense that all systems of meaning are linked to
> socially defined practices that carry more or less privilege and value in society,
> such exploration is also an exploration into power and language. [54]

In this sense, behavior analysis is most likely to gain social and cultural
privilege as it resonates with the existing dominant notions of the medical-
rehabilitative perspective. Therefore, the alignment between both medicine
and science allows the field of behavior analysis to maintain its "scientific
basis" by association without drawing much attention to the challenges, if not
overt threats to its validity that are endemic to behavior analytic research
designs.

Resultantly, the role that pragmatism, or functionality plays in the social
understanding of ASD and its associated "treatments" connects to the dominant discourse of achievement and normality far more than the constructive
platform addressed by humanistic educational approaches. This basic notion
of "function" soon comes to play a vital role in the identity formation, at least
the way practitioners in the field often construct them, of individuals with
ASD. Functionality, in its most common dichotomy of "low" versus "high"
serves as a handy device for categorizing individuals and making predictions

about their responses to behavior analysis. Since "functioning" is presented as a ubiquitous term despite its complete lack of context or operational definition, it allows the field of behavior analysis to "package" what individuals can currently *do*, and what they will likely be able to *do* with enhanced behavior analytic treatment. Of course, the general notion is that "low" functioning individuals will likely achieve normality far less, or at least with the necessity of far "more" treatment, while "high" functioning individuals may well reach "normality" requiring less intervention. In any case, the notion of functioning appears to be very easy to demonstrate, or to at least appear to be demonstrable, with behavior analytic principles. That is, an individual cannot "do" something before treatment, and they can "do" it after treatment. It can be observed, it can be measured, and it can be graphed, so therefore it can be verified. This is another clever rhetorical tool employed by the field of behavior analysis despite its clear violation of being operational. As Nadesan describes:

> Autism . . . is a disorder of the early twentieth century while the high-functioning variants of autism such as Semantic Pragmatic Disorder (SPD), Pervasive Developmental Disorder [Not Otherwise Specified] (PDD-NOS), and Asperger Syndrome (AS) are fundamentally disorders of the late twentieth and early twenty-first centuries. . . . And so the history of autism in all its forms must be contextualized with the evolution and transformation of medical practices, the development of professions such as psychiatry, psychology, social work, and special education. . . . The history of "high functioning" forms of autism must be further understood in the context of new standards of parenting that emerged mid-twentieth century and new economic and social conditions surrounding the purported "information revolution" that began in the 1960s.[55]

Therefore, the only true need to reduce a condition to a set of rules and conditions, as the DSM and the BACB *Guidance* documents clearly do, is to legitimize a particular treatment approach that appears to be in line with the current understanding, or at least diagnostic framework, of that disorder. The approaches that are most successful may not truly be any more effective than others that are disregarded, but rather better represent the zeitgeist of a particular culture and the goals of a particular society. In the case of behavior analysis, remediation and progress toward normality is a popular end point toward which many parents would strive for their children. As Osteen suggests, "[most medical explanations of autism] have sought to erect a monolithic concept of autism in order to promote a particular therapy and buttress a clinician's authority."[56]

It is thus that the rhetoric of behavior analysis serves to maintain separatist notions and indicate the necessity of segregated environments unless integrated environments are earned through achievement of and assimilation to normality. Despite the presence of literature on how behavior analytic interventions increase opportunities for inclusive education (though framed in the same single-subject context explored previously), the condition of inclusion is still contingent on achieving "socially appropriate" status. That is, when the individual is normal enough, he or she can be included. This is a clearly positivistic, if not hegemonic, view of how and why inclusion should happen. As Fitch explains:

> This practice, grounded in scientific positivist assumptions and the biomedical model of disability, continues to legitimate segregation and inequality and justify a dual system of special education and general education. Demonstrating the socially constructed nature of difference/deviance, labeling deviance theory has played a crucial role in challenging this orientation, serving as one of the key conceptual foundations for the disability and inclusive movements.[57]

Ultimately, the behavior analytic perspective employs the positivistic view that facts precede theories, and by delineating the facts, which are universal, the theory, also universal, will thus be yielded, which will, in turn, lead to the antidote (in this case, behavior analytic treatment that is in line with the positivistic medicalized view of ASD). As Hallihan and Kauffman suggest:

> The real issues are the meanings we attach to disabilities, not the fact that we label them. Labels, in and of themselves, are not evil. How they are interpreted by others and by the labeled person determine whether they are harmful or ameliorative.[58]

Therefore, by insisting on a reductive and positivistic view of ASD as a disorder rather than employing a holistic and comprehensive interpretation of the individual both within and beyond ASD as a part of an identity, the individual is maintained as an abnormal being unprivileged to gain access to inclusive environments until he or she can be taught to engage in a more socially appropriate manner, thus earning them the right to do so. This view is to embrace entirely not only the dichotomous distinction between normal and abnormal, but to propagate the legitimacy of ableist practices in schools that should be designed to instill a sense of value in all of its members.

NOTES

1. Wayne Sailor and Matthew Stowe, "The Relationship of Inquiry to Public Policy." *Research & Practice for Persons with Severe Disabilities* 2003, 28(3), 149.

2. Barry Prizant, "Is ABA the Only Way?" Spring 2009 *Autism Spectrum Quarterly*.

3. E. Carr, D. Granpeesheh, and L Grossman. "The Future of Applied Behavior Analysis in Autism Spectrum Disorders." *Autism Advocate*, 2008, 4, 50–58.

4. Prizant, 2009.

5. Frank M. Gresham et al. (1993). "Treatment Integrity in Applied Behavior Analysis with Children." *Journal of Applied Behavior Analysis*, 26(2), 257.

6. Frank Gresham. "Evolution of the Treatment Integrity Concept: Current Status and Future Directions." *School Psychology Review*, 2009, 38(4), 533–40.

7. D.F. Brassert, R.I. Parker, E.A. Olson, and L. Mahadevan (2006). "The Relationship Between Visual Analysis and Five Statistical Analyses in a Simple AB Single-case Design." *Behavior Modification*, 30(5), 531–63.

8. Veronica Ximenes et al. (2009). "Factors Affecting Visual Inference in Single-Case Designs." *Spanish Journal of Psychology*, 12(2) 823–32.

9. Ibid.

10. Anthony Deprospero and Stanley Cohen (1979). "Inconsistent Visual Analyses of Intra-subject Data." *Journal of Applied Behavior Analysis*, 12(5), 573–79.

11. Michele Speckley and Roslyn Boyd (2009). "Efficacy of Applied Behavioral Intervention in Preschool Children with Autism for Improving Cognitive, Language, and Adaptive Behavior: A Systematic Review and Meta-analysis." Journal of Pediatrics, 338–44.

12. Brian Reichow (2011). "Overview of Meta-Analyses on Early Intensive Behavioral Intervention for Young Children with Autism Spectrum Disorders." *Journal of Autism and Developmental Disorders*.

13. Jane S. Howard et al. (2005). "A Comparison of Intensive Behavior Analytic and Eclectic Treatments for Young Children with Autism." *Research in Developmental Disabilities*, 26, 359–86.

14. Ted Schoenberger. "Autism Research Controversy: A Response to Howard et al.'s (2005) Defenders." *Journal of Speech Language Pathology and Applied Behavior Analysis*, 2(2).

15. Philip M. Podaskoff et al. "Common Method Biases in Behavioral Research: A Critical Review of the Literature." *Journal of Applied Psychology* 2003, 88, 5, 879–903.

16. James D. Herbert et al. (2002). "Separating Fact from Fiction in the Etiology and Treatment of Autism: A Scientific Review of the Evidence." *Scientific Review of Mental Health Practice*, 1(1).

17. Schreibman, 2007, as cited by Prizant, 2009.

18. Wyatt and Midkiff (n.d.), as cited by Wakefield, 2006. "Is Behaviorism Becoming a Pseudo-science?: Power Versus Scientific Rationality in the Eclipse of Token Economies by Biological Psychiatry in the Treatment of Schizophrenia." *Behavior and Social Issues*, 15, 202–21.

19. Ibid., 207.

20. Jerome C. Wakefield. "Is Behaviorism Becoming a Pseudoscience? Replies to Drs. Wyatt, Midkiff, and Wong." *Behavior and Social Issues*, 2007, 175.

21. Trevor F. Stokes and Donald M. Baer. "An Implicit Technology of Generalization." *Journal of Applied Behavior Analysis*, 1977, 10, 350.

22. Donald M. Baer, Montrose M. Wolf, and Todd R. Risley. "Some Current Dimensions of Applied Behavior Analysis." *Journal of Applied Behavior Analysis*, 1968, 1(1), 91–97.

23. Steven C. Hayes, Arnold Rincover, and Jay V. Solnick. "The Technical Drift of Applied Behavior Analysis." *Journal of Applied Behavior Analysis*, 1980: 13, 275–85.

24. Ibid., 283.

25. Ibid., 282.

26. Susan Haack. *Defending Science—Within Reason: Between Scientism and Cynicism*, Amherst, NY: Prometheus Books, 2003.

27. Heinz K. Klein and Kalle Lyytinen. "The Poverty of Scientism in Information Systems," from http://ifipwg82.org/sites/ifipwg82.org/files/Klein_0.pdf.

28. Ibid.

29. Ibid.

30. Jay Moore. "On Mentalism, Methodological Behaviorism, and Radical Behaviorism." *Behaviorism*, 9 (1 Spring 1981), 55–77.

31. Skinner, 1945, as cited by Moore, 59.

32. Behavior Analyst Certification Board Task List for Board Certified Behavior Analysts Working With Persons with Autism. From http://www.bacb.com/Downloadfiles/AutismTaskList/708AutismTaskListF.pdf.

33. Wakefield, 2006, 219.

34. Richard M. Ryan and Edward L. Deci (2000). "Intrinsic and Extrinsic Motivations: Classic Definitions and New Directions." *Contemporary Educational Psychology*, 25, 54–67.

35. Ibid.

36. Ibid., 60.

37. Ibid., 56.

38. Ryan and Deci, 2000.

39. Ibid.

40. Edward Deci et al. (1999). "A Meta-Analytic Review of Experiments Examining the Effects of Intrinsic Motivation." *Psychological Bulletin*, 125(6), 627–68.

41. See, Lovaas 1987; Jacobson et al. 2009; Maurice, 1993; Cohen, 1998; Jacobsen, Mulick, and Green 1998; Kotler, 1994; Mulick, 1999.

42. Gina, Green. 1996, 38.

43. Laura Schreibman, 2000, 374.

44. Jacobson, Mulick, and Green, 1998, 204.

45. Glen O. Sallows, T. D. Graupner, and W. E. Maclean. "Intensive Behavioral Treatment for Children with Autism: Four Year Outcomes and Predictors."*American Journal on Mental Retardation*, 2005, 110(6), 417–38.

46. Alicia Broderick. "Autism as Rhetoric: Exploring Watershed Rhetorical Moments in Applied Behavior Analysis Discourse," http://dsq-sds.org/article/view/1674/1597.

47. Ibid.

48. Danforth, 1997, as cited by Broderick, 2009. "Autism, Recovery (to Normalcy), and the Politics of Hope," *Intellectual and Developmental Disabilities*, 47, 4, 263–81.

49. Corinna F. Grindle, H. Kovshoff, R. P. Hastings, and B. Remington. "Parents' Experience of Home-Based Applied Behavior Analysis Programs for Young Children with Autism." *Journal of Autism and Developmental Disorders*, 2009, 39, 42–56.

50. Broderick, 2009, 271.

51. Kephart, 1998, as cited by Broderick, 2009, 276.

52. Thomas Hehir. "Eliminating Ableism in Education," 1–32.

53. Pat Griffin, Madeline L. Peters, and Robin M. Smith. "Ableism and the Curriculum Design," 198–231.

54. Rogers, 2004, as cited by Broderick 2009, 264.

55. Majia Nadesan. *Constructing Autism: Unraveling the Truth and Understanding the Social*. New York: Routledge, 2005, 3.

56. Mark Osteen, as cited by Stuart Murray. "Autism Functions/The Function of Autism." *Disability Studies Quarterly*, 30, 1 (2010), http:///dsq-sds.org/article/view/1048/1229.

57. Frank Fitch. "Laggards, Labeling and Limitations: Reconnecting Labeling Deviance Theory with Deweyan Pragmatism." 2010 Ohio Valley Philosophy of Education Society, http://www.ovpes.org/Fitch.pdf.

58. Hallihan and Kauffman, 1989, as cited by Fitch, 2010.

Chapter Seven

The Polemic for a Comprehensive Approach for Autism Spectrum Disorders

Since there are vast and concerning limitations of viewing programs from a single paradigmatic and methodological perspective, it is incumbent upon the field of educating individuals with Autism Spectrum Disorder to determine how to design a truly comprehensive program that still meets the mandates of evidence basis as well as sound theoretical and philosophical underpinnings. A quote from a well-known behavioral researcher exemplifies the folly in unilateral behavior analytic teaching:

> The biggest problem . . . is that most people think of teaching as an art—but when teaching is an art, then great teaching ends up being accidental. [Behaviorists] think of teaching as a science, and the challenge, in our view, is to educate people that science really works. [1]

This quote suggests a number of erroneous assertions, but of most importance to this treatise, it suggests that any successful teaching outside of "scientific teaching" (of which behavior analysts regard behavior analytic teaching) could only be purely accidental, as art, ostensibly, is haphazardly created while science is constructed intentionally. Implicit in this characterization is that the success comes from the *method*, not the *teacher*, suggesting that anyone can learn to be an effective teacher so long as the science behind the teaching methodology is understood and applied effectively. This is to say that science simplifies, and therefore supersedes, the act (and art) of teaching.

This chapter will focus on proffering a justifiable and evidence-based framework for a comprehensive educational program for individuals with Autism Spectrum Disorder, and provide a deep means of legitimization for the preference of applying such a program in place of a unilateral (specifically, only behavior analytic) approach to educating individuals with ASD. As the treatise has already established, but, as noted is ever worth recapitulation, applied behavior analytic approaches are in no way being disparaged, devalued, or suggested to be eliminated. Quite the contrary, behavior analytic approaches are imperative, if not foundational components of a comprehensive educational program. However, adequate focus on other, equally relevant aspects of individuals with ASD including emotional regulation, relationship development, joint attention, and sensory integration and, resultantly, approaches centered on these components, are also included with equal relevance, importance, and value.

CONSTRUCTING THE PHILOSOPHICAL RATIONALE FOR A COMPREHENSIVE EDUCATIONAL APPROACH

While the purpose of education in general is a concept that extends beyond the scope of this treatise, an exploration of particular philosophical approaches to education is important to determine, at least at a foundational level. Skrtic proposes that there are three general structures in which education can be framed: functionalism, radical structuralism, and radical humanism.[2] It will be suggested that behavior analytic teaching encompasses an entirely functionalist paradigm, ipso facto possessing all of the inherent weaknesses of the paradigm, while a well-designed comprehensive educational program for individuals with ASD represents a radical humanist paradigm, grounded deeply in social justice, inclusiveness, knowledge construction, and individual value.

According to Skrtic, most Western (and in particular, American) schooling, either in the area of special or general education, falls under the category of functionalism. Functional education is characterized as an interpretation of social reality that grounds the knowledge of social science, and claims that reality is objective, inherently orderly, and rational, which leads to the notion that social problems are pathological, warranting containment rather than being directly addressed.[3] In the way that a functionalist approach applies to individuals with exceptionalities, specifically ASD and behavior analytic intervention, the approach grounds itself, quite intentionally and to its own self-declared advantage, deeply in psychology and biology emphasizing accurate diagnosis and prescriptive (or described as behaviorists, "scientific") teaching. From this perspective, progress (or recovery, as some studies designate) is designated in terms of increasing skill acquisition as demonstrated by quantitative performance assessments. Functionalist education is based on four assumptions:[4]

1. Student disability is a pathological condition.
2. Differential diagnosis is objective and useful.
3. Special education is a rationally conceived and coordinated system of services that benefits the diagnosed student.
4. Progress in special education is a rational-technical process of incremental improvements in conventional diagnostic and instructional practices.

Tomlinson describes the functionalist paradigm in this way:

> The way in which children are categorized out of . . . mainstream education and into special education is generally regarded as enlightened and advanced, and an instance of the obligation placed upon civilized society to care for its weaker members.[5]

This characterization fits precisely within the context of the rhetoric of behavior analysis, using the dichotomy of hope versus hopelessness and a progress toward "normality" as the best opportunity for children with ASD, along with being the only truly "evidenced-based" (from a squarely functionalist and positivistic perspective) approach. The persistent pathologizing of the individual with ASD is ever-present in both behavior analytic descriptions as well as intervention protocols, insisting only that maladaptive behaviors are replaced by adaptive ones, yielding a rehabilitative process toward normality. This approach not only accepts, but validates the segregated and achievement-based precept of American school culture, and obliges the individuals to abide by its exclusionary rules.

The second framework, according to Skrtic, is radical structuralism, which takes a macroscopic, objective, and realistic perspective of the social world, accepting the assumption that there is, indeed, a real social world in which conflict, domination, and coercion exists and predominates, yielding discrimination and, in some extreme cases, oppression. As such, the structure and design of society both implements and maintains such practices, engraining them into general society and, specifically, its schooling practices. In the context of education, radical structuralism looks at students in terms of their individual economic value, with the most valuable being given most inclusive and privileged access, and the least valuable being kept most exclusive and segregated.[6] While there are elements of behavior analytic approaches that can be just as equally deemed as radical structuralist, perhaps the most obvious is the implication that progressing toward "normality" yields accruing more "value" and, therefore being more readily (if not permissibly) included in "regular classrooms," or in some cases even self-contained class-rooms in "regular schools."

The third approach, radical humanism, is based on three fundamental tenets:[7]

1. The development of human consciousness and self-consciousness is a paramount achievement, providing the opportunity to engage in ethical reflection leading to ethical action, which is a product of awareness.
2. There is a call for a need to increase, if not maximize, human freedom in order to exercise ethical abilities.
3. Dominant ideologies restrict human development, creating a gap between the appearance of a cultural situation and its reality.

From the radical humanist perspective, many socially based institutions, including schools and other educational and clinical entities, are seen as the most pressing threats to individual freedom and a likely source of maintaining oppressive practices. The behavior analytic perspective contributes to this characterization as a "behavior replacement" technology. That is, often the behaviors that make individuals "autistic" are the behaviors that are most readily and rapidly sought to be replaced regardless of how disruptive these behaviors truly are on individual quality of life. Rather, behaviors that receive the most attention are those that appear to be threatening to the perception of the individual as "normal." The radical humanist approach, then, poses three main questions to education, specifically, of individuals with exceptionalities:[8]

1. What are the consequences for education in relying primarily, if not exclusively, on the functionalist paradigm for the diagnosis and education of children with exceptionalities?
2. How does education in its current state form and shape the idea of exceptionality in the context of education?
3. How does society form and shape the idea of exceptionality in the context of education?

Approaching the education of individuals with ASD from a comprehensive perspective can ensure their human liberties, their right to experience and express their feelings, and their right to be who they are in the inclusive context. Rather than limiting the individual from a reductive perspective of what they "should be," a comprehensive approach will allow for the individual to retain "who they are" while still allowing them to improve in areas that will make environments more readily accessible for successful interaction (though not, under any circumstances, denied) and individual contributive-ness. By focusing equally on skill acquisition as well as emotional regulation, relationship building, and sensory integration processing, individuals are regarded as whole beings rather than compartmentalized clusters of socially and academically deleterious symptoms. This comprehensive focus will allow the teacher (and other relevant parties) to target the underlying aspects of what manifests itself as "Autism Spectrum Disorder" from a less corrective and more nurturing, accepting, and socially just manner than behavior analytic approaches alone. As such, measuring success by quantitative analyses of observable skill acquisition alone is vastly inadequate and reductive. Modes of assessing progress must, by all means, be considered from a holistic and comprehensive perspective.

There is significant methodological and humanistic danger in approaching education for individuals with ASD from a single-mode perspective. With the foundational tenet of special education being the acknowledgment and addressing of the specific needs of the individual, claiming the potential effectiveness of a single mode approach, much less the superiority of one, is not only inaccurate and antithetical to the very basis of special education philosophy and theory, but morally and ethically precarious. This is of particular concern in the context of teacher and clinician education and training programs, which are apt to be one of the main sources of the propagation of the supremacy of behavior analytic approaches. As Scheuermann and colleagues suggest:

> First, training teachers in only one approach to the treatment of children with ASD sends the false message that only one approach will work with all children with the disorder. Individuals with ASD are a heterogenous group, with such a wide variation in severity and types of symptoms that it is virtually impossible to conclude that one method will work with each and every individual with the disorder. Subsequently, training teachers in only one method not only limits their ability to be successful with all children with ASD but also falsely implies that the one approach in which they are trained will work with all children. This false belief that one has been trained in the one and only approach necessary to treat all children with ASD limits teachers' recognition of the individuality of each child with ASD. Teachers should base their teaching methods on what will best meet the needs of each individual child, not on whichever method of instruction they were trained to use.[9]

As clearly explicated, approaching teacher and clinician training from potentially irresponsible and unfounded claims does not only violate the philosophy of special education, but actually detracts from the ultimate quality of teachers and clinicians available in the field to provide the best possible educational services for individuals with ASD. As Scheurmann and colleagues elaborate:

In order to choose the best method of instruction for each child, one must have been trained in more than one approach. Teachers who have limited training may continue with a program because it is the only one they know, despite that fact that the child or children with whom they are working are not benefiting from the methods. This is a detriment not only to the teacher but, most important, to the children whose needs are not being met. In order to meet each child's needs, teachers need a number of approaches from which to choose and the training and confidence in each to be successful. [10]

ESTABLISHING COMPONENTS OF A COMPREHENSIVE EDUCATIONAL PROGRAM IN ASD

Since the argument that there is not only a methodological but also a humanistic need to address individuals with ASD from a comprehensive approach, this section will focus on establishing and defining the main components of a comprehensive approach to teaching individuals with ASD. These methodologies include in the current state (but can and should change as evidence and research findings indicate) those based in relationship development, emotional regulation, behavior modification, and sensory integrative approaches.

The working definition of *comprehensive educational approach* needs significant care and attention before any such argument can take place. While there is no singly accepted definition for the term in the field, there are some indications as to what such an approach should encompass. According to Rogers, comprehensive educational programs use methodology that "seeks to change the nature of the outcome in autism and improve the overall functioning of persons." [11] In a later article Rogers and Vismara revised the definition of comprehensive approach as, "treatments that addressed the core deficits in autism, including language, social, cognition, and play." [12] While it appears the behavioral aspect was neglected in this definition, the concept clearly indicates that comprehensive approach targets a wider array of components then single-mode approaches, such as behavior analytic interventions, that seek to target one main component, despite fitting many others into a liberal definition of that particular component (e.g., the claim that "behavior" encompasses all observable and measurable conditions including overt behavior, language and communication, and academic skills). As further stated, "[a]lthough developmental and behavioral approaches are often discussed as mutually exclusive, in reality they are often blended. . . . Good teaching practices and procedures share many common elements between developmentalists and behaviorists." [13]

Because this dichotomy between "behavioral" and "developmental" or, in many cases, "behavioral approaches" and "non-behavioral approaches" as characterized by the BACB is largely imaginary, there is already a practical tendency in the field of educating individuals with ASD to embrace a comprehensive approach, evidenced by the receipt of many services including speech and language therapy, occupational and physical therapy, and other types of ancillary services in addition to, or in tandem with, behavior analytic interventions. Therefore, the arguments between the behavioral field and the rest of the educational field appear to be largely rhetorical, reflecting little actual bearing on practice. As Simpson states:

> Using a variety of methodologies to identify effective practices for students with ASD appears to be the most sensible and pragmatic path for the ASD field to follow . . . the onus for making responsible methodology decisions falls with teams of professionals and parents. Professionals and parents require access to straightforward information about the efficacy of various methods, as well as supplementary information that will assist them in determining a method's suitability with individual students. Moreover, it is essential that the professionals and parents who are making decisions about which methods to use demonstrate a willingness to use this information in a collegial and collaborative fashion.[14]

As such, a careful balance must be struck between stringency of cautious application of methodologies and monitoring of results of yet untested, under-tested, or not directly outcome evidenced approaches and exclusionary practices of possibly, if not probably, legitimate and valuable methods, such as behavior analytic interventions. Therefore, the following definition is proposed to encompass the working conception of comprehensive educational programs in this treatise. Comprehensive treatment programs:

1. Reflect *both* theoretical and outcome-based evidence for legitimizing the application of such methodologies for individuals with ASD.
2. Does not exclude or include methodologies based solely on anecdotal or philosophical considerations, so long as those considerations do not violate standards of ethical treatment of human beings or entail is proportionate physical or emotional risk.
3. Apply research findings and theoretical applications from peer-reviewed journals in multidisciplinary and interdisciplinary domains including, but not limited to education, psychology, sociology, philosophy, linguistics, and computer information systems.
4. Create educational approaches from a "person-first" perspective, yielding totally individualized programs based primarily on outplay of the individual within his or her environment behaviorally, emotionally, socially, linguistically, communicatively, and sensorially.
5. Are reformed, revised, and adapted at the necessary frequency in order to reflect developments in all related research areas.

Some major points compel emphasis when earnestly considering a comprehensive educational program. First and foremost, a comprehensive educational program is not a platform for methodologies offering quixotic outcomes in the area of cure, recovery, or any other clearly unreasonable domain. The methodologies included in a comprehensive program must only be those approaches that have legitimate theoretical and evidentiary (either established or developing) grounding. As suggested by Prizant, comprehensive strategies are not to be represented by a "patchwork quilt" structure in which portions of different interventions are selectively (and often haphazardly) applied in the name of providing comprehensive interventions.[15] Second, a comprehensive educational program will not regard ASD as the individual's defining characteristic, but rather a component (for some a major one, for others a minor one) of one's identity, along with other related or unrelated emotional, physical, sensory, behavioral, academic, and/or social characteristics. Finally, comprehensive educational programs should, by all means, possess a mechanism for evaluation, assessment, and vetting, though one that is not entirely dependent on outcomes or positivistic means, but also accounts for processes and components that are less easily operationalized. From this perspective, evidence-basis will not be regarded as a dichotomous category of either "effective" or "ineffective," but rather incorporate a spectrum of evidentiary systems and statuses to enable deep and comprehensive analysis, discussion, and decision-making. Based on the growing body of evidence and research findings the program itself will be revised, reformed, and further developed consistently to ensure compatibility with current understandings in all related areas.

FOCUSING ON THE DEVELOPMENT OF MEANINGFUL RELATIONSHIPS

While it has been clearly established that the field of behavior analysis places a clear preference on addressing the behavioral difficulties of individuals with ASD, and widens the expanse of such coverage by denoting everything that can be observed and measured as a behavior, there are multiple theoretical frameworks and respective approaches that focus on other aspects of ASD as central to providing adequate and effective therapeutic intervention. One such area is that of the quality of the relationship between the individual with ASD and others.

Play, which is a multi-factorial activity that is typically regarded as naturally occurring but challenging for individuals with ASD, is an important foundation for such relationship-based approaches. Play, in and of itself, is not only an indication of developmental progress, but an activity that directly affects the development of linguistic, socio-emotional, physical, communicative, and metacognitive skills, among other aspects of higher order thinking and social engagement. For individuals with challenges in any of these areas, engagement and development in play overall, as well as related skills will be inhibited, therefore complicating and denigrating the developmental process.

The focus of play, then, and all of its respective component phenomena, can be regarded, at least in its basic senses, as being initially facilitated by creating and maintaining meaningful and emotionally connected relationships with others. Therefore, interventions focusing on these aspects may be instrumental in addressing many of the core needs of individuals with ASD. This view was pioneered and propagated significantly by Stanley Greenspan and Serena Wieder. Steeped firmly in the tradition of neurological foundations for socio-emotional development and the emotional basis of behavior, Greenspan and Weider suggest that children with ASD, and children who are at risk for developing ASD as babies, appear to lack even the most basic foundations for initiating and developing interpersonal experiences. This is particularly problematic in terms of adequate social, emotional, and behavioral development because, "the child's interactions in relationships and family patterns are the primary vehicle for mobilizing development and growth."[16] Such growth is facilitated by the existence of what Greenspan and Wieder term *Functional Developmental Capacities.*[17] The *Functional Emotional Developmental Level* examines how children integrate the full range of their capacities, including motor, cognitive, linguistic, spatial, and sensory skills in order to carry out emotionally meaningful activities. Among these capacities, children may attend to multisensory affective experience while being able to simultaneously maintain a calm and regulated emotional state (e.g., maintaining visual contact with another individual in a stimulating environment such as a playground), engage with and evidence affective preference and pleasure for a caregiver (e.g., directing smiles or initiating playful interactions), and initiating and responding to two-way presymbolic gestural communication (e.g., sending and returning smiles, pointing, or looking in response and initiation to others). The *Individual Differences in Sensory, Modulation, Processing, and Motor Planning* concept suggests the existence of biologically based individual differences resulting from genetic, prenatal, and maturational variations and/or deficits that can be characterized in four distinct ways: (a) sensory modulation, including hypo-and hyperactivity in each sensory modality including touch, sound, smell, vision, and movement in space; (b) sensory processing in each sensory modality, including auditory processing and language and visuo-spatial processing; (c) sensory-affective processing in each modality (e.g., the ability to process and react to affect, including intentionality to connect through motor planning, sequencing, and use of language and symbols); and (d) motor planning and sequencing, including the ability to sequence actions, behaviors, and symbols in the form of thoughts, words, visual images, and spatial concepts. *Relationships and*

Interactions include developmentally appropriate (or inappropriate) interactive relationships with caregivers, parents, and engagement in family patterns with the ability to negotiate and broaden the range of intentionality and use of affect and emotion for socially relevant purposes.

Based on this comprehensive theory of social-emotional development under typical circumstances, and factoring in potential individual differences based on genetic, neurological, and environmental influences, Weider and Greenspan developed their theoretical framework, known as the Affect Diathesis Hypothesis (ADH); a foundation for understanding the difficulty of social and emotional interactions for children with ASD. Resultantly, they created a corresponding methodology for intervention called the Developmental, Individual-Difference, Relationship Based Model (DIR), with its primary practice known as Floor Time.

The ADH is primarily a psychological framework that is based on (then) current knowledge of brain functioning and neurological development, and can also serve to provide important clues for potential biological, neurological, and even physiological interventions for individuals with ASD. Essentially, the ADH suggests that children with ASD are likely to have a unique type of biologically and neurologically based processing difference which involves the connection between affect and emotion, which is directly related to intentionality, motor planning, and sequencing capacities as well as symbol and symbolic play formation. This difference becomes most evident during the second year of life when, under typical developmental circumstances, individuals begin to display intentional social problem-solving behavior and meaningful language-based interaction, all of which are directly connected to affect and emotional regulation. In children with ASD, this condition often remains unobserved, which may lead to the use of repetitive, solitary, and socially and emotionally dysfunctional behavior.[18] This theoretical framework was, even at the time of its creation, consistent with the current understandings of neural networks in neurological developmental research. In recent years, however, with the increased capacity of brain imaging and the current focus on differences in both brain structure and functionality in individuals with ASD, this hypothesis has gained ever more legitimacy. Since the major difference appears to be in the connection between affect and planning in the area of social and emotional regulation and interpersonal connection, interventions for individuals with ASD should include intent focus on:

> higher level cognitive, social, and motor skills, including creative, logical, and abstract thinking, built on the meaningful (not rote) use of ideas. Meaning is imparted to behavior and ideas through their connection to emotional inclination, intent, or affect.[19]

The Floor Time approach, then, is a well-structured and clearly defined methodology which denotes six essential milestones toward which this therapy is intended to progress: [20]

1. The ability to self-calm and process environmental information
2. The ability to engage in relationships
3. The ability to engage in two-way communication
4. The ability to create complex gestures and connect a series of actions into an elaborate and deliberate problem-solving sequence
5. To create ideas
6. To build bridges between ideas so that they become reality-based and logical

Therefore, this approach utilizes a play-based, child-directed interactive intervention procedure in which developing meaningful emotional relationships is the primary goal. These relationships, which are initially built on simple imitation and playful connection, are intended to develop into meaningful, intentional, and emotionally intimate relationships between the individual with ASD and those engaged with him or her. Most importantly, this intervention is proposed as a component of a larger array of corresponding interventions, establishing once again that there is no requirement of exclusivity for this intervention to be considered effective or implementable. Furthermore, this approach recognizes that individuals with ASD are more than simply "functioners" or "behavers" or "compliers," and seeks not only to identify but to engage with the underlying socio-emotional needs of the individual. Therefore, the process of Floor Time consists of five steps:

1. *Observation*—The caregiver or play partner observes the child's natural facial and bodily expressions and gestures and listens to specific tones of voice, verbal expressions, and vocal patterns in order to determine how he or she may best be approached.
2. *Approach (based on open circles of communication)*—Dependent on the current mood and communicative and behavioral styles of the individual, the caregiver or play partner approaches the child using suitable and familiar words and gestures (based on the observation of the child) which is an attempt to open a "circle of open communication" through the acknowledgment of the child's emotional stage and interest at that particular moment (e.g., doing what the child does is validating, familiar, and unthreatening). Once the approach has been successful, the play partner may establish "creative obstructions" such as moving a preferred item out of the child's reach, for the purposes of capitalizing on the child's greatest interest during this step.

3. *Follow the Child's Lead*—The child is encouraged to guide the activity as the caregiver or play partner provides individualized and sensitive support. During this stage is when the child begins to experience feelings of warmth, connection with others, and being understood (not corrected), yielding a building of self-worth and sense of self, as well as experiencing a sense of influence on his or her environment, as evidenced by the caregiver's imitation of the child's own behavior.

4. *Extend and Expand Play*—The caregiver or play partner makes encouraging comments about the child's play and extends and expands play without being intrusive (for example engaging in a similar behavior and then adding a step to it or by asking questions about objects in the play area), in the hopes that the child will engage in this extended form of creative play. The primary goal of this step is to show the child, by example, that behaviors can be changed, modified, extended, and expanded without threatening the interaction of the play partner or negatively affecting the environment.

5. *Child Closes the Circle of Communication*—The child is seen to have closed the circle of communication when he or she builds on the comments and gestures of the caregiver or play partner with comments and gestures of his or her own. Interactions with the child allow for many different circles of communication to be open and closed, with the circles expanding in length, complexity, and emotional connection.

The theoretical framework of DIR has been instrumental in providing a diametrically different conception both of ASD as a condition as well as potential means of addressing the needs of individuals with ASD in a therapeutic though unthreatening environment. First and foremost, DIR approaches the therapeutic interaction from an approach-based perspective in which the caregiver or play partner enters the space and "world" of the individual, rather than an extraction-based perspective, in which the "teacher" or "therapist" insists on the individual "leaving" their space, deemed dysfunctional and "entering" the therapists' space, deemed socially appropriate and more functional. Allowing the individual to remain in his or her own space, at least initially, provides a number of advantageous environmental circumstances. The child, from this approach-based perspective, is not corrected for his or her preference of behavior, but rather is engaged through imitation, allowing the individual to maintain control while learning that his or her behavior can be effectively used to engage another. Further, the child learns that their behaviors can serve not only a needs-based function, but also a socially and emotionally based function, where gestures and words (or even non-word sounds) can be used to connect with another without the need for any additional external "reward" or "motivation." By maintaining this interaction on the child's terms, the play partner ensures that the child remains in a comfortable and non-vulnerable state. When this interaction is expanded, likely by the play partner, the child is given an opportunity to engage in the expansion at his or her own volition, and is not punished or corrected for violating a social rule or not complying with a direction. Second, the child is regarded as a fully formed human being not only capable of feeling emotion, but able to be taught, albeit under more directional circumstances, to engage in such emotionally intentional activities and behaviors. Instead of ignoring the existence of emotions for their non-observable or measurable qualities or "working through" emotional behaviors such as crying and tantrums to an end of compliance followed by reward, the individual is permitted to orchestrate the social interaction on their own, maintaining that the individual's comfort is not only recognized, but respected and obeyed by the play partner. This allows the individual to maintain control in a potentially adverse environment while being consistently reminded that he or she is not only permitted to engage in their preferred behavior, but that such behavior can actually affect the interactions with the play partner in an emotionally functional way. Third, the DIR approach is designed to be a component of an overall comprehensive approach, indicating clearly that it does not, in any way, purport to be a cure or means for recovery in ASD, but rather a means of addressing an important facet of the developmental and experiential state of individuals with ASD. The framework of the ADH and the methodology of DIR do so by not characterizing or addressing ASD as a "syndrome" or a "condition," but rather relating relevant facets of such individuals' experience to the natural occurrences in individuals without such difficulties and creating environments in which such difficulties can be circumvented or at least minimized, leading to an opportunity to experience intimate emotional relationships.

SCERTS, a concept proposed by Prizant and colleagues, is another theoretical framework with a corresponding methodology that bases its main focuses on both the development of meaningful relationships and the centrality of socio-emotional functioning. One of the foundational tenets of the SCERTS framework is the notion that the label of ASD, in and of itself, is reductive, especially when that label carries with it a connotation of a single mode disorder (such as one that is predominantly affected by a single modality such as behavior or language) with any other corresponding characteristics attributed only to being part and parcel of the overall "main" deficiency. As an alternative to the "syndromic" perception of ASD, the SCERTS framework conceptualizes the experience as a component-based characterization of Language Disability + Emotional Disability + Behavioral Disability (LD + ED + BD). The SCERTS framework, then, attempts to provide a theoretical basis and corresponding methodology for recognizing, understanding, and addressing the social behavioral difficulties of children fitting this phenotype. This research basis is derived directly from empirical studies involving the social and emotional development of children who display both typical and atypical characteristics. [21]

The major contribution of both the theoretical and the methodological framework of SCERTS is that regarding ASD as a "syndromic" or single-complex disorder can detract from the importance of multi-faceted aspects of the individual, causing educational approaches to be designed for the "syndrome" and its associated characteristics as opposed to the individual outplay of specific types of idiosyncrasies that will vary between individuals.

Examinations of research involving language and communication development of children with and without identified disabilities, in many cases, reveal that the preponderance of studies focus on the narrow topics of linguistic skills or social communication skills. However, limiting research questions to these concepts alone results in the tendency to ignore the significance of the specific socio-emotional context in which language is developed and used. Additionally, focusing primarily on overt language skills, these narrow contexts omit the function that language serves in regulating and expressive affective states and in the actual development of relationships themselves. [22] This suggestion is based largely on the finding of Lewis, who distinguished between the concepts of social interaction and social relationships. The distinction, he suggested, is that relationships are developed out of early social acts between caregivers and children. Further, social acts between children give rise to both social and cognitive structures, developing into competency in initiating and developing relationships with others through the processes of self-schema, empathy, and sharing. [23] What is most important about this process is the child's development of a sense of self, a process that is often compromised in children who display LD + ED + BD characteristics. Address of this central area of difficulty is likely to be bypassed entirely by using behavioral approaches alone, which are apt to focus on compliance and behavior replacement rather than the development of meaningful and functional socio-emotional relationships. This negligence can further stunt the child's already compromised ability to develop meaningful social interaction skills.

Through SCERTS, the behavioral approach and the socio-emotional developmental approach can be combined creating a synergistically effective methodology by using initial modes of reinforcement to establish the connection between child and teacher, and maintain interest in such connections, while the emotional connection between the individuals is consistently exercised and developed over time, capitalizing on both extrinsic and intrinsic motivation. Therefore, the goal of such an approach is:

> to enhance the student's language and communicative competence and to promote development of successful relationships with adults and peers . . . promoting use of language for self- and interactive regulation, developing vocab-

ulary to express emotions, enhancing temporal awareness and organizational abilities, developing knowledge of the language of school discourse and peer interactions, and developing metalinguistic awareness and prosocial skills.[24]

Incumbent upon this goal are a number of implications. First, teachers must accept the notion that student self-esteem and self-confidence is, in itself, a means of communication, though one that is more tacitly expressed and dependent on the "listener" to perceive. Therefore, these components should be addressed not only in terms of functionality or behavior replacement, but also in the context of encouraging control and regulation over one's environment initiated by oneself, not only out of compliance to teacher instructions. Second, teachers must recognize that socio-communicative problems are not uni-dimensional, and encompass both past experience and persistent misinterpretations of environmental and social information and how such information affects social experience and language. Third, teachers must accept the legitimacy of students' feelings regardless of their ability to express them in socially appropriate ways, and respect the right of students to feel and express negative emotions without requiring them to "work through" such behaviors to gain appropriate social status, social response, or external reinforcement. Finally, there is a distinct need for input from a multidisciplinary team in order to provide various legitimate perspectives that can address all single and interactive aspects of individuals who display characteristics of LD + ED + BD.[25]

The corresponding methodological framework of SCERTS, then, can be introduced by indicating the meaning of the acronym. It is a methodology that is focused on the concepts of social communication (SC), emotional regulation (ER), and transactional support (TS). This methodology, created out of a rich history of multidisciplinary research, represents an important development in the field of educating individuals with ASD from a comprehensive perspective. As Prizant and colleagues explain:

> Efforts to increase communicative and socioemotional abilities are widely regarded as among the most critical priorities and growth in these areas are closely related to prognosis and long-term positive outcomes. However, some widely disseminated approaches are not based on the most contemporary developmental research on social and communication development in children with and without disabilities, nor do they draw from current understanding of the learning style of children with ASD.[26]

This characterization falls directly in line with the earlier critique of single mode interventions, especially those of behavior analysis, and reiterates the deep need for the field to embrace methodological programs that reflect multiple areas of research, respecting the developments across disciplines as relevant and contributive to the implementation of effective teaching strategies. It also provides a means of actually incorporating areas of research that are derived from varying disciplinary backgrounds and even, in some cases, varying philosophical foundations into a well-designed, well-structured, and truly comprehensive methodology. By embracing this level of multi-modal yet empirically legitimate methods of practice, a model such as SCERTS can aptly be applied to individuals across the spectrum of ASD regardless of the severity of each mode of difficulty. As Prizant and colleagues explain:

> In this manner, the model reflects a new conceptualization of education/treatment that most closely addresses the core deficits observed in ASD, and therefore represents an example of what we believe to be the "next generation of treatment approaches for ASD."[27]

The most notable question still remains, however: Why are relationship-based approaches still regarded as, at best "promising" and, from many behavior analytic positions, non-evidence based? The answer remains simple. There is still an extremely powerful sense of authority and territoriality held by the behavioral community in the realm of ASD, much of which is maintained by an almost compulsive output of articles, maintaining the over-reliance on outcomes-based quantitative results only. This hyper-focus on quantitative results only, coupled with the legitimacy ascribed to methodologies which possess simply "large numbers" of studies somewhat regardless of the quality of such studies appears to have been effective at keeping these effective and theoretically sound methodologies marginalized in the vast mainstream of education and ASD.

FOCUSING ON DEVELOPMENT OF JOINT ATTENTION AND EMOTIONAL REGULATION IN ASD

Because, in many ways, the initial identification and diagnosis of ASD in young children remains largely based in deficits of typical language and social development as well as unusual indications of behavioral functioning, a deep knowledge of social, emotional, and linguistic development as well as behavioral processes is imperative to identify and address the specific needs of individuals with ASD. One such central clinical marker in the area of social development is joint attention, conceptualized specifically in such areas as proto-declarative pointing, showing objects to others, and pretend play.[28] Research interest and emerging evidence in this area has allowed the field to improve its clinical identification of individuals who are potentially at risk for ASD as these appear to be apparent earlier than those of overt behavioral markers. What makes these pre-linguistic conditions so important is that rapidly expanding research indicates that such actions serve to actually coordinate attention between social partners in an attempt to share an awareness of objects or events, which reflects the emergence of social-cognitive processes, thus creating a foundation for the acquisition of verbal language and communication skills.[29] Since the development of these skills under natural conditions in typical language development appears to be so pivotal in later language development and effective communication, it stands to reason as well as ethical practice that they should be explicitly included in any comprehensive educational approach for children with ASD. Therefore, since these inconsistencies in pivotal social attention attributes can potentially be identified earlier than behavioral markers, interventional changes to the child's educational program and environment that nurture joint attention will play an integral role in the development of socio-emotional communication.[30]

Joint attention is defined as, "three-way exchanges that involve another, self, and object and may be expressed in the form of referential looks between people and objects, pointing and showing gestures."[31] Deficits, which emerge early in this area, play an important role in both the detection and development of individuals with ASD. As Kasari and colleagues describe:

> Deficits in the ability to share affective states with others constitute another important component of the social deficits displayed by young autistic children. . . . Moreover, we have hypothesized that joint attention deficits among autistic children may be associated with deficits in affect expression among these children. This hypothesis is based in part on research on the normal development of joint attention skills.[32]

The centrality of joint attention skills in the area of both linguistic and emotional development must therefore not be ignored or limited, as it often is in the context of behavior analytic approaches due to the difficulty in devising quantifiable and observable definitions. As such, measures of joint attention in behavior analysis often focus predominantly on "manding" behaviors, or requesting environmentally present objects from a caregiver, or making simple declarative statements that are not likely all that different from simple tacts (such as pointing out objects in the absence of any true socially connective function). Joint attention in its true sense, however, is a much broader and deeper socio-emotional process than simply requesting items from another or pointing out aspects of the environment. As Bruner indicates, "there must be some primitive mood marking procedure to distinguish indicating from commanding or requesting."[33] That is, joint attention serves more to facilitate emotional connection rather than fulfill a functional demand.

Therefore, nurturing joint attention is a vital component in contributing to the development of effective interpretive and emotional state sharing capabilities and intentionality. The child's capability of engaging a social partner for not only needs-based communication, but also for social and emotional intentions is a central component to developing competency in socio-emotional interactions. According to Prizant, there are four distinct areas of challenge in the social-communicative profile of children with ASD:[34]

1. Limitations in coordinating attention and affect which result in:

   a. Orienting and attending to a social partner
   b. Shifting gaze between people and objects in order to monitor another's attentional focus and intentions
   c. Sharing emotional states with another person
   d. Following and drawing another person's attention toward objects or events for the purpose of sharing experiences
   e. Participating in reciprocal interactions over multiple turns in a social exchange

2. Limitations in sharing intent which result in:

   a. Directing signals to others to express intentions
   b. Gaining another's attention when initiating either gestural, vocal, or linguistic communication
   c. Communicating intentionality at a rate necessary to maintain reciprocal interaction

3. A restricted range of communicative functions resulting in:

   a. Reduced frequency of communication for more social purposes, such as social interaction, calling attention to oneself for social reasons
   b. Reduced frequency of joint attention activities such as commenting on and sharing experiences
   c. Reduced frequency of expressing emotions

4. Difficulties inferring another's perspective or emotional state resulting in:

   a. Problems in monitoring the appropriateness of verbal and nonverbal discourse
   b. Selecting appropriate topics
   c. Providing sufficient background information
   d. Reading and responding appropriately to others emotional expressions

The research regarding the concept of Theory of Mind (ToM) provides important information in the connection between developing joint attention skills and emotional regulation. The concept of ToM was first introduced by Premack and Woodruff in 1978 in the context of cognitive psychology. While a deeper look at the theory will be entertained in a later section of this chapter, ToM is a significant and applicable idea to the development of individuals with ASD. Basically, ToM, known also as meta-representation process, is the process that "mind readers" employ in order to infer others' "mental states" on the basis of certain contextual emotional clues such as crying, laughing, facial expressions, and body language, among others. Theory of Mind, however, is not to be thought of as a "theory" that has been constructed externally; rather, it is a theory in the sense that it is inherently employed by primates, including humans, when the necessary neurological faculties are intact.[35] Contextualized by Humphreys, ToM can be thought of as a matter of "social chess" by which individuals living in a complex society have to combine both social and intellectual skills in order to predict the "moves" of others when planning one's own "moves," being ever willing to re-evaluate and re-strategize in order to meet the changing needs of the interaction.[36] According to Humphreys:

> In evolutionary terms it must have been a breakthrough. . . . Imagine the biological benefits to the first of our ancestors who developed the ability to make realistic guesses about the inner life of his rivals; to be able to picture what another was thinking about and planning to do next; to be able to read the minds of others by reading his own.[37]

This concept is particularly important in the context of ASD because many skills which appear to be troublesome for such individuals, such as socially appropriate and emotionally connected relationships, meaningful play, and emotional regulation may likely be attributed to challenges in the ability to engage in ToM activities. As proffered by Leslie, in order to successfully negotiate between social understanding and understanding of pretense the proclivity for meta-representation, or the ability to represent the aspects of others' minds in one's own mind, is necessary. As such, ToM is a prerequisite to imaginative and symbolic play. Children with ASD have difficulty being able to infer important mental states such as knowing that other people *can* know, think, want, feel, and believe things, potentially elucidating the seemingly inherent lack of development of and engagement in pretend play.[38] Essentially, this link becomes solidified with joint attention as, in order to share attention with another beyond simply fulfilling demands, ToM would need to be intact in order to make sense of initiating and maintaining such social connection.

A relatively ingenious means by which some facets of ToM have been investigated in children with and without ASD is the Sally-Anne test, an interactive assessment possessive of multiple variations. Basically, the Sally-

Anne test requires respondents to recognize a difference between their own knowledge and the knowledge of others, and distinguish how that difference in knowledge will affect the goal-oriented behavior of others. In the test, a marble (or some other object) is placed in either a box or a basket with two dolls present, one named Sally, the other named Anne. One of the dolls takes leave and the other doll moves the marble to a different location. The respondent is then asked where the doll that left will look for the marble. A respondent with ToM intact would naturally respond that the doll would look for it in the original placement, since they would be aware of the fact that the doll does not "know" it was moved even though the respondent does. Children with ASD consistently show a lack of success on these tasks, indicating that they have difficulty with distinguishing between what they know as being different with what the doll "knows." As such, this tendency may be an indication that there is a failure to implement ToM to discern that they have "extra information" that the doll does not, and therefore cannot attribute this difference in knowledge to a difference in behavior. It is, however, important to note that a low percentage of individuals with ASD do demonstrate accurate engagement with ToM, and this difficulty cannot, therefore, be seen as a fundamental issue.[39]

The role that ToM plays in the emotional and social outplay of children with ASD is particularly important, and is beginning to reveal some interesting findings. Two principal emotions that are associated with ToM have been identified as embarrassment and shame, which are based on two main social requirements: (a) the ability to understand that behavior has social consequences in the eyes of others in the social environment and; (b) an understanding of social norms and what potential violations are. Findings of studies suggest that children with ASD perform significantly more poorly than children without ASD on tasks that involve identifying self-conscious emotions (embarrassment, hurt, shame, humiliation, etc.), while they do not differ on identifying non-self-conscious primitive emotions (happy, sad, excited). Therefore, applying the findings of such research in the connection between joint-attention, relationship-development, and emotional regulation to a comprehensive educational approach is absolutely imperative.

Connected to the concept of ToM and one's capability of reconciling their emotional states and corresponding behavior with the demands of the social environment is the concept of emotional regulation, also a key factor in the development and maintenance of meaningful relationships. Emotional regulation is, "the intra and extra organismic factors by which emotional arousal is redirected, controlled, modulated, and modified to enable an individual to function adaptively."[40] Extending what behavior analysts often call self-stimulatory behavior, a perpetuation of behavior based on some "internal" or "biologically automatic" reinforcement, the notion of emotional regulation addresses the core socio-emotional capacities and needs of individuals with

ASD rather than dismissing it as simply "non-functional" behavior that is, more often than not, socially inappropriate. As Prizant describes it:

> Through the process of emotional regulation children strive to maintain an optimal state of arousal that matches the social and physical demands of their environments and allows them to respond adaptively.[41]

Therefore, emotional states and their concurrent needs for modulating regulation are influenced by multiple conditions including environmental characteristics such as types and intensity of sensory and emotional stimulation, social contexts such as the availability of familiar communicative partners, and internal variables such as wellness or illness, level of fatigue, anxiety, or personal comfort.[42]

FOCUSING ON SENSORY PROCESSING AND INTEGRATION

Though interventions involving sensory processing or sensory integration are often dismissed as being, at best, non-evidence-based or, at worst, blatant quackery, a closer examination of both the research involving the theory and the methodology would reveal clearly that there is a scientifically supported theoretical framework for the approach, stemming mostly from the ever advancing neuroscientific research. Posited first by Ayres in the early 1970s, the concept of sensory integration suggests that, for individuals with sensory dysfunction, or the inability to process and integrate sensory information from the environment, sensory integration therapy can facilitate speech-language acquisition by enabling more efficient sensory processing. This processing, occurring mainly at the brain stem level, when consistently stimulated will lead to more complex cortical processing, including central auditory processing, a vital component of language development.[43] As Ayres explains:

> Sensory integration is the neurological process that organizes sensation from one's own body and from the environment and makes it possible to use the body effectively within the environment. The spatial and temporal aspects of inputs from different sensory modalities are interpreted, associated, and unified. SI is information processing . . . the brain must select, enhance, inhibit, compare, and associate the sensory information in a flexible, constantly changing pattern; in other words the brain must integrate it.[44]

Expanding on Ayres's definition some years later, Fisher and Murray specify the three foundations of sensory integration therapy:

> The first major postulate specifies that normal individuals take in sensory information derived from the environment and from movement of their bodies,

process and integrate these sensory inputs within the central nervous system (CNS), and use this sensory information to plan and organize behavior. The second postulate specifies that deficits in integrating sensory input result in deficits in conceptual and motor learning. The third major postulate guides intervention and specifies that the provision of enhanced sensory experiences, provided within the context of a meaningful activity and the planning and production of an adaptive behavior, results in enhanced sensory integration, and in turn, enhanced learning.[45]

Underlying these postulates are three main notions about the brain: (1) the brain operates holistically; (b) there is an interdependent relationship among the sensory systems, in terms of both development and function; and (c) portions of the brain interact with other portions for individuals to function. Though suggested without much evidence by Ayres in the early 1970s, all of these presumptions have been shown to be accurate and strongly evidenced by neuroscientific advances, especially in the area of neuroimaging. Further, sensory integration is centered on the idea that the brain has capability of plasticity, or can increase function despite structural and functional anomalies, by providing extensive sensory stimulation, which is also empirically supported by neuroscientific advances.[46] The aim of sensory integration therapy, then, is to develop primitive forms of sensation, which is seen as a prerequisite to all perceptual motor activity, in the context of developing the ability to organize purposeful motor activities for visual, auditory, and olfactory processes, as well as in the area of vestibular (spatial orientation principally in the area of balance), proprioceptive (the individual's awareness of one's own position in space), and tactile (to the touch) sensations.[47] Because all perceptual motor activity, including reading, writing, and speaking pragmatically are dependent on the ability to appropriately integrate sensory integration, this skill is imperative to target in any educational program. With consistent stimulation in these areas, individuals improve in the areas of "lower level" integration, which are the basic and primitive functions such as the filtering and refining of sensory information, as well as the "higher level" of integration which analyzes precise details of related sensory information allowing for abstraction, perception, reasoning, as well as language and learning.[48] Proponents of the sensory integration are also careful to emphasize that it can, and in fact should, be used in conjunction with other approaches, again displaying the willingness of other approaches recognizing the importance of comprehensive educational programs.

As such, the purpose of sensory integration techniques is to provide sensorially meaningful activities that combine both sensory activities as well as engage cognitive processes that facilitate motor and spatial planning. These activities must be based on what are seen as the three basic senses: (a) tactile; (b) vestibular; and (c) proprioceptive; the integration of these three basic senses, when harnessed appropriately and meaningfully, are foundational in the development of more complex abilities such as hand-eye coordination, auditory-linguistic connections, and environmental interaction that enhance communicative skills. Therefore, the typical examples used to debunk sensory-based theories such as brushing a student's hands or providing weighted apparel on its own indicates a vast and foundational misunderstanding of what sensory integration approaches seek to do. For example, if an individual with visual integration challenges were to be tasked to select five green balls from a ball pit full of multi-colored balls and place them in a nearby bucket before he or she may leave the ball pit, this would be a well-structured visual integration activity as it requires the individual to both process the sensory information of color, as well as plan the necessary motoric elements such as scanning for the balls, picking them up using hands, and placing them in a central location (not to mention a function of negative reinforcement if the individual does, indeed, wish to escape the ball pit). Furthermore, the criterion of five balls to be deposited before the task is deemed completed engages multiple process. Therefore, there are at least three distinct sensory, motor, and cognitive processes being engaged in a task such as this, clearly demonstrating the versatility of sensory integration approaches. In the case of musical or visual art approaches, these methodologies should be applied in the same way, ensuring that those are required to engage in such activities do so either entirely for pleasure or in a way that engages multiple facets of their central nervous system.

One potential reason for the skepticism involving Sensory Integration Therapy (SIT) is a lack of a solid or even generally accepted definition of the methodology. A significant clarification must be made before addressing this issue more deeply, however: sensory integration therapy is tailored to the individual's particular needs. Therefore, there is no prescriptive method of SIT that can be applicable to all individuals. Rather, multiple activities depending on the location and frequency of service, the severity of need, and the personal sensitivities are designed and implemented to address particular needs of individual children. As such, the purpose of SIT is less about the actual activity or methodology, and more about the effectiveness with which it stimulates or de-stimulates the particular areas of the brain that need to be addressed under controlled and well-structured sensory input activities.

However, the empirical evidence for SIT is not entirely absent, though there is indeed a dire paucity; the methodology is in clear need of better controlled studies and more validated means of investigation. As such, the field's biggest challenge is not as much a lack of evidence-basis, but rather a lack of methodologically sound studies that are capable of demonstrating its potential effectiveness, which can undoubtedly be observed amongst trained and capable practitioners. Such flaws include, but are not limited to, poor means of evaluating the effects of therapy, poor control over potentially confounding conditions, lack of baseline conditions, being a practitioner dominated as opposed to a researcher dominated field, as well as potential bias stemming from both pro and anti-SIT paradigms creating the existence of illegitimate and politically based articles disguised as studies.[49] Research over the last few decades has been showing increasingly better methodology applied in studies and, as a result, more convincing research. Focus on research areas in the field of neuroscience heavily supports the theoretical underpinnings of SIT as well as the potential benefits becoming much clearer and more convincing.

Adding to the legitimacy of the importance of sensory integration issues outside of direct outcome studies of SIT is the increasingly validated empirical evidence involving executive dysfunction and weak central coherence amongst individuals with ASD. Executive function is generally a "catch-all" term to describe functions such as planning, working memory, impulse control, inhibition, and mental flexibility, among other potential components, which may be incorporated by an individual singly or in any permutation of simultaneous functioning. Many components of executive functions are implicated as being dysfunctional, or at least significantly challenged amongst individuals with ASD. According to Hill:

> For the executive dysfunction account of autism to be valid as a cognitive account of the primary symptoms, these difficulties must be a universal feature of autism, that is they must be a characteristic of every affected individual. . . . Studies focusing on a range of executive functions, as well as those reflecting naturalistic situations need to be investigated. Not only will this help clarify the universality of executive dysfunction to autism, but also the impact of social aspects of tasks that could cause increased difficulty in autism. Of additional benefit will be an empirical demonstration of the ways in which different aspects of executive performance correlate and fractionate in autism and whether this maps clearly onto the patterns seen in the normal population.[50]

These hypotheses involving executive dysfunction and what will eventually be termed weak central coherence can address and abate the limitations of ToM, which are more likely to explain the "triad" based challenges in individuals with ASD, but account for little beyond. As such, though ToM can help the individual identify how one is feeling toward the attainment of goal-oriented action, it is not likely to assist the individual in discerning how such an action toward a goal can actually be attained. For this to take place, executive function must be engaged. Whether ToM is a component of executive functioning or is a consequential process is highly debated, and is beyond the scope of this work. It appears clear, however, that the limitations of ToM can likely be addressed by the introduction of executive function (or dysfunction, in the case of ASD).

A logical extension of this research, then, indicates that a more robust theory would have to account for both ToM factors as well as executive function factors. This more comprehensive theory was purported by Frith as "weak central coherence." Weak central coherence accounts for both the social issues in ASD, as addressed by ToM, as well as the non-social features, which may be addressed by executive functioning. Therefore, the weak central coherence theory contends that non-social features of autism in terms of both assets and deficits extend from tendencies to process local information rather than global information, leading to a failure to process incoming stimuli within context. That is, individuals with ASD perceive parts with far more aptitude than wholes, hyper-focusing on details while disregarding the "big picture." Evidence for this tendency has been indicated in various visually based perception studies.[51] The importance of this theory is that it accounts for aspects of even the earliest descriptions of autism that are dismissed by many intervention approaches, especially those of behavior analysis. For example, Kanner's original description suggested:

> A situation, a performance, a sentence is not regarded as complete if it's not made up of exactly the same elements that were present at the time the child was first confronted with it. If the slightest ingredient is altered or removed, the total situation is no longer the same and therefore is not accepted as such. . . .[52]

It is important to note, however, regarding weak central coherence theory, that connoting a "weakness" cannot be distinctly characterized as a deficit, but rather may indicate a superior ability in the area of local processing, or potentially a processing bias. That is, it is not necessarily the case that individuals with ASD *cannot* process globally, but rather that they *choose*, or at least prefer, to process locally.[53]

NEUROLOGICAL EVIDENCE FOR COMPREHENSIVE EDUCATIONAL APPROACHES IN ASD

From a positivistic point of view, many of the methodologies described in the above section would have already been discounted based on a narrow, outcomes-based view of evidence-basis. However, this narrow perspective is insufficient in capturing the value of a comprehensive approach based on the unnecessary stringency of its purview. However, as aforementioned, theoretical evidence, especially those from well-established empirical fields such as neuroscience can provide a wealth of support for the theoretical foundation and practical implications of relationship-based, emotional regulation, joint attention, and sensory-integration based methodologies. This section will delineate specific findings within the field of neuroscience that adds empirical credence to the inclusion of these methodologies in a comprehensive approach in educating individuals with ASD. The purpose of this section is not, in any way, to act as a primer on any aspect of neuroscience, including neurological structure or function, nor is it to be presented as anything near an exhaustive investigation of the actual workings of the brain in the area of ASD. It will, however, present a formidable body of evidence such that establishes the legitimacy of conducting further earnest evaluation of the aforementioned components of a comprehensive educational program for individuals with ASD. In the field of neuroscience there appears to be somewhat unilateral agreement that no approach for educating individuals with ASD could truly be validated without the unification of educational sciences with neuroscience. As suggested by Nicolson and Szatmari:

> It seems likely, however, that specific and uniformly effective treatment will not be realized without a clear understanding of the disorder's underlying neurological and genetic causes. Hopefully, interventions aimed at the brain-level biochemical and structural changes leading to autism will result in long-lasting and significant improvement. [54]

Similarly suggested by Belmonte, one of the foremost and well-respected researchers in the area of Autism Spectrum Disorders:

> It has been said that people with autism suffer from a lack of "central coherence," the cognitive ability to bind together a jumble of separate features into a single, coherent object or concept. Ironically, the same can be said of the field of autism research, which all too often seems a fragmented tapestry stitched from differing analytical threads and theoretical patterns. Defined and diagnosed by purely behavioral criteria, autism was first described and investigated using the tools of behavioral psychology. More recent years have added brain anatomy and physiology, genetics, and biochemistry, but results from these new domains have not been fully integrated with what is known about autistic behavior. The unification of these many levels of analysis will . . . provide therapeutic targets for prevention and remediation of autism. . . ." [55]

Though specific investigations into specialized brain areas will demonstrate evidence for each individual component, a brief exploration of general brain differences that are likely to be found amongst children with ASD will provide a sturdy foundation upon which more specific evidentiary claims can be built. Findings from multiple neuroimaging studies indicate that the brain volume of individuals with ASD appears to be between 5 and 12 percent larger than those children without ASD, and experience disproportionately excessive acceleration of head circumference growth in the first two years of life. [56] Furthermore, a number of other studies report both an enlarged amygdala in contrast to a reduced number of neurons functioning within the structure for individuals with ASD, a seemingly contraindicative finding. The amygdala is thought to be largely correlated with emotional, social, and communicative functioning; an area of clear challenge for individuals with ASD.[57]

Furthermore, there is a global issue of neural connectivity apparent in the brains of individuals with ASD, indicating that differences in brain structures alone cannot account for all differences, but also that the communication capacities between regions of the brain, even if structurally intact and developed, can also be responsible for some of the clear differences in neurological functioning and its resultant behavior. These research findings have been increasingly supported in the last decade.[58] These issues, though increasingly well-identified, can be a result of a multitude of atypical developmental processes from prenatal neuronal migration establishing both correct positioning and patterning of neuronal connectivity between brain structures, as well as potentially postnatal features including development of dendrites and synapses.

As such, the evidence from neuroscience appears to support the notion that ASD is not a result of a single structure or even single system within the brain, but rather a complex and global series of anomalies between multiple systems and structures. This coincides with the finding that multiple structures and systems within the brain have been implicated as significantly atypical in ASD including the cerebellum, brainstem, frontal and temporal lobes, as well as the limbic system and other emotional regulatory systems. Further complicating matters is the vast heterogeneity of behavioral, social, and emotional outplay amongst individuals with ASD, potentially indicating a heterogeneity of underlying neurological contributors as well. Therefore, distinguishing between structures, connectivity, and systems involved is critical.[59]

Because the previous section established that Theory of Mind (ToM) is a central system for the appropriate development of many levels of social and emotional communication and is likely challenged to at least some degree in most individuals with ASD, albeit some exhibiting far more significant challenges than others, an exploration of neuroscientific findings involving brain structures that are thought to be associated with ToM is imperative. While still seminal, a rapidly advancing discovery of a class of neurons called "mirror neurons," discovered first in the brains of macaque monkeys, are contributing important information that can potentially lead to a deeper understanding of the existence of ToM in humans, and its potential dysfunction amongst individuals with ASD. Mirror neurons, in the context of macaque monkeys, are visuomotor neurons that respond both when a particular action is performed by the monkey itself and when the same action is observed in another monkey. These cells appear to play a key role in the neurological recognition of goal-oriented behavior, regardless of who is actually engaging in it. The next phase of investigation, which has already been implicated, is that mirror neurons contribute to the more complex action of mind reading in humans.[60] These discoveries, though clearly demonstrated neurologically in monkeys, have led to a variety of different theories and interpretations of how ToM is likely to work in humans. Two of these perspectives are known as "theory theory (TT)" and "simulation theory (ST)." According to TT, mental states are represented as inferred ideas in a naïve theory, positing that people without atypical neurological development and function can engage in mind reading by using a commonsense theory of mind, which is either inherently possessed or tacitly acquired during the developmental process. In this context, mental states of other people are conceptualized as unobservable and theoretical posits which are utilized to both explain and predict others' behavior.[61] ST, on the other hand, suggests that mind reading occurs as a function of adopting others' perspectives by tracking or matching others' mental states with comparative mental states of one's own. In this process, mind readers utilize their own familiar mental states in order to perceive those of others, requiring as much self-awareness as other-awareness for ToM to be functional.[62] The main difference between the two is the implication of the role of self-awareness. That is, from the TT perspective, mind reading is a detached theory without use for self-awareness, whereas ST actively engages both self-awareness and other-awareness in order to engage in mind reading effectively.

While the neuroscience behind mind reading is in no way comprehensive or exhaustive even under typical circumstances, much less atypical circumstances, emerging studies will be able to provide a vast groundwork of understanding in order to observe and compare atypical development and functioning amongst individuals with ASD. Since there is a clearly behavioral occurrence of a functional difference in these areas amongst individuals with ASD, comparative neuroscientific studies can elucidate neurological differences, thereby creating a means by which educational interventions can be better informed.

A logical extension, or perhaps even prerequisite, of ToM is the notion of emotional connection and regulation in individuals with ASD, for which a vast body of neurological research exists. Much research indicates that individuals with ASD not only have difficulty attributing others' emotional and mental states, but also have trouble understanding and expressing their own in a functional or regulated way. Therefore, it is imperative for comprehensive approaches to not only address the connection between social and emotional behavior in an external sense, but also the individual's awareness of his or her own social and emotional needs, especially in ever-changing environments outside of the classroom or therapeutic setting. Much of the research in this area implicates the function of the amygdala. The amygdala is located deep within the temporal lobe of the brain. As a vital part of the brain's limbic system, the amygdala plays a key role in the processing of emotions, especially raw emotions such as fear and pleasure. Both the structural differences in terms of size and functional differences, such as quantity of neurons present in the amygdala, are integral in understanding the likely role of the amygdala in the behavioral, social, communicative, and emotional outplay of ASD. Because there is clear evidence that individuals with ASD have different tendencies in understanding, expressing, or regulating social-emotional behavior, it follows that one of the main neurological structures involved in such activities is likely affected, which has been demonstrated. [63]

The role of the amygdala also appears to be closely related to the actions involved with ToM, adding credence to the notion that individuals with ASD are not likely able to naturally engage in the behavioral consequences of ToM, such as modifying behavior or emotional states in order to match those of others when appropriate in a given social setting. In a neuroimaging study by Baron-Cohen and colleagues, the amygdala in individuals of ASD did not activate comparably when they were asked to make mentalistic inferences from another's eyes as compared to individuals without ASD, who did show amygdala activity. Because the amygdala is thought to be neurologically connected to several other brain structures involved in drive-related behavior such as the prefrontal cortex and the hypothalamus, it is thought to be an area of significant importance in potential neurobiological influences in ASD. Adding to this proposition is the finding that patients with lesions in their amygdala show impairments in social judgment and behaviors that are similar to those in ASD, warranting the description of some pathologists as "acquired autism." [64]

Sensory-based differences, while widely defined and difficult to capture in anything resembling parsimonious terms can be regarded, at least for the purpose of this examination, as information that is gathered from the environment through any sensory modality, be it sight, hearing, touch, taste, or smell. For the most part, however, the research involving the differences in sensory processing for individuals with ASD focus primarily on visual and auditory, and in some cases, though much rarer, tactile issues. While sensory integrative differences have comprised a key feature of descriptions of ASD from the very beginnings of its identification by Down, Kanner, and Asperger, behavior analytic approaches have almost entirely dismissed its importance. Neurophysiological research clearly implicates a variety of structural and functional differences that can be indicative of atypical sensory processing. In general, many ideas in sensory integration processing suggest that individuals with ASD have difficulty, or complete inability, to filter and process stimuli from visual, auditory, and tactile channels that are presented simultaneously, potentially resulting in any number of behaviors, from over-stimulation, such as jumping or vocalizing, to avoidant behaviors such as retreating, eloping, or ear-covering. These difficulties do not remain in the realm of sensory reactivity, however, and have also been shown to be related to adequate development of speech and communication as well as comprehension of social and academic stimuli.[65] As described by Marco:

> Given the ubiquitous nature of sensory behavioral differences for individuals with autism, understanding the neural underpinnings of basic sensory processing in autism spectrum disorders is an important task. Furthermore, as the neurophysiologic data mount, we suggest that differences in sensory processing may actually cause core features of autism such as language delay (auditory processing) and difficulty with reading emotion from faces (visual processing).[66]

One of the more widely cited difficulties for individuals with ASD involves visual processing, namely facial recognition. Because recognition processes are largely, if not entirely, neurological in nature, it is suggested that certain regions of the brain are implicated to possess either structural or functional differences. As such, it is reasonable to infer that a facial recognition problem is not entirely a social problem, but may also indicate a visual perceptual problem as well. Evidence for the visual perceptual issues for individuals with ASD is exemplified through difficulties in identifying same from different in visual tasks, perceiving differences between facial features, as well as difficulty distinguishing between emotional expressions. Some neuroimaging studies suggest that these differences may not be attributable only to hypo-activation of relevant brain regions (such as the fusiform gyrus), but also hyper-activation of brain regions that are not typically activated during such tasks, indicating a potential system connectivity issue in sensory processing, similar to that which was suggested for emotional regulatory processing.[67]

The issue in facial recognition, however, may not be entirely visual, indicating also a systemic disconnectivity basis. As one theory suggests, faces do not have intrinsic emotional salience to individuals with ASD, leading to an inability to be socially motivated to engage with them, an idea much akin to that described in Theory of Mind. As a result, people with ASD may not look at faces as much as those without ASD, finding generally less need or use for them resulting in a decreased necessity for recognition. These aspects of difficulty in visual processing lend credence to the notion of weak central coherence, for which there is likely a multi-faceted and complex composition of processes leading, quite likely, to some of the symptomatology that is thought of as being "autistic." As suggested by Bertone:

> It is reasonable to hypothesize that at least some of the behavioral manifestations of autism are due to neural dysfunction that affect perceptual processing. An important function of perceptual systems is to provide the brain with accurate and meaningful internal representations of our external environment. Neural representations underlying our perception of events and subsequent association of these events with appropriate affect are necessary for higher level cognitive functioning to occur. If the construction of internal representations

based on complex perceptual information is compromised in autism, it is possible that subsequent social behaviors necessitating the recognition of internal representations may be affected and manifested by characteristic "negative" autistic behaviors.[68]

Though it is clear that neuroscientific research is not the *coup de grace* of research in Autism Spectrum Disorders, the vast advances indicate clearly, if not inarguably, that there must be a multi-faceted and comprehensive educational approach to individuals with ASD that extends beyond simply applied behavior analytic methods. To continue to pursue such uni-dimensional approaches would be not only unfounded, narrow-minded, or ignorant of advances in other fields, but entirely unethical. The reality is that ASD, if it can even be considered a single condition, is heterogenous in its etiology and outplay. Though behavior analytic intervention and research has contributed, and continues to contribute, significantly in terms of framing particular interventions and monitoring progress and effectiveness in the context of those interventions, its tendency to be almost entirely dismissive of the clearly empirical evidence implicating the multitude of other issues in ASD beyond simply behavioral differences leaves it entirely lacking in credibility as the most effective or, more extremely, the only effective intervention for individuals with ASD. A comprehensive approach only can be deemed as even potentially most effective as it seeks to employ a heterogenous methodology for a heterogenous condition.

NOTES

1. R. Douglas Greer, "Include Me In." *TC Today*, Spring/Summer 2013, 61.

2. Thomas M. Skrtic, "Disability and Democracy: Reconstructing (Special) Education for Postmodernity." Teachers College Press: New York, 1995.

3. Ibid.

4. Ibid.

5. Sally Tomlinson, "A Sociology of Special Education," in T. Skrtic, *Disability and Democracy*, 5.

6. Skrtic, 1995.

7. Ibid.

8. Ibid.

9. Brenda Scheuermann et al. "Problems with Personnel Preparation in Autism Spectrum Disorders." *Focus on Autism and Other Developmental Disabilities*, 18(3), 199–200.

10. Ibid., 200.

11. Sally Rogers, "Empirically Supported Comprehensive Treatments for Young Children with Autism." *Journal of Clinical and Child Psychology*, 1998, 27(2), 168–69.

12. Sally Rogers and L.A. Vismara, "Evidence-Based Comprehensive Treatments for Early Autism." *Journal of Clinical Child and Adolescent Psychology*, 2008, 37(1).

13. Ibid.

14. Richard L. Simpson, "Evidence-Based Practices and Students with Autism Spectrum Disorders." *Focus on Autism and Other Developmental Disabilities*, 2005, 20(3), 142–43.

15. Barry Prizant, Amy W.Wetherby, Emily Rubin, Amy C. Laurent. "The SCERTS Model: A Transactional, Family-Centered Approach to Enhancing Communication and Socioemotion-

al Abilities of Children with Autism Spectrum Disorder." *Infants and Young Children*, 16(4), 296–316.

16. Stanley Greenspan and Serena Wieder, "A Functional Developmental Approach to Autistic Spectrum Disorders." *JASH*, 1999, 24(3) 147–61.

17. Ibid.

18. Ibid.

19. Ibid., 153.

20. Ibid.

21. Lauren J. Hummel and Barry M. Prizant, "A Socioemotional Perpsective for Understanding Social Difficulties of School-Age Children with Language Disorders," *Language, Speech, and Hearing Services in Schools*, 1993, 24, 216–24.

22. Ibid.

23. Ibid.

24. Ibid., 221–22.

25. Ibid.

26. Barry Prizant et al., "A Transactional, Family-Centered Approach to Enhancing Communication and Socioemotional Abilities of Children with Autism Spectrum Disorder." *Infants and Young Children*, 16(4), 296.

27. Ibid., 299.

28. Sanra Maestro et al., "Attentional Skills During the First 6 Months of Age in Autism Spectrum Disorder." *Journal of the American Academy of Child and Adolescent Psychiatry*, 41(10) October 2002, 1239–45.

29. Peter Mundy et al. "A Longitudinal Study of Joint Attention and Language Development in Autistic Children," *Journal of Autism and Developmental Disorders*, 20, 115–28.

30. Geraldine Dawson, "Early Social Attention Impairments in Autism: Social Orienting, Joint Attention, and Attention to Distress." *Developmental Psychology*, 2004, 40, 271–83.

31. Connie Kasari et al., "Affective Sharing in the Context of Joint Attention Interactions of Normal, Autistic, and Mentally Retarded Children." *Journal of Autism and Developmental Disorders*, 20, 1990, 88.

32. Ibid., 88

33. Bruner, 1981, as cited by Kasari et. al., 1990, 89.

34. Prizant, 2003, 300–301.

35. Uta Frith and Francesca Happe, "Autism: Beyond 'Theory of Mind.'" *Cognition*, 50, 1994, 115–32.

36. Simon Baron-Cohen, *Mindblindness: An Essay on Autism and Theory of Mind*. Cambridge, MA: MIT Press, 1997.

37. Ibid., 21.

38. Frith and Happe, 1994.

39. Simon Baron-Cohen et al., "Does the Autistic Child Have a Theory of Mind?" *Cognition*, 21, 1985, 37–46.

40. Cichetti et al., 1991, as cited by Prizant, 2003, 304.

41. Prizant, 2003, 304.

42. Ibid.

43. Mona R. Griffer, "Is Sensory Integration Effective for Children with Langauge-Learning Disorders: A Critical Review of the Evidence." *Language, Speech, and Hearing Services in Schools*, 1999, 30, 393–400.

44. Ayres, 1979, as cited by Daria M. Mauer, 384.

45. Ibid., 384.

46. Ibid.

47. Hoehn and Baumeister, 1994.

48. Ibid.

49. Jane E. Roberts, et al., "Behavioral Indexes of the Efficacy of Sensory Integration Therapy." *American Journal of Occupational Therapy*, September/October 2007, 61, 555–62.

50. Elisabeth L. Hill, "Executive Dysfunction in Autism." *TRENDS in Cognitive Sciences*, 8, 2004, 30.

51. Francesca Happe, "Studying Weak Central Coherence at Low Levels: Children with Autism do not Succumb to Visual Illusions. A Research Note." *Journal of Child Psychology and Psychiatry*, 37, 1996, 873–77.

52. Kanner, 1943, as cited by Happe and Frith, 2006.

53. Francesca Happe and UtaFrith, "The Weak Central Coherence Account: Detail Focused Cognitive Style in Autism Spectrum Disorders." *Journal of Autism and Developmental Disorders*, 2006, from http://www.ucp.pt/site/resources/documents/ICS/GNC/ArtigosGNC/AnaMariaAbreu/D_HaFr06.pdf.

54. Rob Nicolson and Peter Szatmari, "Genetic and Neurodevelopmental Influences in Autistic Disorder." *Canadian Journal of Psychiatry*, 48, 2003.

55. Matthew K. Belmonte et al., "Autism and Abnormal Development of Brain Connectivity." *Journal of Neuroscience*, 2004, 24(42) 9228–31.

56. Eric Courchesne, "Mapping Early Brain Development in Autism." Neuron, 56, 2007, 399–413.

57. Ibid.

58. Daniel H. Geschwind and Pat Levitt. "Autism Spectrum Disorders: Developmental Disconnection Syndromes." *Current Opinion in Neurobiology*, 17, 2007, 103-111.

59. Jocelyne Bachevalier and Katherine A. Loveland, "TheOrbito-frontal-amygdala Circuit and Self Regulation of Social-Emotional Behavior in Autism." *Neuroscience and Biobehavioral Reviews*, 30, 2006, 97–117.

60. Vittorio Gallese and Alvin Goldman, "Mirror Neurons and the Simulation Theory of Mind Reading." *TRENDS in Cognitive Sciences*, 2(12), 1998.

61. Ibid.

62. Ibid.

63. Bachevalier and Loveland, 2006.

64. Simon Baron-Cohen et al. (2000). "The Amygdala Theory of Autism." *Neuroscience and Biobehavioral Reviews*, 24, 355–64.

65. Elysa Jill Marco, "Sensory Processing in Autism: A Review of Neurophysiologic Findings," *Pediatric Research*. 2011, 69, 48R–54R.

66. Ibid., 51R.

67. Marlene Behrmann et al., "Seeing it Differently: Visual Processing in Autism." *TRENDS in Cognitive Sciences*, 10, 2006, 258–64.

68. Armando Bertone et al. "Motion Perception in Autism: A Complex Issue." *Journal of Cognitive Neuroscience*, 15, 218–25.

Chapter Eight

Facilitating the Viability of Evidence-Based Comprehensive Approaches in ASD

The philosophy and theory behind the legitimacy and ethicality of fostering, creating, and implementing comprehensive approaches in teaching individuals with ASD has been well-established in the previous chapter. The overall purpose of this concluding chapter is to propose a foundation upon which well-structured and evidence-based comprehensive approaches may be built. To be clear, this chapter is *not* intended to be construed as a full guide to constructing comprehensive educational programs by any means, nor is it intended to propose an actual model for a comprehensive approach. Rather, it is to identify important components that, when implemented, will be instrumental in leading to the establishment of such an approach. It is ever maintained that individual comprehensive approaches must themselves maintain their own progress toward and achievement of the standards outlined in this chapter, as well as any other standards the program, itself, establishes and uses for evaluation in order to make model, center, or individually based decisions for theoretical or methodological revision or reform based on their own data collection and analysis systems. As such, the information contained in this chapter is intended for groundwork and framework only, not modeling. The focus of this chapter will rely on three main avenues of exploration. First is the importance of teacher education and preparation programs being established in the context of critical and constructivist philosophies as opposed to a positivist perspective. Second is a deeper explanation into the four tenets outlined in chapter 7 by which a program can be considered as evidence-based. Third, and finally, a proposition for a means of actually evaluating a comprehensive approach will be offered.

BUILDING THE FRAMEWORK FOR COMPREHENSIVE EDUCATIONAL APPROACHES IN ASD

Grounding in Critical and Constructivist Teacher Education

An area of significant contention as well as clash of ideologies and philosophies lies in the appropriate and most effective ways to educate and/or train pre-service and in-service teachers. Indeed, these debates extend from individual classrooms and schools, through school administrations, higher education, and into the highest offices of state and federal governments. The field has been through a multitude of teacher education initiatives and reformations, leading even to state and federal policies and products of legislation in an attempt to improve the means by which teachers are trained and prepared for classroom practice. For quite some time much of the policy has been, and continues to be, focused on positivistic views of teacher education. That is, identifying specific, definable, and measurable skill sets that all teachers must possess in order to be effective. While at face value this approach may seem reasonable and even desirable, there are a multitude of problems which abound from such a perspective.

Before the foundations and tenets of constructivist educational methods are investigated, it is equally as important to discuss the nature of critical education, an important foundation upon which constructivist programs may be built. Critical teacher education addresses educational methodologies that regard teaching not as a passive translational process; that is, an act of embedding information into students, but rather as a political, social, and transformational process, imbuing the notions of social change, social justice, and self-determination into the realities of their students and classroom environments from a cultural sharing perspective as opposed to an authoritative imperative. In order to do this effectively, teachers must have a solid grounding in various aspects of teaching practices that include positivist practices focused on measurement and observability of behavioral change, but also a multitude of other perspectives. With such an arsenal of comprehensive potential pedagogical practices, teachers will be far more apt and able to decipher individual and collective learning needs that affect the social and cultural well-being of their students' lives and address them in a way that is more universal to the differing needs of each student.[1] Grounding a teacher education approach from such a diverse and critical perspective allows for teachers to develop a more sophisticated ability to engage in observation and means of addressing the individual needs in their teaching environment. By understanding that there can be multiple interpretations of social and educational situations and interactions, there are multiple means of addressing them, each leading toward differing or similar goals. As Kincheloe explains:

A critical complex empiricism understands that knowledge about humans and their social practices is fragmented, diverse, and always constructed by human beings coming from different contexts. Such a form of knowledge does not lend itself to propositional statements—i.e., final truths. Indeed, a critical complex empirical knowledge does not seek validation by reference to universal truths. Rather it remains somewhat elusive, resistant to the trap of stable and consistent general conceptions of it and its relationship with ever-changing contexts. Thus, our conception of empirical knowledge is more dialectical than propositional. Simply put, there is not one single answer to any research question and non one question is superior to all others. Particular empirical descriptions will always conflict with others, tensions between accounts will persist, and alternative perspectives will continue to struggle for acceptance.[2]

In this context, all potential truths, and there can be multiple, are legitimate fodder for research and investigation, as even those ideas that are presently accepted as "Truth" (capital T) were, at one point, likely deemed taboo, or even heretical. The revolutionary nature of science and knowledge must be respected not as a "thing-in-itself" as Kincheloe suggests, but as a consistently and persistently protean process, and it should remain that way. Allowing teachers to develop this value of not ever really "knowing" while maintaining a persistent desire to continuously question is the only true way to ensure that progress in education, society, and culture is preserved at its very source: the critical classroom. From such an approach, there are no subjects and questions that are avoided and deemed unfit and unworthy for investigation regardless of how alternative or even counter-intuitive they may appear. As Kincheloe further elucidates:

All educational programs and curricula are built on a foundation of normative knowledge—even if such knowledge is hidden or even not fully understood. This is what is so often not understood in teacher education and in schooling. Thus, a key dimension of the work of teacher education is to bring these norms, these ethical and moral assumptions, these visions to the light of day so they can be analyzed and discussed. Because many in teacher education have not conceptualized and talked about normative knowledge, those operating within a positivist culture of neutrality often view this analytical process with great discomfort.[3]

Framing Teacher Education in Autism Spectrum Disorders within a Constructivist Perspective

While grounding in critical teacher education provides a frame of thought for which information should be presented and organized from a philosophical point of view, it does not, in and of itself, address which methodologies or methodological standpoints should actually be included in the curricula. It is clear that a positivistic, overtly behavioral framework alone would not meet the needs of a teacher education program designed to foster a comprehensive approach in ASD. A constructivist framework, however, would be conducive to exploring diverse and differing intervention strategies, theories, and philosophies, as it allows inclusion of multiple perspectives and interpretations of the matters that need to be addressed in such a curriculum. While the constructivist approach is open to and accommodative of multiple understandings and methodologies of curricular delivery it should not, by any means, be considered eclectic and haphazard, as its tenets and the methodologies included in the curricula must be based either in well-designed research or within a theoretically sound foundation with a sound future of well-designed research. That is, such programs would not entertain methods promising quixotic results or charlatanic approaches that are misguided. Rather, its openness lies in the ability to incorporate a multitude of sound methodologies all of which must factor in cognitively and developmentally relevant aspects such as self-esteem, morality, social interaction, and child-directed media.[4] According to Piaget, one of the theorists after whom constructivist methodology is closely designed, describes the main idea in the following terms:

> Pedagogy is very far from being a mere application of psychological knowledge. Apart from the question of the aims of education, it is obvious that even with regard to technical methods it is for experiment alone and not deduction to show us whether methods such as that of work in groups and of self-government are of any real value. For, after all, it is one thing to prove that cooperating in the play and spontaneous social life of children brings about certain moral effects, and another to establish the fact that this cooperation can be universally applied as a method of education. This last point is one which only experimental education can settle. Educational experiment, on condition that it can be scientifically controlled, is certainly more instructive for psychology than any amount of laboratory experiments, and because of this experimental pedagogy might perhaps be incorporated into the body of the psycho-sociological disciplines. But the type of experiment which such research would require can only be conducted by teachers or by the combined efforts of practical workers and educational psychologists. And it is not in our power to deduce the results to which this would lead.[5]

One of the more important aspects of constructivism as compared to positivism is the focus on using increasing levels of interpersonal understanding and functioning, an element that is, in most cases, entirely overlooked by behavior analytic interventions in ASD or, when addressed, reduced to only their observable and measurable elements such as initiation and responding. As such, one of the more striking differences between constructivist practices and behavior analytic practices is the act of coercion. To be clear, the word coercion is not intended to be connoted negatively in this context, but rather as a means of expressing motivation. That is, from constructivist approaches intrinsic motivation is utilized (as per Deci and Ryan) as opposed to extrinsic motivation, used almost exclusively in behavior analytic approaches. As such, the following two themes are central to constructivist approaches:[6]

1. Children construct knowledge in that the child's subjective experience must be the focus of all educational efforts because the child is construed as the active constructor of knowledge, personality, and morality.
2. Children are unable to attain autonomy intellectually or morally when authoritarian relations are fostered with adults. Children must learn to follow and respect rules out of personal obligation based on conviction and commitment, not because they are simply compliant to a set of rules superimposed on their morality.

Piaget explains it in this way:

> If [the child] is intellectually passive, he will not know how to be free ethically. Conversely, if his ethics consist exclusively in submission to adult authority, and if the only exchanges that make up the life of the class are those that bind each student individually to a master holding all power, he will not know how to be intellectually active.[7]

Equally as important to constructivist theory is Vygotsky, whose notion of the zone of proximal development (ZPD) is central to its tenets. ZPD is defined as:

> The distance between the actual developmental level as determined by independent problem solving and the level of potential development as determined through problem solving under adult guidance or in collaboration with more capable peers.[8]

The ZPD is directly related, then, to the development of the child's language, which is used far more than to just implement demands upon the environment from adults who have provisional capabilities (as in mands), but is to be seen as equally as important as the result of the speech itself. It is at this point where the role of language becomes not only goal-directed in terms of attaining desired objects or activities from gate-keeping adults (as mands do), but when children understand that language can be used for themselves in order to plan, connect, and understand their own experiences in terms of that language. As Vygotsky states:

> The greatest change in children's capacity to use language as a problem-solving tool takes place somewhat later in their development, when socialized speech (which has previously been used to address an adult) is turned inward. Instead of appealing to the adult, children appeal to themselves; language thus takes on an intrapersonal function in addition to its personal use.[9]

The tenets and framework of constructivist education now being understood, it is essential to determine how these approaches can be applied to best address a comprehensive model of educating individuals with ASD. This issue has been addressed regarding disability studies in general:

> Constructivism, and therefore constructivist pedagogy, is consistent with the aim of disability studies to confront the oppression and marginalization of people with disabilities, particularly with regard to their right to define who they are and their liberty to speak for themselves. [10]

As expressed further by Linton:

> Disability studies take for its subject matter not simply the variations that exist in human behavior, appearance, functioning, sensory acuity, and cognitive processing but, more crucially, the meaning we make of those variations. The field explores the critical divisions our society makes in creating the normal versus the pathological, the insider versus the outsider, or the competent citizen versus the ward of the state. [11]

The current problem in the preparation of teachers in ASD specifically is aptly described by Scheurmann and colleagues, as related in chapter 7:

> First, training teachers in only one approach to the treatment of children with ASD sends the false message that only one approach will work with all children with the disorder. Individuals with ASD are a heterogenous group, with such a wide variation in severity and types of symptoms that it is virtually impossible to conclude that one method will work with each and every individual with the disorder. Subsequently, training teachers in only one method not only limits their ability to be successful with all children with ASD but also falsely implies that the one approach in which they were trained will work with all children. This false belief that one has been trained in the one and only approach necessary to treat all children with ASD limits teachers' recognition of the individuality of each child with ASD. Teachers should base their teaching methods on what will best meet the needs of each individual child, not on whichever method of instruction they were trained to use. . . . Second, in order to choose the best method of instruction for each child, one must have been trained in more than one approach. Teachers who have limited training may continue with a program because it is the only one they know, despite the fact that the child or children with whom they are working are not benefiting from the methods. . . . In order to meet each child's needs, teachers need a number of approaches from which to choose and the training and confidence in each to be successful. [12]

Constructivist structures for teacher education programs are the most apt means by which the issues addressed by Scheuermann and colleagues as well as the numerous other issues identified in this treatise can be resolved. At its basis, modeling teacher education programs for ASD within a constructivist framework would reestablish such education as a part of the greater educational purview as opposed to a specialized service divorced from teacher education, necessitating clinicians functioning as teachers. From behaviorally based perspectives, teacher education programs work to reproduce clinical methodologies delivered within a classroom, creating a highly deliberate and entirely unnatural form of educating students with ASD, regardless of whether such programs are housed in public schools amongst neighboring general education classrooms or within separate specialized schools intended only for individuals with disabilities. By teacher education programs in ASD being structured upon constructivist methodologies, teacher preparation becomes far less prescriptive and clinical, allowing the teacher to not only explore various methodologies for educating individuals with ASD, but also learning to regard individuals with ASD as *students* needing *education*, as opposed to *patients* needing *therapy* and *rehabilitation*. As such, teachers learn to be comfortable with the notion that teaching, as an act, is a continually developing and reforming process facilitated by consistent restructuring within the context of the classroom, relegating it as a formative, rather than a prescriptive process. [13]

DEFINING AND EVALUATING COMPREHENSIVE EDUCATIONAL APPROACHES IN AUTISM SPECTRUM DISORDERS

Defining the Term "Comprehensive Educational Approach"

The term "comprehensive" has been used extensively in this treatise, but a deeper exploration of what this could mean practically is ever pressing. As such, the following represents what a comprehensive approach should include:

1. Multiple facets of the individual are addressed within the educational framework on a regular basis, including behavioral, socio-emotional, sensory, and linguistic.
2. No single approach is favored over another as a general rule, rather, the distribution of attention and approach is dictated by the individual receiving the educational services.
3. The focus of the educational services and its corresponding data collection and analysis is equally distributed between the process and the outcome, considering not only what skills are being enhanced or what the level of compliance is, but also how the individual appears to feel and engage with the curriculum.

4. The role of motivation is distributed between intrinsic and extrinsic as appropriate for the individual student, ensuring that compliance is not the only measure by which progress is gauged.

One potential difficulty of a comprehensive approach, and a challenge that is highlighted by antagonists to the idea, is how intangible aspects of an individual, such as emotion or intrinsic motivation, can be "taught" or "transmitted" into a teaching practice. By allowing room for such important though elusive components into a teaching program, an educational program can extend the gauging of progress or success beyond simply the exhibition of "changed behaviors" or observably "acquired skills" and into a program that values the emotional state of both the teacher and the student as additional indicators of success.

The first component involves the methodological protocols, which asks "what do you do?" With any educational approach, the methodological soundness of each approach, including the allowable level of "drift" or "modification" is essential. How these approaches are practiced will affect both the fidelity of implementation and the allowable margin for individualization. Striking a balance between remaining true to the findings and tenets of the theoretical frameworks as well as establishing an allowable margin within which individualized accommodations, adjustments, and accommodations can be made is imperative. The second is that of a teacher reflective component, which asks "how does the teacher feel while engaging in the educational interactions?" Because a comprehensive approach must account for both operational and intangible (or at least, less readily operational phenomena), the instinct, "gut feeling," an artistic intuition of any good teacher is an invaluable indication of whether or not a teaching approach has "gut validity." It must be made unmistakably clear that this component is in no way intended to be an overarching standard nor should it be considered evaluative in and of itself, but can be distinctly informative qualitatively. When teachers teach, it is imperative that the positive emotions they are feeling are transmitted through their interactions. Finally, there is the student dignity component which asks, "how does the student report or appear to feel while engaging or being engaged by the teacher?" Because many overly behavioral approaches that rely exclusively on extrinsic motivation gauges progress only by compliance with commands or demonstration of observable skills that are expected to be acquired without the consideration of how the individual may feel while engaging, or what is the level of understanding of "why" they are engaging (if possible). Because it is of utmost importance for teachers to centrally consider the effect that their teaching has on their students, paying close attention to their apparent emotional states is an essential means of gauging appropriateness and attention to dignity. For example, if compliance and engagement is maintained as the only measure of success or progress, clear indications of disconcert or outright agitation may be easily disregarded, creating a relatively common approach of "working through the behavior." That is, the agitation is of secondary importance to the compliance or demonstration of a target behavior. This is questionably ethical and dismissive of personal dignity.

Evaluating Comprehensive Approaches for Comprehensive Evidence Basis

Because the establishment of evaluative means of truly measuring progress for the whole person includes, but is not limited to outcomes-based data analysis, there is an equal need to establish a sensible and empirically based means of evaluating the effectiveness of comprehensive data-based approaches. This section will delineate a working set of criteria by which such programs should be evaluated, each of which will be explored in greater detail:

1. Multi-level evaluation including analysis at the overall model level, the variation level, and the individual component level.
2. Use of theoretical-based evidence, formative-based process evidence, and outcomes-based summative evaluation in the designing and implementation of approaches, as well as multi-disciplinary research from all related areas including, but not necessarily limited to, educational research, psychological research, neuroscience research, speech and language developmental research, and occupational and physical therapy research.
3. Individualized, student-driven instructional and interventional methodologies that seek to define methodologies based only on particular student needs, not allegiance to a paradigm or prescriptive learning theory.
4. Use of instruction-based data collection for each individual, rather than superimposition of externally "validated" models upon the methodologies within the classroom that utilizes well-structured means of both quantitative and qualitative data collection and analysis methodology, seeking to account for both opeartionalized and non-operationalized phenomena.
5. Avoidance of use of methodological titles (such as ABA, SIT, etc.), but rather describing and conceptualizing individual approaches in terms of need and component-based descriptions (e.g., auditory integration focused methodology, Theory of Mind focused methodology, overt behavior based methodology, etc.).
6. Use of evaluators that are qualified in terms of training and experience in multiple approaches of methodology, multiple means of evaluation,

non-dominating allegiance to a paradigm, and familiarity with legitimate multi-disciplinary research.

7. A full description of all philosophies, theories, and methodologies applied in the program from well-structured standpoints that are sensitive to evolution, reformation, and revision.

Multi-level evaluation including analysis at the overall model level, the variation level, and the individual component level.

In order to ensure that methodologies are being validated from practice-based and non-allegiant perspectives as well as from data collected and analyzed directly from the individuals who are receiving such approaches, multiple levels of evaluation are necessitated. Because it is meaningful for some comprehensive programs to establish a model-based definition, those that do must maintain a body of model-based research in order to legitimize the conceptualization of that approach, whatever it may be. This level of evaluation allows the program to retain its theoretical-based validity, contributing to the veracity of its overall educational and interventional philosophy. Analysis at the variation level includes exceptions and reorganizations of the overall theory for particular types of individuals in whatever manner the program determines typology, if it does, or any other means of organizing or characterizing variations in approach. In order for such variations to remain legitimate theoretically, this level of analysis is imperative. Finally, at the individual component level, the exact methodologies used with the individual students themselves are analyzed in terms of individual progress as well as comparative progress on well-founded means, if necessary or appropriate. Individually based analysis is important in order to maintain the practice-based legitimacy of model-level or variation-level theories. That is, if the theory which guides the practice is demonstrated to be effective as evidence by comprehensive qualitative and quantitative evidence, this lends veracity to the soundness of the theory, an essential characteristic of true evidence-basis. If models are based on multiple components addressing multiple aspects of the individual, component analysis can lend both specific evidence for each isolated component as well as the comprehensive model overall. This allows for a sophisticated and sound methodology of analysis.

Use of theoretical-based evidence, formative-based process evidence, and outcomes-based summative evaluation in the designing and implementation of approaches, as well as multi-disciplinary research from all related areas including, but not necessarily limited to, educational research, psychological research, neuroscience research, speech and language developmental research, and occupational and physical therapy research.

Because comprehensive methodologies use approaches that are not necessarily sensitive to only outcomes-based data collection systems but are verifiable by more sophisticated types of qualitative data analysis, a variety of data collection methodologies are required. As stated above, a multiple-level means of evaluation can serve to validate the methodologies from the theoretical level to the practice level, advancing the robustness of the methodology. In order to attain such robust veracity, however, a variety of data-collection and analysis methods are necessitated as each can address particular research questions and variables more precisely and accurately than others. Therefore, well-grounded methodologies from qualitative perspectives can lend credence to the overall theory of the approach, mixed methodological formative-based evaluation systems can vet the particular instructional processes, and quantitative-based outcomes research can verify individual acquisition of skills and behaviors at individual levels. Furthermore, since ASD is a complex and multi-factorial condition, progress in multi-disciplinary areas of research is absolutely imperative for comprehensive approaches. By limiting only particular fields or particular methodologies of research to inform both practice and theory, a limited and incomplete body of evidence is applied leaving the analysis of the approach resultantly incomplete. The issues that affect individuals with ASD have been investigated using various means from a multitude of perspectives, each of which is contributive to the comprehensive understanding of not only the condition itself, but the experience that each individual identified as having the condition undergoes. The ability for a program to be legitimized from multiple perspectives and by multiple theories only lends global credence to that approach both theoretically and practically well-established.

Individualized, student-driven instructional and interventional methodologies that seek to define methodologies based only on particular student needs, not allegiance to a paradigm or prescriptive learning theory.

Because comprehensive approaches are particularly wary of paradigmatic allegiances, a commitment of the comprehensive model must include dedication not to prescriptive or titular approaches, but rather to the individual needs of each student and the root issue associated with each aspect of the methodology. That is, if a student's classroom experience indicates a type of approach that may use practices and theories from an unfamiliar or previously unused area, the need of the student and the potential effectiveness of the approach supersedes the prescriptive or theoretical misgivings stemming from a paradigmatic belief (for example, behavior analytic approaches tend to be generally dismissive of sensory integrative approaches due to their incompatibility with its theory and perceived "empirical ineffectiveness"). Therefore, practitioners of a comprehensive approach must be willing to implement strategies from theoretical perspectives that may challenge, if not even entirely contradict their own, based on the notion that children are different and, therefore, need different methodological approaches. Because comprehensive approaches, if implemented correctly, continuously undergo comprehensive validation, the evaluation process will reveal whether or not such approaches are, indeed, effective and will, *ipso facto* inform the veracity of the overall theory. By this means, it is the evidence that determines the value of including the approach, not individual ideologies or philosophies which may be biased.

Use of instruction-based data collection for each individual, rather than superimposition of externally "validated" models upon the methodologies within the classroom that utilizes well-structured means of both quantitative and qualitative data collection and analysis methodology, seeking to account for both operationalized and non-operationalized phenomena.

Because there appears to be a tendency of programs that claim "evidence-basis" of their approaches based on external validations (that is, since ABA is shown to be evidence-based then any program that implements ABA is, by default, evidence-based), it is imperative that individual programs maintain their own body of data based on their own institutional findings as well as research conducted in the greater field in order to inform their practice. It is sensible to use externally validated approaches as a justification for trying such approaches within the model, however, it is incumbent on the approach to self-validate the approach based on their own consumers rather than resting on the laurels of supposed established "evidence-basis." This is achieved by implementing well-structured and grounded data collection and analysis from both quantitative and qualitative methodologies. Since the vast literature on both forms of data analysis methodology, when interpreting it from a non-biased perspective, is clear that neither can be seen as superior to the other but rather can answer different types of questions in different ways, it is important that both methods are used. The legitimacy of the data collection and analysis methodology depends less in its categorization as quantitative or qualitative and more on its ability to maintain a well-structured, well-grounded, and systematically implemented means of data collection and analysis. While quantitative data collection and analysis is more useful when analyzing operationalized variables that can be well-defined as discretely measured as observable responses, qualitative data collection and analysis is more applicable to capture less operational phenomena that are reliant on careful and detailed description in order to be understood and interpreted. Because comprehensive approaches value the legitimacy of both observable and unobservable (or less observable) phenomena, the utility of both approaches is central to its grounding in evidence-basis.

Avoidance of use of methodological titles (such as ABA, SIT, etc.), but rather describing and conceptualizing individual approaches in terms of need and component based-descriptions (e.g., auditory integration focused methodology, Theory of Mind focused methodology, overt behavior based methodology, etc.).

Because comprehensive educational approaches place far more value on *what* an approach *targets* and from *what* an approach is *built on* as opposed to *what* an approach is *called*, there must be a general wariness of using titular labels to define components (or totalities) of an approach. Labels are often deeply rooted in paradigmatic allegiances which, as has been claimed, can be distinctly detrimental to ethical practices in education. As such, labels, by their very nature, seek to delineate clear inclusive and exclusive components (e.g., Applied Behavior Analysis warrants the necessity of something to be considered a "behavior," which in turn necessitates that behavior to be observable and measurable). This creates a focus on methodological definition rather than individual need. Therefore, because emotional regulation is not easily observed or measured, it would not qualify for inclusion in an ABA methodology based simply on its theoretical groundings. However, it is vastly clear that ASD is a complex and multi-component condition that undoubtedly requires attention to many different variables. In order to preserve the allegiance to the individual *need* rather than the theoretical *device*, specific references to components and needs are used. For example, if an individual with ASD is engaging in hand-flapping, the approach will not simply look to reduce and/or replace the behavior from an acquisition standpoint, which is preferable from a behavior analytic perspective due to its clear operationalization, but rather look to address not only the function of the *behavior*, but rather the sensorial, physiological, or neurological composition of the individual that necessitates it regardless of its observability or measurability. It is important to note that this limitation in using methodological titles applies to all such titles regardless of whether its underlying philosophy is, indeed, recognized and addressed in the comprehensive educational approach.

Use of evaluators that are qualified in terms of training and experience in multiple approaches of methodology, multiple means of evaluation, non-dominating allegiance to a paradigm, and familiarity with legitimate multi-disciplinary research.

Apropos of the above description detailing the risks of paradigmatic allegiances and titular indications, it is necessary for true comprehensive educational approaches to utilize both practitioners and evaluators that are both qualified and experienced in multiple areas of methodology as well as multiple areas of evaluation (e.g., both quantitative and qualitative analysis) remaining allegiant only to the effectiveness of practice for each student, not any particular paradigm or methodology. Furthermore, familiarity, if not, preferably, expertise in multi-disciplinary approaches to ASD research will allow the evaluator to not only remain unbiased, but also current in progress across the broader contributive field. By these means, the legitimacy of the theory and practice of the specific comprehensive approach as applied to the individual student is perpetuated. Therefore, the continuation of the model as a whole or any individual components of the model are not determined based on tangentially related, if not entirely unrelated research or, worse, maintenance of a body of invalid or outdated beliefs, but rather on robust and unbiased direct evaluation and research.

A full description of all philosophies, theories, and methodologies applied in the program from well-structured standpoints that are sensitive to evolution, reformation, and revision.

Because theoretical and philosophical basis and the openness and sensitivity to multi-disciplinary research advancement is essential in the legitimacy of a comprehensive-based educational approach, it is necessary for all comprehensive educational approaches to devise and actively evaluate a manifesto with full descriptions of all philosophies, theories, and methodologies that are applied in the approach. Stagnation of research and insistence on maintaining claims of old and un-replicated bodies of research is an immediate disqualifier for evidence-basis. Furthermore, because there is a vastly heterogenous makeup of individuals with ASD, any approach that seeks to develop a theoretical basis must be, by nature, evolutionary and sensitive to almost constant change and revision. With advances in vast areas across the field being reported regularly, approaches that are to remain relevant and effective must, without fail, actively seek to incorporate these findings while maintaining their own means of data collection and analysis. As such, combining information from widely based research with localized findings can only be facilitated through a dedication to not only apply, but embrace rapidly changing information from a multiplicity of perspectives. By engaging constructively with such changes, approaches can ensure that both their theoretical and practical bases remain current, well-informed, and effective.

A SKETCH OF COMPONENTS FOR A COMPREHENSIVE EDUCATIONAL PROGRAM FOR INDIVIDUALS WITH ASD

Because this work aims primarily to set up a philosophical and theoretical framework legitimizing efforts toward establishing a comprehensive educational approach for individuals with ASD, it extends the scope to proffer a full indication as to what such a classroom would look like for multiple reasons, the most significant being that such an approach is not intended to be a "model," but rather an ad hoc but ever evaluative and reflective process that is individualized to the needs of particular students, varying even within single classrooms. However, in order to provide a sense of how such a program may take shape, a "sketch" will be offered in an attempt to do just that.

As aforementioned, a comprehensive approach for individuals with ASD must be based within a constructivist framework in which multiple interpretations of social and educational situations and interactions can be applied. That is, there is no correct way to interpret and address a given situation, but multiple ways that can lead to a variety of outcomes allowing for various approaches to be applied in any number of permutations. In order to allow this sketch to play out, the example of a somewhat common physical behavior amongst individuals with ASD will be used: hand flapping. For the purpose of satisfying a more stringent approach (likely that of behaviorism), the behavior of hand flapping will be operationally defined as the slow or fast-paced motion of waving hands either in front of one's face or next to one's ears, at times accompanied by bouncing with both feet and/or concurrent vocalizations of either real words or non-word sounds.

Maintaining this example, it is important to surmise how each individual approach may be apt to interpret such a behavioral occurrence (that is, how the behavior itself is interpreted), leading to a potential difference in how this occurrence is likely to be addressed. From a *behavioral perspective*, a functional behavior assessment would be necessitated, allowing the analyst a means to determine the "reason" that the behavior is occurring. That is, what purpose does engagement in the behavior serve (an attempt to access a tangible, an attempt to escape or avoid a demand, an attempt to gain social attention, a means of self-stimulatory or automatic reinforcement, or, in rarer and less workable situations, a medical function that is explained by some extraneous biological factor)? Once this is determined, the behavior analyst may determine a means by which the inappropriate behavior (hand flapping) can be reduced and replaced by a behavior deemed more appropriate by serving the same function, or providing access to the same functional reinforcer. Ultimately, the behavior will be changed or at least modified based on the availability and accessibility of external reinforcers or, in some cases, punished also by external punishing stimuli. From a *sensory integrative perspective*, the activity of hand flapping likely indicates some sort of sensory imbalance or over/under-stimulation: that is, there is an aspect (or multiple aspects) of the environment that causes over/under-stimulation as a result of difficulty or inability to process and integrate the stimuli. Because this can hyper-activate or hypo-activate neurological responding, excitatory behaviors are likely to result (such as hand flapping). The *socio-emotional perspective* would likely regard the behavioral occurrence of hand-flapping similarly to that of the sensory integrative, but place the root of the behavioral outplay on an imbalance of emotional reactions or responses leading to an "emotional overload," thus resulting in the excitatory behavior. The *linguistic perspective* is more protean to capture as it can be easily adapted to any and all of the above stated approaches as a means of regulating the behavior from whichever perspective. That is, if use of language can assist in accessing the functional reinforcer, it can be applied to the behavioral perspective; if use of language can be used to communicate what aspect or element of the environment is likely to cause the sensory imbalance, then it can be applied to the sensory perspective, as is similar to the socio-emotional perspective if the language leads to the ability to communicate emotional situations and reactions leading either to individual changes or changes in others' responses or behavior.

Determining differences in the interpretation of the behavioral occurrence itself, however, is not a complete indication of the role and benefit of comprehensive educational approaches for individuals with ASD. However, the difference in the response and addressing of the behavioral outplay (and the underlying reasons or causes for such outplay) is equally as important. It is essential to note, however, that the frameworks within which each approach *may* address the behavioral outplay and a corresponding example will be provided, though these suggestions and accompanying examples are not intended, by any means, to be seen as the only potential interpretation or methodological or instructional practice available. Since, from a *behavioral perspective* the behavior is likely to be regarded as being displayed as a result of a behavioral function, once the function is determined the behavior analyst will design an intervention plan that both decreases the "inappropriate behavior" (hand flapping) while increasing an "appropriate behavior" as a replacement (to be determined by the behavior analyst). When the "appropriate" behavior is displayed it will be followed by the availability of some sort of reinforcement (primary or secondary), thus increasing the probability that the "appropriate" behavior will occur as opposed to the "inappropriate behavior," which does not lead to the access of a reinforcer and may lead to a punishment (if the contingency plan provides for such a measure). Therefore, from this perspective, the level of analysis centers on the "function" that the behavior serves (based on the FBA), and applying the use of environmental consequences to decrease one behavior while increasing another. The interpretation of the behavioral occurrence from a *sensory perspective* is likely to lead to a different approach; however, it may be one that is not as isolated in terms of addressing a specific behavior, but rather addressing the sensory environment as a whole. Since the sensory integrative perspective is likely to target the sensory stimuli in the environment as playing the main role in such behavior, the environment as a whole is likely to be addressed rather than the single behavior or individual reaction to some stimuli in the environment. This can be facilitated in a variety of ways. To proffer only two of them, the sensory stimuli in the environment can be changed (reduced or enriched) to provide the sensory input needed (for example, if the individual may become over-stimulated or under-stimulated by stillness, a fan may be set up next to the individual to provide spatial stimulation). Second, sensory integrative exercises or stimuli may be included or incorporated into the individual's curriculum to ensure that a consistent provision of sensory stimulation is provided (for an example of stimuli, the individual may sit on an inflatable and textured seat cushion providing both proprioceptive and tactile input while engaging in academic tasks; for an example of exercises, an individual may engage in a "sensory obstacle course" intermittently and non-contingently such as finding only "red maracas" throughout the room, shaking them each for twenty seconds at three or four different stations along with music coming through headphones before returning to work). Finally, from a *socio-emotional perspective* the individual is seen as engaging in the behavioral occurrence as a result of some sort of emotional imbalances. Because addressing emotional imbalances can be particularly difficult amongst individuals with an inability or difficulty in expressing emotions linguistically (or any other way than behaviorally), an approach may be to simply engage in the behavior along with the individual to provide a sense of understanding, compassion, and permissibility to express whatever intends to be expressed by the behavior. While this may not result in a reduction of the behavior (at least immediately), it does provide for an environment and a kinship with another individual in which the person with ASD is not sent the message that what they are doing is "inappropriate" or, worse, "wrong," but that it is both understood and permitted in the environment.

All of these approaches are indicative of potential effectiveness as well as potential challenges. None of them, alone, is indicative of an entirely holistic and satisfactorily complete means of addressing the complex needs of individuals with ASD. As such, using them in combination with one another, to be differed and adapted between individuals and changed within individuals as often or as seldom as necessary is the most appropriate, ethical, and likely effective way to address the vast and multi-faceted needs of individuals with ASD. As aforementioned, since all of these approaches can be monitored using various forms of data collection and analysis (some more quantitative and outcomes-based, some more qualitative and process-based), a far more complete understanding of all aspects of the educational process can be interpreted and analyzed yielding a far more complete understanding of the dynamic interactions involved in teaching individuals with ASD.

SOME CAUTIONS IN IMPLEMENTING A COMPREHENSIVE EDUCATIONAL PROGRAM FOR INDIVIDUALS WITH ASD

As is the case with any new idea or any change in a framework, especially those intended to be an application for human beings, there are a number of cautions that must be considered before and during such approaches are being practiced. Comprehensive approaches are not just equally as vulnerable, but likely more vulnerable as the structure of such approaches can be easily misused or ill-suited, if approached haphazardly, to account for such dangers. First and foremost is to maintain the establishment of the true definition of a comprehensive approach. That is, a comprehensive approach is not a means by which any methodology, sensible or not, can be applied and accepted. While more opportunity for less "quantitatively accepted" methodologies exists within comprehensive approaches in order to provide a fair and viable grounds upon which less traditional approaches can be applied, observed, and analyzed, this does not mean that quixotic or "magic pill" approaches are welcome. No approaches within a comprehensive program are to be seen as supreme, and any approaches that straddle ethical boundaries by making false promises, creating false hope of recovery, or any other similar component of the many examples of quackery that exists within the field will be entertained. Ensuring that each approach incorporated into a comprehensive program is accurately and systematically monitored using some form of legitimate data collection and analysis system will prevent such practices from becoming a part of a true comprehensive program. Similarly, comprehensive programs are often in danger of becoming overly complex and, therefore, less applicable in a classroom setting. Because comprehensiveness calls for total individualization, such classrooms may be harder to set up and maintain without the proper organization. Therefore, the necessary amount of organization, supervision, and administration must be built into the very program in order to maintain its integrity.

A second potential concern lies in the area of vastly different theoretical and philosophical frameworks being applied in a single program. This can be dangerous from any avenue, whether the fundamentalist is from the behavioral, sensory integrative, or socio-emotional paradigm. Any single paradigmatic approach is a cantankerous element to a truly comprehensive program. Therefore, there must be an understanding that only participants who are not paradigmatic or fundamentalist are included in the application or, if individuals who are paradigmatic are included they are required to bracket their fundamentalism in the program design process as well as application. This can be particularly hard, so careful considerations and provisions must be built directly into the infrastructure to detect, account for, and address such an occurrence.

Third and potentially most hazardous is the danger of the tendency for an applied field to be "model-centric" and, thus, transform a framework (what a comprehensive program is intended to be) into a model (what applied settings often look for in terms of ease of practicability and administration). The reduction of a comprehensive program into a model-based approach would be terminal to its very integrity. From a total individualization perspective, models (at least strict models) cannot be applied or there enters a distinct risk of over-simplification and superimposition. As such, each program in whatever setting it functions must take care to build this idea into its manifesto, and determine, design, and implement an infrastructure that is capable of maintaining total individualization and prevent a "model mentality" from being incurred.

As such, to design and implement a comprehensive program is a complex undertaking enriched with potential benefits and rife with vulnerabilities. The only means by which a comprehensive program can truly be applied is through careful, systematic, and closely supervised and monitored planning and implementation. It cannot be a "train and hope" mentality as this type of application is doomed to failure. Rather, it must employ an active consistent practice of research, application, analysis, and revision from multiple perspectives. This is the only way by which the complex and multi-factorial needs of individuals with ASD can be addressed while still providing an environment in which they are able to maintain their dignity and not be seen as "pathological defects," rather as human beings with as much value as any other.

NOTES

1. Joe Kincheloe, "The Knowledges of Teacher Education: Developing a Critical Complex Epistemology," *Teacher Education Quarterly*, Winter 2004.

2. Ibid., 53.

3. Ibid., 56.

4. RhetaDeVries, "What is Constructivist about Constructivist Education?" Retrieved from http://www.uni.edu/coe/regentsctr/Publications/what%20is%20constructivist.pdf.

5. Piaget, 1932/1965, as cited by Devries, 2002, 406.

6. Rheta DeVries, "What Does Research on Constructivist Education Tell Us about Effecting Schooling?" Iowa Academy of Education Occasional Research Paper #5, June 2002.

7. Piaget, 1932/1965, as cited by Devries, 2002, 107.

8. Vygotsky, 1987, as cited by Chaiklin, 2003.

9. Vygotsky, 1978, as cited by Jones and Brader-Araje, 2002.

10. Deborah J. Gallagher, "The Importance of Constructivism and Constructivist Pedagogy." For Disability Studies in Education, *Disability Studies Quarterly*, Spring 2004, 24, 2, retrieved from http://dsq-sds.org/article/view/489/666.

11. Linton, 1998, as cited by Gallagher, 2004.

12. Schuermann et al., 2003, 200.

13. Sam Hausfathe, "Where's the Content? The Role of Content in Constructivist Teacher Education." *Educational Horizons*, 2001, 15–19.

Bibliography

Alberto, Paul, and Anne C. Troutmann. *Applied Behavior Analysis for Teachers*. Upper Saddle River, NJ: Pearson.

Bachevalier, Jocelyne, and Katherine A. Loveland. "The Orbitofrontal-amygdala Circuit and Self-Regulation of Social Emotional Behavior in Autism." *Neuroscience and Biobehavioral Reviews*, 2006: 30, 97–117.

Baron-Cohen, Simon. *Mindblindness*. New York: Bradford, 1997.

Baron-Cohen, Simon, Alan M. Leslie, and Uta Frith. "Does the Autistic Child Have a 'Theory of Mind'" *Cognition*, 1985: 21, 37–46.

Baron-Cohen et al. "The Amygdala Theory of Autism." *Neuroscience and Biobehavioral Reviews*, 2000: 24, 355–64.

Behrmann, Marlene, Thomas Cibu, and Kate Humphreys. "Seeing It Differently: Visual Processing in Autism." *TRENDS in Cognitive Sciences*, 2006: 10, 258–64.

Belmonte, Matthew K. et al. "Autism and Abnormal Development of Brain Connectivity." *Journal of Neuroscience*, 2004: 24, 9228–31.

Bertone, Armando et al. "Motion Perception in Autism: A 'Complex' Issue." *Journal of Cognitive Neuroscience*, 2003: 15, 218–25.

Brantlinger, Eileen et al. "Qualitative Studies in Special Education." *Exceptional Children*, 2005: 71, 195–207.

Breland, Keller, and Marian Breland. "The Misbehavior of Organisms." *American Psychologist*, 1961: 16, 681–84.

Broderick, Alicia A. "Autism as Rhetoric: Exploring Watershed Rhetorical Moments in Applied Behavior Analysis Discourse." *Disability Studies Quarterly*, 2011: 31.

———. "Autism, 'Recovery (to Normalcy),' and the Politics of Hope." *Intellectual and Developmental Disabilities*, 2009: 47: 263–81.

Brownell, Mary T. "Critical Features of Special Education Teacher Preparation: A Comparison with General Education Teacher Education." *Journal of Special Education*, 2005: 38, 242–52.

Buckley, Kerry W. *Mechanical Man: John Broadus Watson*. New York: Guilford Press, 1989.

Carr, James E., and Amanda M. Firth. "The Verbal Behavior Approach to Early Intensive Behavior Intervention for Autism: A Call for Empirical Support." *Journal of Early Intensive Behavioral Intervention*, 2005: 2, 18–27.

Case-Smith, Jane, and Marian Arbesman. "Evidence Based Review of Interventions for Autism Used In or of Relevance to Occupational Therapy. *American Journal of Occupational Therapy*, 2008: 62, 416–29.

Chung, Man Cheung, and Michael E. Hyland. *History and Philosophy of Psychology*. Oxford, UK: Wiley-Blackwell, 2012.

Courschesne, Eric. "Mapping Early Brain Development in Autism." *Neuron*, 2007: 399–413.

Curren, Randall R. *Aristotle on the Necessity of Public Education*, Lanham, MD: Rowman & Littlefield, 2000.

Dawson, Geraldine. "Early Social Attention Impairments in Autism: Social Orienting, Joint Attention, and Attention to Distress." *Developmental Psychology*, 2004: 40, 271–83.

Dawson, Geraldine et al. "Neurophysiological Correlates of Early Symptoms of Autism." *Child Development*, 1998: 69, 1276–85.

Deci, Edward L., and Richard M. Ryan. "Self-Determination Theory: A Macrotheory of Human Motivation, Development and Health." *Canadian Psychology*, 2008: 49, 182–85.

Deci, Edward L. et al. "A Meta-Analytic Review of Experiments Examining the Effects of Extrinsic Rewards on Intrinsic Motivation." *Psychological Bulletin*, 1999: 125, 627–68.

DeProspero, Anthony, and Stanley Cohen. "Inconsistent Visual Analysis of Intrasubject Data." *Journal of Applied Behavior Analysis*, 1979: 12, 573–79.

Dillonburger, Karola. "The Emperor's New Clothes: Eclecticism in Autism Treatment." *Research in Autism Spectrum Disorders*, 2011: 5, 1119–28.

Drake, Robert E. et al. "Implementing Evidence-Based Practices in Routine Mental Health Service Settings." *Psychiatric Services*, 2001: 52, 179–82.

Duit, Reinders, and David F. Treagust. "Learning in Science: From Behaviourism Towards Social Constructivism and Beyond." In *International Handbook of Science Education*, B.J. Fraser and K.G. Tobin (Eds.). New York: Kluwer American Publishers, 1998, 3–25.

Fairbanks, Sarah et al. "Response to Intervention: Examining Classroom Behavior Support in Second Grade." *Exceptional Children*, 2007: 73, 288–310.

Ferster, C.B. "Positive Reinforcement and Behavioral Deficits of Autistic Children." *Child Development*, 1961: 32, 437–56.

Ferster, C.B., and M.K. DeMeyer. "The Development of Performances in Autistic Children in an Automatically Controlled Environment. *Journal of Chronic Diseases*, 1961: 31, 312–45.

Feuer, M.J. et al. (2002). "Scientific Culture and Educational Research." *Educational Researcher*, 2002: 31, 4–14.

Fitch, Frank. "Laggards, Labeling, and Limitations: Reconnecting Labeling Deviance Theory with Deweyan Pragmatism." *Ohio Valley Philosophy of Education Society*, 2010.

Fletcher, P.C. et al. "Other Minds in the Brain: A Functional Imaging Study of 'Theory of Mind' in Story Comprehension." *Cognition,* 1995: 57, 109–28.

Foxx, Richard M. "Applied Behavior Analysis Treatment of Autism: The State of the Art." *Child and Adolescent Psychiatric Clinics of North America*, 2008: 17, 821–34.

Frith, Uta, and Francesca Happe. "Autism: Beyond 'Theory of Mind.'" *Cognition*, 1994: 50, 115–32.

Gallese, Vittorio, and Alvin Goldman. "Mirror Neurons and the Simulation Theory of Mind Reading." *Trends in Cognitive Sciences*, 1998: 12, 493–501.

Gardner, Howard. *The Mind's New Science: A History of the Cognitive Revolution.* New York: Basic Books, 1987.

Geschwind, Daniel H., and Pat Levitt. "Autism Spectrum Disorders: Developmental Disconnection Syndromes." *Current Opinion in Neurobiology*, 2007: 17, 103–11.

Gilgun, J.F. "The Four Cornerstones of Evidence-Based Practice In Social Work." *Research on Social Work Practice*, 2005: 15, 52–61.

Greenspan, Stanley J., and Serena Wieder. "A Functional Developmental Approach to Autistic Spectrum Disorders." *JASH*, 1999: 24, 147–61.

Gresham, Frank M. "Evolution of the Treatment Integrity Concept: Current Status and Future Directions." *School Psychology Review*, 2009: 38, 533–40.

Griffer, Mona. "Is Sensory Integration Effective for Children with Language-Learning Disorders?: A Critical Review of the Evidence." *Language, Speech, and Hearing Services in Schools*, 1999: 30, 393–400.

Guba, Egon. *The Paradigm Dialog.* Thousand Oaks, CA: Sage, 1990.

Haack, Susan. *Defending Science—Within Reason: Between Scientism and Cynicism.* Amherst, NY: Prometheus Books, 2003.

Happe, Francesca G.E. "Studying Weak Central Coherence at Low Levels: Children with Autism Do Not Succumb to Visual Illusions: A Research Note." *Journal of Child Psychology and Psychiatry*, 1996: 7, 873–77.

Happe, Francesca G.E., and Uta Frith. "The Weak Coherence Account: Detail-focused Cognitive Style in Autism Spectrum Disorders." *Journal of Autism and Developmental Disorders*, 2006: 36, 5–25.

Hausfathe, Sam. "Where's the Content? The Role of Content in Constructivist Teacher Education." *Educational Horizons*, 2001: 15–19.

Hayes, Steven C., Arnold Rincover, and Jay V. Solnick. "The Technical Drift of Applied Behavior Analysis." *Journal of Applied Behavior Analysis*, 1980: 13, 275–85.

Heerey, Erin A., Dacher Keltner, and Lisa M. Capps. "Making Sense of Self-Conscious Emotion: Linking Theory of Mind and Emotion in Children with Autism." *Emotion*, 2003: 3, 394–400.

Heikler, Paul. "Autism, Rhetoric, and Whiteness." *Disability Studies Quarterly*, 2012: 32.

Herbert, James D., Ian R. Sharp, and Brandon A. Gaudiano. "Separating Fact From Fiction in the Etiology and Treatment of Autism: A Scientific Review of the Evidence." *Scientific Review of Mental Health Practice*, 2002.

Hergenhahn, B.R. *An Introduction to the History of Psychology.* Belmont, CA: Wadsworth, 2009.

Hill, Elisabeth. "Executive Dysfunction in Autism." *TRENDS in Cognitive Sciences*, 2004: 8, 26–32.

Hockenbury, Don H., and Sandra E. Hockenbury. *Psychology.* New York: Worth Publishers, 2008.

Hoehn, Theodore P., and Alfred A. Baumeister. "A Critique of the Application of Sensory Integration Therapy to Children with Learning Disabilities." *Journal of Learning Disabilities*, 1994: 30, 383–92.

Holburn, Steven. "A Renaissance in Residential Behavior Analysis? A Historical Perspective and a Better Way to Help People with Challenging Behavior." *Behavior Analyst*, 1997: 20, 61–85.

Homme, L.E. et al. "Use of the Premack Principle in Controlling the Behavior of Nursery School Children." *Journal of the Experimental Analysis of Behavior*, 1963: 6, 544.

Howard, Jane et al. "A Comparison of Intensive Behavior Analytic and Eclectic Treatments for Young Children with Autism." *Research in Developmental Disabilities*, 2005: 26, 359–83.

Hummel, Lauren J., and Barry M. Prizant. "A Socioemotional Perspective for Understanding Social Difficulties of School-age Children with Language Disorders." *Language, Speech, and Hearing Services in Schools*, 1993: 24, 216–24.

Jack, Jordynn. "'The Extreme Male Brain' Incrementum and the Rhetorical Gendering of Autism." *Disability Studies Quarterly*, 2011: 31.

Jacobson, John W., James A. Mulick, and Gina Green. "Cost-benefit Estimates for Early Intensive Behavioral Intervention for Young Children with Autism—General Model and Single State Case." *Behavioral Interventions,* 1998: 13, 201–26.

Jahoda, Gustav. *A History of Social Psychology: From the Eighteenth-Century Enlightenment to the Second World War.* Cambridge, UK: Cambridge University Press, 2007.

Jones, M. Gail, and Laura Brader-Araje. "The Impact of Constructivism on Education: Language, Discourse, and Meaning." *American Communication Journal*, 2002: 5.

Joseph, Robert M., and Helen Tager Flusberg. "The Relationship of Theory of Mind and Executive Functions to Symptom Type and Severity in Children with Autism." *Developmental Psychopathology*, 2004: 16, 137–55.

Kasari, Connie et al. "Affective Sharing in the Context of Joint Attention Interactions of Normal, Autistic, and Mentally Retarded Children." *Journal of Autism and Developmental Disorders*, 1990: 20, 87–100.

Kazdin, A. "Mediators and Mechanisms of Change in Psychotherapy Research." *Annual Review of Clinical Psychology*, 2005: 3, 1–27.

Kincheloe, Joe. "The Knowledges of Teacher Education: Developing a Critical Complex Epistemology." *Teacher Education Quarterly*, 2004: 31, 49–66.

Korthagen, Fred A.J. "In Search of the Essence of a Good Teacher: Towards a More Holistic Approach in Teacher Education." *Teaching and Teacher Education*, 2004: 20, 77–97.

Linan Thompson, Sylvia. "The Response to Intervention of English Language Learners at Risk for Reading Problems." *Journal of Learning Disabilities*, 2006: 39, 390–98.

Lovaas, O. Ivar. "Behavioral Treatment and Normal Educational and Intellectual Functioning in Young Autistic Children." *Journal of Consulting and Clinical Psychology*, 1987: 35, 3–9.

Lovaas, O. Ivar et al. "Some Generalization and Follow-Up Measures on Autistic Children in Behavior Therapy." *Journal of Applied Behavior Analysis*, 1973: 63, 131–66.

Maestro, Sandra et al. "Attentional Skills During the First 6 Months of Age in Autism Spectrum Disorder." *Journal of the American Academy of Child and Adolescent Psychiatry*, 2002: 41, 1239–45.

Maloney, Gerald, and Frida Perales. "Using Relationship-Focused Intervention to Enhance the Social-Emotional Functioning of Young Children with Autism Spectrum Disorders." *Topics in Early Childhood Education*, 2003: 23, 77–89.

Marco, Elysa Jill. "Sensory Processing in Autism: A Review of Neurophysiologic Findings." *Pediatric Research*, 2011: 69, 48–54.

Martin, Gary, and Joseph Paer. *Behavior Modification: What It Is and How to Do It.* Upper Saddle River, NJ: Prentice Hall, 1996.

Mastrangelo, Sonia. "Play and the Child with Autism: From Possibilities to Practice." *International Journal of Play Therapy*, 2009: 18, 13–30.

Mauer, Daria M. "Issues and Applications of Sensory Integration Theory and Treatment with Children with Language Disorders." *Language, Speech, and Hearing Services in Schools*, 1999: 30, 383–92.

Maurice, Catherine, Stephen C. Luce, and Gina Green. *Behavioral Intervention for Young Children with Autism.* Austin, TX: Pro-Ed, 1996.

Mills, John A. *Control: A History of Behavioral Psychology.* New York: NYU Press, 1998.

Modgil, Sohan, and Celia Modgil. *B.F. Skinner: Consensus and Controversy,* Philadelphia, PA: Falmer Press, 1987.

Moore, Jay. "On Mentalism, Methodological Behaviorism, and Radical Behaviorism." *Behaviorism,* 1981: 9, 55–77.

Morris, Edward K. "The History of Behavior Analysis: Some Historiography and a Bibliography." *Behavior Analyst,* 1990: 13(2), 131–58.

Mundy, Peter, Marian Sigman, and Connie Kasari. "A Longitudinal Study of Joint Attention and Language Development in Autistic Children." *Journal of Autism and Developmental Disorders,* 1990: 20, 115–28.

Murray, Stuart. "Autism Functions/The Function of Autism." *Disability Studies Quarterly,* 2010: 30.

Nadesen, Majia. *Constructing Autism: Unraveling the Truth and Understanding the Social.* New York: Routledge, 2008.

Nedelcu, Cristina-Maria. "Play Therapy and Autism." *ARPCAPA,* 2010: 4, 52–57.

Nelson, Catherine, and Dixie Snow Huefner. "Young Children with Autism: Judicial Responses to the Lovaas and Discrete Trial Training Debates." *Journal of Early Intervention,* 2003: 26, 1–19.

Nicolson, Rob, and Peter Szatmari. "Genetic and Neurodevelopmental Influences in Autistic Disorder." *Canadian Journal of Psychiatry,* 2003: 48, 526–37.

Nyikos, Martha, and Reiko Hashimoto. "The Constructivist Theory Applied to Collaborative Learning in Teacher Education: In Search of ZPD." *Modern Language Journal,* 1997: 81, 506–17.

Odom, Samuel L. et al. "Evaluation of Comprehensive Treatment Models for Individuals with Autism Spectrum Disorders." *Journal of Autism and Developmental Disorders,* 2010: 40, 425–36.

———. "Evidence-Based Practices for Young Children with Autism: Contributions for Single-Subject Design Research." *Focus on Autism and Other Developmental Disorders,* 2003: 18, 166–75.

———. "Research in Special Education: Scientific Methods and Evidence-Based Practices." *Exceptional Children,* 2005: 2, 137–49.

O'Donohue, William T., and Kyle E. Ferguson. *Handbook of Behaviorism*, William O'Donohue and Richard Kitchener (Eds.). Thousand Oaks, CA: Sage, 2001.

Ozonoff, Sally, Bruce F. Pennington, and Sally J. Rogers. "Executive Function Deficits in High Functioning Autistic Individuals: Relationship to Theory of Mind." *Journal of Child Psychology and Psychiatry*, 1991: 32, 1081–1105.

Podsakoff, Philip M. et al. "Common Method Biases in Behavioral Research: A Critical Review of the Literature and Recommended Remedies." *Journal of Applied Psychology*, 2003: 88, 879–903.

Prizant, B. M, Wetherby, A. M., Rubin, E., Laurent, A. C., and Rydell, P. J. (2006). *The SCERTS Model: A Comprehensive Educational Approach for Children with Autism Spectrum Disorders* (Volume 1–Assessment; Volume 2–Educational Program Planning and Implementation), MD: Paul Brookes Publishers.

Prizant, Barry. "Is ABA the Only Way." *Autism Spectrum Quarterly*, 2009.

Prizant, Barry M. et al. "The SCERTs Model: A Transactional, Family-Centered Approach to Enhancing Communication and Socioemotional Abilities of Children with Autism Spectrum Disorder." *Infants and Young Children*, 2003: 16, 296–316.

Ray, Dee et al. "The Effectiveness of Play Therapy: Responding to the Critics." *International Journal of Play Therapy*, 2001: 10, 85–108.

Reichow, Brian. "Overview of Meta-Analyses on Early Intensive Behavioral Intervention for Young Children with Autism Spectrum Disorders." *Journal of Autism and Developmental Disorders*, 2011: 42, 512–20.

Reynolds, Cecil R., and Sally E. Shaywitz. "Response to Intervention: Ready or Not? Or, From Wait-to-Fail to Watch-Them-Fail." *School Psychology Quarterly*, 2009: 24, 130.

Richards, Graham. *Putting Psychology in its Place: Critical Historical Perspectives*. New York: Routledge, 2010.

Roberts, Jane E., Linda King-Thomas, and Marcia L. Boccia. "Behavioral Indexes of the Efficacy of Sensory Integration Therapy." *American Journal of Occupational Therapy*, 2007: 555–62.

Robinson, Daniel R. *An Intellectual History of Psychology*. Madison: University of Wisconsin Press, 1995.

Rogers, Sally. "Empirically Supported Comprehensive Treatments for Young Children with Autism." *Journal of Clinical Child & Adolescent Psychology*, 1998: 27, 168–79.

Rogers, Sally, and Vismara, L.A. "Evidence-Based Comprehensive Treatments for Early Autism." *Journal of Clinical Child & Adolescent Psychology*, 2008: 37, 8–38.

Rosenwasser, Beth, and Saul Axelrod. "The Contributions of Applied Behavior Analysis to the Education of People with Autism." *Behavior Modification*, 2001: 25, 671–77.

Ryan, Richard M., and Edward L. Deci. "Intrinsic and Extrinsic Motivations: Classic Definitions and New Directions." *Contemporary Educational Society*, 2000: 25, 54–67.

Sackett, D.L. et al. "Evidence-Based Medicine: What It Is and What It Isn't." *British Medical Journal*, 1996: 312, 71–72.

Sailor, Wayne, and Matthew Stowe. "The Relationship of Inquiry to Policy." *Research & Practice for Persons with Severe Disabilities*, 2003: 28, 148–52.

Scheuermann, Brenda et al. "Problems with Personnel Preparation in Autism Spectrum Disorders." *Focus on Autism and Other Developmental Disabilities*, 2003: 18, 197–206.

Schneider, Susan M., and Edward K. Morris, "A History of the Term Radical Behaviorism: From Watson to Skinner." *Behavior Analyst*, 1987:10 (1), 27–39.

Schreibman, Laura. "Intensive Behavioral/Psychoeducational Treatments for Autism: Research Needs and Future Directions." *Journal of Autism and Developmental Disorders*, 2000: 30, 373–78.

Shakespeare, Thomas. "Disability, Identity, and Difference." In *Exploring the Divide*, Colin Barnes and Geof Mercer (Eds.). Leeds, UK: Disability Press, 1996.

Simpson, Richard L. "Evidence-Based Practices and Students with Autism Spectrum Disorders." *Focus on Autism and Other Developmental Disabilities*, 2005: 20, 140–49.

Skrtic, Thomas. *Disability and Democracy: Reconstructing (Special) Education for Postmodernity*. New York: Teachers College Press.

Smith, S. et al. "Effects of Sensory Integration Intervention on Self-Stimulating and Self-Injurious Behaviors." *American Journal of Occupational Therapy*, 2005: 59, 418–25.

Spreckley, Michelle, and Roslyn Boyd. "Efficacy of Applied Behavioral Intervention in Preschool Children with Autism for Improving Cognitive, Language, and Adaptive Behavior: A Systematic Review and Meta-Analysis." *Journal of Pediatrics*, 2009: March, 338–44.

Stanfield, Andrew C. "Towards a Neuroanatomy of Autism: A Systematic Review and Meta-Analysis of Structural Magnetic Resonance Imaging Studies." *European Psychiatry*, 2007: 23, 1–11.

Stokes, Trevor F., and Donald M. Baer. "An Implicit Technology of Generalization." *Journal of Applied Behavior Analysis*, 1977: 10, 349–67.

Sundberg, Mark L., and Jack Michael. "The Benefits of Skinner's Analysis of Verbal Behavior for Children with Autism." *Behavior Modification*, 2001: 25, 698–724.

Sundberg, Mark L., and James E. Partington. *Teaching Language to Children with Autism or Other Developmental Disabilities*. Concord, CA: AVB Press, 1998.

Tachibana, Koji. "How Aristotle's Theory of Education Has Been Studied in Our Century." *Studida Classica*, 2012: 3, 21–67.

Tatto, Maria Teresa. "The Influence of Teacher Education on Teachers' Beliefs About Purposes of Education, Roles, and Practice." *Journal of Teacher Education*, 1998: 49, 66–77.

Thomson, Rosemary Garland. *Extraordinary Bodies: Figuring Physical Disability in American Culture and Literature*. New York: Columbia University Press, 1997.

Tomlinson, Sally. *A Sociology of Special Education*. London: Routledge & Kegan Paul, 1982.

Ullman, Leonard P., and Leonard Krasner (Eds.). *Case Studies in Behavior Modification*. New York: Holt, Rinehart & Winston, 1965.

Uttal, William R. *The War Between Mentalism and Behaviorism: On the Accessibility of Mental Processes*. Mahwah, NJ: Psychology Press, 1999.

Virués-Ortega, Javier. "Causes of Unity and Disunity in Psychology and Behaviorism: An Encounter with Arthur W. Staats' Psychological Behaviorism." *International Journal of Clinical and Health Psychology*, 2005: 5(1), 161–173.

Vogeley. V. "Mind Reading: Neural Mechanisms of Theory of Mind and Self-Perspective." *NeuroImage*, 2001: 14, 170–81.

Wakefield, Jerome C. "Is Behaviorism Becoming a Pseudo-science?: Power Versus Scientific Rationality in the Eclipse of Token Economies by Biological Psychiatry in the Treatment of Schizophrenia." *Behavior and Social Issues*, 2006: 15, 202–21.

———. "Is Behaviorism Becoming a Pseudo-science?: Replies to Drs. Wyatt, Midkiff, and Wong." *Behavior and Social Issues*, 2007: 160, 170–89.

Wanzek, Jaenne, and Sharon Vaughn. "Response to Varying Amounts of Time in Reading Intervention for Students with Low Response to Intervention." *Journal of Learning Disabilities*, 2008: 41, 126–42.

Wetherby, Amy M. et al. "Early Indicators of Autism Spectrum Disorders in the Second Year of Life." *Journal of Autism and Developmental Disorders*, 2004: 34, 473–93.

Wolf, Montrose, Todd Risley, and Hayden Mees. "Application of Operant Conditioning Procedures to the Behavior Problems of an Autistic Child." *Behaviour Research and Therapy*, 1964: 1, 305–12.

Ximenes, Veronica M. et al. "Factors Affecting Visual Inference in Single Case Designs." *Spanish Journal of Psychology*, 2009: 12, 823–32.

Zelazoa, Philip David et al. "The Relation Between Theory of Mind and Rule Use: Evidence from Persons with Autism Spectrum Disorders." *Infant and Child Development*, 2002: 11, 171–95.

Index

About the Author

Eric Shyman currently serves as assistant professor on the faculty of the Child Study Department at St. Joseph's College in Patchogue, New York. Dr. Shyman received his certification in special education in 2003 and his Doctorate of Education in Intellectual Disability and Autism Studies, with a specialization in Instructional Leadership from Teachers College, Columbia University in 2009. Recently, Dr. Shyman received the Early Career Award from Teachers College. In addition to being a full-time professor, Dr. Shyman has served as a teaching assistant, a lead teacher, a staff trainer, curriculum developer, consultant, a lecturer, and workshop leader locally and nationally. Dr. Shyman's research currently focuses both on designing and evaluating teacher preparation program curriculum as well as issues in enhancing social justice and inclusive opportunities for students with various disabilities in public school regular education classrooms. He lives in New York with his wife, two sons, and dog, Dixie.